THE GILDED AGE

A Reappraisal

THE GILDED AGE

A Reappraisal

H. WAYNE MORGAN

Editor

SYRACUSE UNIVERSITY PRESS 1963

This work has been published
with the assistance of a
Ford Foundation grant.

LIBRARY OF CONGRESS
CATALOG CARD: 63-13886

First printing, 1963
Second printing, 1964
Paperback edition, 1964
Second printing, 1966
Third printing, 1967
Fourth printing, 1968

Manufactured in the United States of America

Preface

The editor has organized this project to examine critically the historical facts and interpretations available on the period in American history generally known as the Gilded Age. Dates are always arbitrary, but we have taken this period to be roughly the generation that followed the Civil War, or approximately the years 1865 to 1890.

This book is not a general survey; such is not its purpose. The contributors hope by bringing new attention, new interpretations, and fresh materials to several topics especially relevant to the Gilded Age, to arouse interest in further study. Above all, we hope to show where and how we feel the facts and interpretations concerning these topics specifically and the period generally have been misused or misunderstood. Our chief purpose always has been to arouse interest, believing that further study will give a more adequate and more accurate view of the Gilded Age.

A symposium such as this encompasses much labor, but we represented here feel well rewarded with the results. Our thanks go, without egotism, to each other and to the many institutions and persons who have helped us singly and collectively.

H. WAYNE MORGAN

Austin, Texas
December, 1962

Contents

PREFACE v

1. An Age in Need of Reassessment: *A View Beforehand*
   H. WAYNE MORGAN 1

2. The Robber Baron in the Gilded Age: *Entrepreneur or
   Iconoclast?* JOHN TIPPLE 14

3. The Worker's Search for Power: *Labor in the Gilded
   Age* HERBERT G. GUTMAN 38

4. Spoilsmen and Reformers: *Civil Service Reform and
   Public Morality* ARI HOOGENBOOM 69

5. The Republican Party Revisited, *1877–1897*
   VINCENT P. DE SANTIS 91

6. Greenbackers, Goldbugs, and Silverites: *Currency
   Reform and Policy, 1860–1897*
   PAOLO E. COLETTA 111

7. Rumblings Beneath the Surface: *America's Outward
   Thrust, 1865–1890* MILTON PLESUR . . 140

8. Gilt, Gingerbread, and Realism: *The Public and Its Taste*
   ROBERT R. ROBERTS 169

9. The Search for Reality: *Writers and Their Literature*
   ROBERT FALK 196

10. New Men and New Ideas: *Science and the American
    Mind* PAUL F. BOLLER, JR. 221

NOTES TO CHAPTERS 245

CONTRIBUTORS 279

INDEX 283

THE GILDED AGE

A Reappraisal

1

An Age in Need of Reassessment
A View Beforehand
H. WAYNE MORGAN

THE picture is compelling; one sees it half in mirth and half in a muffled pity. There is Colonel Beriah Sellers, surrounded by doting or incredulous townsfolk, plotting with a magisterial wave of a well-tailored arm the future of an inland empire. Its seat will be at this unlikely spot, to be named after a great historical event or man. A gilt cane marks out in the muddy ruts the streets and avenues of riches and success. Here, he says grandly in the overblown rhetoric the age loves so well, will converge the river traffic, despite the absence of rivers soon to be remedied by a huge canal grant from an all-wise national government. Here will be the railroad, despite the hopeless terrain. Here will sit the city, ablaze with color and aglow with the lights of wealth and power, rising from these unlikely dunes and hills. And from here the glory of America will radiate outward toward lesser peoples who may yet come to partake of this bounty at a reasonable price.

The picture is familiar. It is the Gilded Age, or at least it is the stereotype of the bloated dreams, foolish optimism, seedy rhetoric of the generation which followed the Civil War, and no man caught that side of it as well as Mark Twain, who named it. No human vanity, no pomposity, no trace of the overblown or flatulent escaped his pen. In drawing Colonel Sellers and his compatriots, Twain delineated a view of the whole generation, throwing it into a relief that is compelling almost a century later.

Though this view of the age may be partly discounted because it is fiction, there is too often the sterner stuff of facts to corroborate it. The generation that emerged from the Civil War embarked upon a seemingly endless development of America's natural resources, commercial riches, and opportunities for equality in most spheres

1

of life, to stage what Vernon Parrington called "the Great Barbe-cue." The feast of material plenty was set at the national table for everyone, who purchased this bonanza only at the price of bad taste, corruption in politics and economics, and dangerous refusals to face the harder and deeper facts of life. Yet whether these facts be true or false, the age presents a compelling charm in many of its aspects. It was a time of peace, of relative prosperity, of growth and change which seemed the more important and exciting because they occurred in a vacuum of international affairs when the United States could afford the luxury of self-interest. Moreover, the age believed in itself, something its successors cannot always claim. Optimism, a belief in progress, however foolish it may sometimes have become, was the keynote of the time.

A famous jurist once said that the Constitution is what the judges say it is. By the same token, history is often what the historians say it is, and the Gilded Age has fared poorly in that light. Only in very recent years has it begun to emerge in detailed studies which reveal it in true relation to its own time and its successors. For three gen-erations of viewers and students, the era has been either a result of one thing, the Civil War, or a prelude to something better and dif-ferent in the twentieth century. It seems lifeless in historical print. It is something standing between the huge mountain range of the Civil War and the lesser plateaus of Populism and the Progressive movement. It is popular to call it a watershed, and historical water-sheds seem to have no life of their own. Few students have seriously attempted to view it in proper perspective, as it was to itself, and for the things that it produced in itself.

The stereotype picture of the Gilded Age, presented in almost all secondary studies, is the result of the work of relatively few scholars. Chief among these is one of America's most celebrated critics and scholars, Vernon Lewis Parrington, whose *The Begin-nings of Critical Realism in America* sets a tone which few sub-sequent students have materially altered.[1] Though primarily literary criticism and cultural history, Parrington's widely read study pro-foundly influenced historians and scholars interested in American culture. To Parrington, a man of acute social consciousness, reared in the traditions of Progressive America, the Gilded Age seemed an appalling low in national morals and manners. It was to him frankly and crassly materialistic, a spectacular national feast labeled "the Great Barbecue." It surrendered the country's affairs into the hands of a few men of business who looted, overbuilt, and ultimately almost ruined the economy and political and social system: "With no social conscience, no concern for civilization, no heed for the future of democracy it talked so much about, the Gilded Age threw itself into the business of money-getting." [2]

From Parrington's view, the era's chief fault was the transfer of power from the people to the economic masters. With this, the Jacksonian agrarian frontier of freedom and mobility disappeared, and in its stead came the monolithic and oppressive grandeur of an industrial system producing many goods, but devouring labor and wasting materials while building fortunes and power for the wrong men. America was on the road to economic plenty and social goodness in the Gilded Age, but not until some distant future date would they become real. In the meantime, the generation of the Gilded Age was an interregnum of waste, corruption, and inefficiency.[3]

The evil of corrupt politics and lopsided economics was compounded by a nadir of taste. "It was in the seventies that good taste reached its lowest ebb," Parrington wrote, without explaining either his own view of good taste, or what the seventies thought of taste, good or bad.[4] With his blanket condemnations, qualified now and then by a reserved, hopeful prognostication for the future, Parrington set the tone for dealing with the Gilded Age. His thesis, covered in the bright gloss of a happy style, lent itself to quotation for two generations of college students and serious scholars who also liked to smash idols. The glamor of much of his theory and the widespread appeal of his thinking lie largely in the ease with which they are repeated, as a generation of uncritical historians should know. Parrington saw the age from a special viewpoint; in many ways he was the last great agrarian critic among American scholars, and inevitably he did not take kindly to a generation or a morality that overthrew his ideal.

Of the other major figures who dealt with the period, Charles A. Beard is easily the most important.[5] Perhaps because he was a trained historian presumably with a broader view and deeper knowledge, or perhaps because his purposes were different, Beard produced a critical and biased yet more substantial and even commentary on the era. Though he too viewed history within a famous framework, "the economic interpretation," Beard had the common sense, at least in the 1930's, not to become totally imprisoned in his theories at the expense of the facts of history.

Like Parrington, Beard deplored the waste of resources and the gravitation of power into the hands of the economically minded few. But he also saw that the period was far more complex than Parrington sketched it. He saw that the urban middle class, growing wealthy from the Civil War and the industrial and transportation system it produced, ruled society; but he also saw that this class was greatly expanded in a bloodless revolution. The new culture it produced was "without form and void" save for the older parts of the East. Money ruled, "the cash nexus pure and simple," but the wealth was more widely spread and far more easily obtained than in the prewar era. The age was ruled by "the onrushing plutocracy"; yet that plutocracy was not fixed or hereditary, and the nation avoided revolution because of its innate conservatism and flexible social structure. "Among American working classes, all save the most wretched had aspirations; there was a baton in every tool kit." [6]

His criticism no less strong than that of others, Beard also saw much that other students missed, much that redeemed the age and helped its children forgive its sudden and massive interest in boundless wealth and power. Not all men were blind to the era's faults; there were reformers and reform movements in most spheres of life, and political criticism was especially harsh. After all, it was the age of E. L. Godkin, Thomas Nast, and free-wheeling editorializing on a scale later generations might not accept. Beginnings are not always what men desire, but they are beginnings nonetheless. The Gilded Age witnessed pioneer efforts in education, when a few of the "Robber Barons" endowed institutions of higher learning; when most major eastern cities established art galleries; when states began to expand their educational systems and social services, forming molds which the twentieth century would expand. How curious and how often overlooked is the fact of great scientific and philosophical development in the period; it was the age of Charles S. Peirce, William James, and the Social Darwinists.[7]

Doubtless because of its materialism, the energy it showed among its people, and its fascinating studies in power, the Gilded

Age has lent itself to deterministic analysis. No recent student approached the era with more bias than did Matthew Josephson, three of whose works have remained standard interpretations of the period for a generation.[8] Frankly Marxist in his approach, Josephson saw the period in terms of economic, political, and social exploitation of the many by the few, for whom he coined the telling phrase "Robber Barons." He dealt with the period in terms of stark power, showing vividly how within his interpretive framework the late nineteenth century was a breeding ground for tyranny and corruption in every sphere of American life. His black-white interpretation of the period, chosen largely because of the ease of its generalizations, has influenced many, but on the whole it has presented no total view of the period or its actors.

Few if any students of the period have chosen to see it as it saw itself. Any historical problem or person should be approached in two stages: first, the student must decide how it appeared at the time of the event; second, using analysis and hindsight, he must determine its relevance and importance in the mainstream of its time and circumstance. This test has been applied without consistency to the Gilded Age. Because of its activity and transitional nature it does not lend itself to accurate, easy generalizations.

The nation's pent-up forces and emotions, focused by the tragic but compelling events of the early 1860's, burst forth with peace in the Gilded Age to seek wealth, power, and general material advancement. Of the great institutions that touched daily life, politics was doubtless the most real and most immediate to Americans of the Gilded Age. This may well have been the last generation of Americans who freely indulged a national taste for personal participation in the rough and tumble sport of American politics. Free from formal polls, advertising techniques, and what a later generation calls "the Madison Avenue approach," our grandparents and great-grandparents participated freely and often with vehemence in the picnics, rallies, parades, stump speaking, and public dealings that marked the progress of elections, whether state or national. Politics was not only more strongly emphasized by, but more important to the men of this period. If, as most historians have judged, the parties of the era avoided the issues of the day and were in fact as much alike as peas in a pod, how explain this great public interest in such

long-dead issues as the tariff, currency reform, and internal improvements? One answer must surely be that the parties were not
alike to the people of the time, and that the issues were fully as
diversified, clear, and different as those of a later generation.

It is true that much of these political fireworks and most of these
issues seem distant and even unreal today, but that does not invali-
date their earlier appeal. Some of these issues—the currency and
the tariff, for instance—survive in modified form to arouse interest
among politicians and constituents alike.

The importance of politics to Americans of that period showed
the vitality of the democratic spirit. Public interest in government
was very much alive, working within a viable tradition of changing
party politics. No one can blink away the massive corruption in
many areas of politics in the period, especially in city and state government; but these festering sores, many of which were healed
during the Gilded Age, should not blind students to the real accomplishments in politics. The closeness of all the national elections
of the period illustrates the degree and kind of labor necessary for
any party's victory and the extent to which it could marshal support among constituents. The Gilded Age and its interest in government and politics, whatever its faults in both spheres, must not be
forgotten when the accounts are cast up for an analysis of democratic rule in the American party system.

Few generations produced a more striking set of party leaders,
contrary to the views of many scholars who portray it as an age of
drab issues and dull men. The Republicans, long dominant on the
national scene, could count on a host of glamorous if not always
wise or successful military heroes to fill its rosters. The defeated
South after 1876 could return its men in grey to public office with
equal fanfare, if often with worse results. Few are the generations
that can match for political effectiveness and appeal such figures
as Grant, James G. Blaine, "Lord Roscoe" Conkling and his New
York cohorts, or the Boys in Blue. There were also the less colorful
but perhaps more effective men like Hayes, Arthur, McKinley, and
a powerful senatorial group. Nor were the reformers silent. Thomas
Nast, Horace Greeley, E. L. Godkin, Henry and Brooks Adams,
Peter Cooper, and others raised the standard of reform in many
fields. Public and private probity and integrity were never eclipsed,

no matter to what depths certain departments of government fell under some men. Newspaper reporting and editorializing were merciless. It was also a time of free-wheeling third party movements in both politics and labor—the Greenbackers, Socialists, Anarchists, Prohibitionists, and even a few early Communists kept the pot of political change simmering, if not at times boiling.

Contrary to accepted textbook clichés, the Republican party was a vital organization, composed of more than retired colonels and grafting politicians. Fighting for its life and for the consolidation of the great gains made under Lincoln, it dominated the White House during most of this era. It controlled most of the northern and western states by adopting and enacting the greatest program of nationalism and government spending since Federalism. Far from fearing strong central government, the Republicans of this era wrote into law most of Hamilton's theories, arguing that whatever their faults, their merits were greater when viewed in the context of the whole nation's welfare. This centralization, repugnant to many unsuspecting latter-day Republicans, accounted for the party's success and also for much of lasting good within the country's economic and social structure. Its cost, as is the case with any program, is another matter, largely of alternatives available at the time. Perhaps it is not too much to say that the country as a whole benefited more quickly under this Republican theory than it would have under a Democratic administration committed largely to states' rights and the trappings of prewar theory.

And what of the society of the time, its culture, taste, manners, and morals? Was it, as most students would believe, made up of the gauche mob now risen to affluence and to new middle-class status on the war's wealth and the postwar period's endless opportunities? How familiar is the standard historical picture of the age: the tasteless reading matter, the lack of interest in the arts and music, the garish architecture rearing up on avenues of small country hamlets as well as proud cities, and the aping of English and French manners and style. Where, critics then and later asked, was the native American architecture, art, music, manners? It was an age of extremes—of low wages and huge dividends, of garish display and of poverty, of opulent richness in one row of houses and of degrading poverty a block away. Socially the gulf between the haves and the have-nots was greater than our generation would recognize. Who can forget the huge balls and parties thrown by the gentry, and who can visit Newport, Saratoga Springs, or Greenbriar without staring in awe at the "cottages" and hostelries built to house the idle rich?

But is this the whole story, this stereotype dealing in extremes? The answer, as Professor Roberts judiciously reminds us, is not quite so clearly cut and dried. It seems a human failing to expect the worst of mankind. Students of the Gilded Age have fastened upon popular culture as proof of the period's tastelessness, ignoring or forgetting the rich vitality which the arts and culture displayed in many fields. The Chautauqua, for instance, was not the thing of chaff and wind depicted by many, and like the lyceum before the Civil War, served a real educational purpose. That it sought basically to perpetuate the manners and morals of the age hardly condemns it, for all such institutions do likewise. That it dealt largely with accepted themes should not blind us also to the new ideas and attitudes it brought to countless towns, large and small alike, enlivening with a combination of entertainment and culture the isolated and dull existence of a predominantly rural nation.

It is easy also to forget the amount of good or at least respectable literature both written and read, the flourishing and often culturally important magazines and newspapers, and the popular interest in both applied and theoretical science. This generation supported more intellectual organs of print than a far richer twentieth century does. The arts were by no means stagnant. The theater, music, the opera all drew large and appreciative audiences, presented tasteful and great works, and reflected new developments as well as their counterparts did elsewhere in the world. Surely there was bad taste, especially among the crassest *nouveaux riches*. But there was also a solid stratum of good taste, intellectual ferment, and artistic endeavor to redeem at least some of the more public and therefore better remembered faults and lapses.

It is easy also to forget the writers and artists, the thinkers and scientists of the period, who seem somehow unreal or small in stature compared to successors. Literature was not limited to women's fiction, Horatio Alger, or the cruder humor of Mark Twain. There was William Dean Howells, the nascent school of realism centering on Hamlin Garland, Edward Eggleston, and others. There were the many solid monthlies and quarterlies that found ready audiences for heavy wares, which would doubtless die today. In the light of cold criticism, the popular fiction devoured by schoolboys and swooning maidens was probably no worse, if such standards there be, than that imbibed by the same groups today.

In the sciences it was a remarkable period, producing a number of distinguished philosophers, educators, experimenters, and theologians. Any generation that can boast William James, Charles Peirce, and Josiah Royce need not hang its head in shame. But there were the lesser known figures of equal import such as the men who founded the Johns Hopkins University, other men who renovated the curriculum at Harvard and Yale, the growing scientific faculties at most important schools. Many of the ideas these men set in motion came full circle only later, but as prophets before their time, they were at least free to work and theorize in the Gilded Age. The development of the nation's school system, both public and private, was a great boon to the spread of new ideas, and a gradually expanding and vital curriculum meant better education for life and living.

But granted that this solid foundation of innovation and continuity lie beneath the age's public and historical front, what of the corruption—the Whisky Ring, the Indian Frauds, the Star Routes, the Credit Mobilier—that hangs like a bad odor over the whole period? Was corruption in politics and business as general as it has been depicted? Professor Hoogenboom answers no, pointing out, while not excusing or ignoring these great public scandals, that the attention paid them has obscured the presence of a civil service board under Grant which was not entirely ineffective. It seems unlikely that any substantial portion of the federal civil service was corrupt or inefficient, despite the usual lurid picture of public malfeasance. And while no one denies the presence of governmental and political chicanery, the people of the time were at least aware of it. Few periods have had so articulate a set of reformers with so many organs open to them for disseminating their views; their voice is measured by the degree to which their protests have overemphasized the age's corruption. There is no evidence, furthermore, that the public was more tolerant of corruption than before or after the Gilded Age.

Of all fields of endeavor, none has suffered more from this

picture of general corruption than business and finance. Black Friday, the Erie War, "watered stock," all stand in the shadows of such men as Commodore Vanderbilt, "Jubilee Jim" Fisk, "Uncle Dan'l" Drew, the genial Andrew Carnegie, the bloodless Jay Gould, and the grimmest but most potent of all the Robber Barons, John D. Rockefeller. Wresting billions from a complacent and tolerant public, corrupting legislatures, dominating senates and presidents, wasting a nation's resources, pursuing no ethic save self-advancement—such is the standard portrait of their lives and works.

Like most stereotypes, there is enough truth in these assertions to give appeal to the total picture. It is hard to justify in twentieth-century terms the economic development of the nation in this generation. Yet, as Professor Tipple says with felicitous common sense, the generation involved thought relatively little of the antics of the stock exchange and wheat pit. They had always been unregulated and were part of the philosophy of free enterprise and go-getting that supposedly supported the American system. The color and publicity of the corporate jerry-building obscured solid gains and lasting achievements of lesser figures. For every Daniel Drew there was a smaller man in local industry and finance with at least a little more sagacity or less abandon. And, as we often forget, the era's economic opportunists were sometimes considered radicals by their compatriots, attacking as they did the hallowed American institution of competition, revealing a contradiction that most Americans had not seen—individualism devouring itself until further individualism was impossible.

It would be easy to insist that the end result of this economic activity was good, bringing standardization of products, settled prices, less waste, and consolidation that made the economy more sound. But such a conclusion smells of whitewash. Suffice it to say that the stereotype of the Robber Baron is much overdrawn. It must be balanced with a fuller picture, showing the new technology he often brought to his industry, the wealth and resources he developed for the economy in general, the social good he sometimes did with his money, offsetting the bitter fact that he paid little in taxes. Some might argue that the government should have regulated, taxed, and controlled business in more sane channels of development, that it should perhaps have participated in the economy; but this was not at the time a feasible alternative. Moreover, there was amid all the greed and overbuilding, an inevitable if unseen social return on the investments of the Gilded Age. And perhaps the tax favors, gifts of public domain, and government grants to business were not as exorbitant as they seem.

For labor this also had advantages. Most working men could aspire with some shred of logic to emulate Rockefeller and Carnegie, themselves fulfillments of the "rags to riches" myth. They could also feel that in the long run their wages rose, their hours of labor shortened, their working conditions improved, and their general economic security expanded. They would not recognize the benefits their grandchildren enjoy under highly organized labor, but by pre-Civil War standards, there is no doubt that the worker like the businessman advanced during the Gilded Age. Labor's gains do not seem as vivid as those of capital. The worker's story is written too largely, however, in the lurid phrases of strikes and depressions, while the prosaic statistics that record real growth and progress, though apparently slow to a later generation, lie forgotten in the dust of faulty memory.

Henry Adams the man disliked the age's crass materialism and often questionable morality, but he was a prescient observer and, when cast in the role of historian, saw its deeper accomplishments. As the century ended and the whole long process of growth and change fell into some pattern, he could say of these developments: "How much they cost was another matter; if the public is ever driven to its last resources and the usual remedies of chaos, the result will probably cost more." [9] Perhaps the most important development in recent American history has been the peaceful and steady narrowing of the gap between the extreme haves and the have-nots, the very rich and the very poor. There is much irony in realizing that while the men and measures of the Gilded Age seemed to widen this gap by piling fortune upon fortune, they also helped close it. They brought amelioration of the divisive issues of the day in the economy, the political system, and society that would have wrecked a less flexible and optimistic system. The belief in progress, savored with enough evidence to make it compelling to the masses of Americans, and the nation's widespread wealth gave the lie to those who predicted that the arrogance of riches would soon clash bloodily with the resentment of poverty. In this watershed period, it was no small accomplishment to ease those great tensions peacefully, despite periodic flurries of violence in hard times, and to provide safety valves for their future reduction.

And the hard, welcome fact remains that the nation *did* grow stronger in all spheres. The foundations for future expansion as a world power economically second to none were laid during this period. The questionable practices, rapid growth, and waste did not triumph over hard work and common sense. Whatever else may be said of the age, it built.

And what to say of that America, provincial in tone, isolated from the world's events, yet sure in her own heart of her innate strength and coming greatness? What became of the confident men with mustaches and beards? Why the sad and solemn ruins of the ornate houses and the heavy but charming furniture? And where did the era's confident hopes go? Memory falls like a veil over much of the generation, softening in the glow of nostalgia the angular faults, hiding the steep places in a desire to return to the "good old days." Whatever its shortcomings, its friends argue, the age was confident, it was peaceful, even if provincial. The dangers of wishing to return are all too clear; Professor Plesur reminds us that though the nation was relatively isolated, it was a time of preparation for American entry into the tangles and bitter responsibilities of world affairs.

This nostalgic appeal is magnetic, and yet who upon reflection would exchange the social gains, the political progress, the economic and material rewards of the mid-twentieth century for the Gilded Age? The choice is personal, but the fact remains, nostalgia aside, that the Gilded Age has not received its just due from either a neglecting public or distorting historians. Any serious student of the period is struck on close examination by several things. First, it was a time of prodigious energy, buttressed by political and diplomatic isolation and lack of armed forces to drain strength away from productive labor. Americans turned inward to develop their virgin wilderness, to raise up a manufacturing plant to rival those of older nations, and to present a society of curious fluidity despite its extremes of wealth and poverty that attracted millions and then tens of millions to its shores. Second, it was a generation of transition, when the industrial revolution came full circle, touching and changing all aspects of life—labor, investment, even geography, politics, and society. Its rapidity and the rate of change of this revolution were again heightened by the absence of foreign responsibilities, which magnified domestic affairs. Third, it was a time of growth and change, progress if one wishes, in almost all spheres of life and labor. Accomplished often with what later generations would call dubious means, yes, but accomplished nonetheless. In the long run this period and its changes and growth may well be the source of American vitality and growth in the critical decades that followed. The generation had a life of its own, achieved enduring and significant things in most spheres of life. That is the pattern we should explore and understand in justice to ourselves and to the Gilded Age.

And so we turn the circle, returning to Colonel Sellers, who stands in memory and imagination on this dividing line between the old and new, the fast and slow, the pure and impure, the realistic and naïve. How well he symbolizes his time, holding as he does so many conflicting ideas and attitudes, posing so many questions about his direction, accomplishments, and ethics. What to say of him and his fellows? They were not adequate always to their tasks, but this is true of all generations; they achieved much for their country's good. If these points of departure are sharpened for further study, we who have written this book will be well rewarded. Perhaps it would be wise merely to see the good Colonel, confident of tomorrow, full of plans and energy, poised for a flight of rhetoric, as a general symbol for the period. Not altogether true, to be sure, but a symbol of great validity nonetheless. What a challenging, vital, and charming way to approach him and the Gilded Age.

2

The Robber Baron in the Gilded Age

Entrepreneur or Iconoclast?

JOHN TIPPLE

*I*T IS more than coincidence that the beginning of the Robber Baron legend, the portrayal of the big businessman as a warlike brigand cheating and plundering his way to millions, was contemporaneous with the inauguration of the corporation as the major instrument of business control in the United States. After the Civil War, the large corporation had begun manifestly to dominate the American economic scene; and in those same years, Charles Francis Adams, Jr., launched his first assault against the "Erie robbers," and his brother, Henry Adams, warned of the day when great corporations, "swaying power such as has never in the world's history been trusted in the hands of mere private citizens," would be controlled by one man or combinations of men who would use these new leviathans to become masters of the nation.[1]

Such dangerous potentialities had not been recognizable earlier because prior to the Civil War the majority of businesses had operated as local enterprises, usually as individual proprietorships, partnerships, or as small closed corporations in which ownership and control were almost invariably synonymous.[2] Under usual circumstances, the power and influences of the businessman had been limited to the immediate environs of operation and, at the very most, seldom extended beyond state boundaries. Equally important was the fact that there existed among most businessmen of prewar days a nearly universal desire and a practical necessity for community esteem, and this governed their conduct, keeping their ventures well within the limits of individual responsibility and tending to restrain any untoward actions or irresponsible profiteering on their part. Ante-bellum criticisms of the businessman, therefore, were few and sporadic. What disapproval there was usually focused on the speculator or stock gambler, and was no doubt often inspired by an agrarian distrust of big-city ways.[3]

The bloody struggles of the Civil War, however, helped bring about revolutionary changes in economic and political life. The war needs had created almost insatiable demands for manufactured goods—arms, munitions, clothing—and had offered some manufacturers unsurpassed opportunities to make vast fortunes. More important than the immediate profits, however, was the stimulus of massive military demands, leading the entrepreneur to new concepts of the power and possibilities of large-scale enterprise: "The great operations of war, the handling of large masses of men, the influence of discipline, the lavish expenditure of unprecedented sums of money, the immense financial operations, the possibilities of effective cooperation, were lessons not likely to be lost on men quick to receive and apply all new ideas." [4] Though the war prevented general economic expansion, the new ideas were profitably applied to the peacetime economy which followed.

With the rich resources of the trans-Mississippi West lying open to private exploitation, the businessman had singular opportunities for achieving vast wealth. Before him spread an immense untapped continent whose riches were his virtually for the taking; and, most opportunely, new means to turn this stupendous wealth to profitable account were at hand. A host of new inventions and discoveries, the application of science to industry, improved methods of transportation and communication were ready to assist the businessman in his ventures, but all of these aids would have been valueless to him had he not had the effective means to put them to work. The practical agency to meet these unprecedented entrepreneurial demands on capital and management proved to be the corporation, for the stockholding system provided immense capital beyond the reach of any individual and, at the same time, the corporate hierarchy presented a feasible solution to the greatly augmented problems of management.

Certainly the corporation was no novelty in this country. It had served political as well as economic purposes in seventeenth-century America, and as an instrumentality of business its use antedated the discovery of this continent. Seldom before, however, in the history of the United States had the corporation been put to active use on such a large scale. From a relatively passive creature of legalistic capitalism, it was transformed by fusion with technics into a dynamic system spearheading American economic expansion.

The impact of the newborn corporation on American society was almost cataclysmic. Although in the first few decades of its existence the modern corporate system probably enabled this nation to develop more wealth than in any other period since the discovery of America, it also brought about a revolution of tremendous potential, menacing not only hallowed economic theories and usages but threatening to ride like a great tidal wave over the traditional social and political beliefs of American democracy. Its size alone was sufficient to change fundamental social and economic relationships; by sheer magnitude the large industrial corporation overshadowed the society around it. Of the newly formed United States Steel Corporation an awed commentator wrote at the turn of the century: "It receives and expends more money every year than any but the very greatest of the world's national governments; its debt is larger than that of many of the lesser nations of Europe; it absolutely controls the destinies of a population nearly as large as that of Maryland or Nebraska, and indirectly influences twice that number." [5] Most significantly, this enormous concentrated economic power normally gravitated into the hands of a few, raising up a corporate ruling class with almost unlimited authority.[6]

Though the meteoric rise of the so-called Robber Baron to unheralded positions of power was inseparably bound to the large corporation, there were other factors behind his sudden emergence into popular view as the outstanding phenomenon of nineteenth-century business life. One of the most important of these was a stable government dedicated to the preservation of private property and devoted to an ambiguous concept of laissez faire. Through political alliances, principally with the Republican party, the big businessman consolidated his economic triumphs. Although in the past the commercial and manufacturing interests of the North had received favors from the federal government in the form of bounties to fisheries and protective tariffs, after the defection of the South they were in the envied position of a pampered only child; and a dotingly partisan Congress bestowed upon them, among other things, new and higher tariffs and a series of favorable banking acts.

The economic supremacy of the North had been guaranteed by military victory in 1865, but it was doubly insured by the actions of the radical Republicans during the process of southern reconstruction. The Fourteenth Amendment, whether intended for such purposes or not, was used by the courts to protect the corporation and to prevent attempts by the states to undermine its position of power.[7] The election of General Grant to the presidency in 1868 and 1872 backed by the leading representatives of the business community, the great financiers and speculators, politically secured the issue of northern prosperity. Despite the panic of 1873, there were obvious signs that the business of the country had, as the *Nation* put it, "adapted itself to the situation created for it by Republican legislation."[8] Within this artificial paradise, private profits were sacred. The inheritance tax had expired in 1870, the income tax was abandoned in 1872, and an attempt to revive it in 1894 was invalidated by the Supreme Court in 1895.[9] Corporate or excess profits taxes did not exist, and by 1890, the bulk of the revenue of the United States government was derived from customs duties and excises on liquor and tobacco, all taxes upon the nation's consumers.[10] Under such idyllic conditions, stock market volume attained the million share mark in December, 1886, and industrial capital almost doubled itself every ten years.[11]

In an untrammeled preserve for self-seeking such as the United States in the late nineteenth century afforded, the dedicated businessman could make money on an unprecedented scale. Though John D. Rockefeller never quite became a billionaire, his fortune in 1892 reportedly amounted to $815,647,796.89.[12] Andrew Carnegie did nearly as well. The profits from his industrial empire in the decade 1889 to 1899 averaged about $7,500,000 a year and, in 1900 alone, they amounted to $40,000,000.[13] In the following year he sold out his interest for several hundred million dollars.[14] Such fortunes, exceptional even for those days, emphasized the prolific wealth available to the big businessman in the United States. In 1892, two New York newspapers engaged in a heated contest to count the number of American millionaires, the *World* uncovering 3,045 and the *Tribune* raising it to 4,047.[15] Regardless of the exact total, millionaires were becoming fairly common. By 1900, for instance, the Senate alone counted twenty-five millionaires among

its members, a fact which was an invitation to some suspicious folk
to dub that august body the "Rich Man's Club" and the "House of
Dollars." [16]

This sudden leap of big businessmen into new positions of
wealth and power caught the public eye, and to the American mind
accustomed to thinking primarily in terms of individuals, the big
businessman stood out as the conspicuous symbol of corporate
power, in his popular image encompassing not only his personal
attributes and failings but combining also the more amorphous
and impersonal aspects of the business organization by which he
had climbed to fortune. Just as Adolph Hitler and Joseph Stalin
were held later to typify their respective countries, so the diminu-
tive Andrew Carnegie came to represent the entire steelmaking
complex of men and decisions which bore his name, the lean,
ascetic John D. Rockefeller to personify Standard Oil, the bulbous
nose and rotund figure of J. P. Morgan to signify the whole of
Wall Street with its thousands of operators, its ethical flaws, and its
business virtues. When big businessmen came under attack as Robber Barons, they were attacked not for their personal failings,
though they had them as well as the lion's share of wealth, but as
the recognizable heads of large corporations. It is perhaps notable
that when Carnegie and Rockefeller gave up their business careers
and became private citizens taking no active part in corporate affairs,
the rancor against them almost ceased. Instead of being censured
for their past actions, which had been widely and vehemently criticized, they were praised as benefactors and good citizens. Public
castigation of the steel trust was lifted from "Little Andy" to fall
upon the broader shoulders of Charles Schwab, and the odium of
monopoly which had surrounded his father was inherited by John
D. Rockefeller, Jr. Only as the active and directive heads of great
corporations, and not as subordinates or members of a business elite,
were big businessmen branded "Robber Barons" and indicted for
alleged crimes against society.[17]

If the big businessman was not resented as an individual but as a
power symbol wielding the might of the great corporation, the
provocative question arises why there was such resentment against
the corporation. The answer is that the large industrial corporation
was an anomaly in nineteenth-century America; there was no place

for it among existing institutions and no sanction for it in traditional American values.

In this country all the institutions and values had been built about the social and political concept of the free individual. Born to the natural rights of life, liberty, and property, he was originally subject only to the law of nature. By being or becoming a member of society, the individual did not renounce his natural rights because this gift of God could not be alienated, but submitted to certain restraints beyond those imposed by nature for the evident good of the whole community. The basis of this ideology was of course the presumed constancy of nature in moral as well as physical operations, and the universal efficacy of its laws. By asserting that these inevitable laws of nature constituted truth and by setting out from the will of God or nature, eighteenth-century Americans sought to erect an inviolable system proceeding from natural causes and therefore not subject to human error. Fanciful as they may seem, these were nonetheless the accepted premises of government and society inherited by Americans of the nineteenth century.

Obviously in such a closed system there was no ready place for the large industrial corporation which was neither an individual nor a natural manifestation. As an artificial person created by charter and comprising many individuals and their wealth, the corporation not only was not an individual but was infinitely greater in size and power than the isolated individual about whom American society had been conceived. Unlike the individual, moreover, the corporate body was not ordinarily exposed to natural hazards of decay and death, having in effect been guaranteed immortality by the society which fathered it; hence where individual accumulation of wealth and power was limited to a lifetime, corporate possibilities were almost limitless—freed from death, and incidentally from death dues and inheritance taxes, the corporation was in a position to wax strong upon the accumulated lifetimes and earnings of many individuals. A further complication, the hazard of which increased directly in proportion to corporate size and power, was that the corporation as an unnatural creation was born without natural reason—"the common rule and measure God hath given mankind"—and was therefore not intrinsically subject to the governance of nature. In ideological terms, the corporation, since it could not be counted upon to follow the moral precepts of nature, was an outlaw to the society which spawned it.

What was to be done with such a monster? Either the corporation had to be made to conform to American institutions and principles, or those institutions and principles had to be changed to accommodate the corporation. This was the dilemma first seriously confronted by Americans during the Gilded Age and the issue that set off the great movement of introspection and reform which was to activate and enrapt the American people for the next fifty years.

Most flagrantly apparent to Americans of the post-Civil War era was the destructive effect of the large corporation upon free competition and equal opportunity. According to the accepted theory, which was a projection of the doctrines of liberal democracy into the economic sphere, the ideal economy—the only one, in fact, sanctioned by nature—was made up of freely competing individuals operating in a market unrestricted by man but fairly ruled by the inexorable forces of natural law. Just as the ideal polity was achieved by bargaining among free and equal individuals under the benevolent eye of nature, so it was assumed that in economic affairs impartial rivalry between individual entrepreneurs, free competition, would automatically serve the best interests of society as a whole by preventing anyone from getting more than his fair share of the wealth. And in early nineteenth-century America, this self-regulating mechanism did seem to work. Where businesses and factories were small, prices and output along with wages and profits did rise and fall according to supply and demand, and every man appeared to have equal opportunity to compete with every other man. Even after the war, the individual businessman in the interests of self-preservation was forced by and large to observe the common rules of competition. Ordinarily his share of the market was too small to permit any attempt at price control unless he joined with others in a pool, a trade association, or another rudimentary price-fixing agreement. Usually, however, the average businessman eschewed trade agreements, not out of theoretical considerations, but for the practical reason that such coalitions did not work very well, suffering as many of them did from mutual distrust and the pursuit of centrifugal aims. But what was true in a world of individual proprietors and workers was not necessarily true for the giant corporation which possessed greater unity of control and a larger share of the market and was therefore in the powerful position either to dictate prices or to combine successfully with one or two other corporations in monopolistic schemes. Indicative of what often happened was the terse statement appearing in the *Commercial and Financial Chronicle* in 1886: "Representatives of the various coal companies met at the house of Mr. J. Pierpont Morgan this week, and informally decided to limit coal production and maintain prices." [18] Thus by bringing to bear superior economic force which to a great extent invalidated the customary tenets of the free market, the large organization put the big businessman in the favored position of operating in an economy dedicated to the idea of freely competing individuals, yet left him unhampered by the ordinary restrictions. Under such auspicious circumstances, it is not surprising that he soon outdistanced his unorganized rivals in the race for wealth.

This markedly unfair advantage did not go unchallenged. As the earliest of the large corporations in the United States, the railroads were also the first to come under concentrated attack. The immense extension of the railways after the Union victory in 1865 and the crucial nature of their operations as common carriers to the nation exposed their activities to the widest public scrutiny and subjected their mistakes or misdeeds to considerable publicity. Popular resentment against the railroads in the early 1870's grew hottest in the farming states of the Midwest, but indignant reports came from all over the country accusing the railroads of using their monopoly power to the impediment of equal opportunity. A most frequent criticism, common to both East and West, was that railway superintendents and managers showed unreasonable favoritism by discriminating between persons and places, offering rate concessions to large shippers, charging more for short than long hauls, and giving preferential treatment to large corporations in the form of secret rebates and drawbacks. That these preferential rates might sometimes have been forced upon the railroads by pressure from business made little difference. The popular consensus was not only that this elaborate system of special rates denied the little man equal opportunity with the rich and influential, breaking the connection between individual merit and success, but that the ultimate effect was to extend further monopoly by preventing free competition among businesses where railway transportation was an important factor.[19]

The Standard Oil Company was generally conceded to be the outstanding example of a monopoly propagated in this manner, the charge being that the determining factor behind Rockefeller's spectacular conquest of the oil business had been this railway practice of secrecy and favoritism which had aided his company and ruined others. By collecting rebates on their own shipments and drawbacks on those of their competitors, Standard had gained virtual control of oil transportation and was therefore in a position to regulate the prices of crude and refined oil, with the detrimental result, so Henry Demarest Lloyd charged, that by 1881, though the company produced only one-fiftieth of the nation's petroleum, Standard refined nine-tenths of the oil produced in the United States and dictated the price of all of it.[20]

As the whipping boy among trusts, Standard undoubtedly had more than its share of criticism; and yet, by contemporary standards of competition, it would seem that the corporation was fairly adjudged a monopoly. Through the testimony of H. H. Rogers, an executive of the company, the Hepburn Committee in 1879 was able to establish the fact that 90 to 95 per cent of all the refiners in the country acted in harmony with Standard Oil.[21] In 1886, the monopolistic proclivities of the oil trust were attested to by the Cullom Committee:

> It is well understood in commercial circles that the Standard Oil Company brooks no competition; that its settled policy and firm determination is to crush out all who may be rash enough to enter the field against it; that it hesitates at nothing in the accomplishment of this purpose, in which it has been remarkably successful, and that it fitly represents the acme and perfection of corporate greed in its fullest development.[22]

Similar convictions were expressed by a New York senate committee before which Rockefeller and other executives testified in 1888.[23] Four years later, in 1892, the Supreme Court of Ohio declared that the object of the Standard Oil Company was "to establish a virtual monopoly of the business of producing petroleum, and of manufacturing, refining and dealing in it and all its products, throughout the entire country, and by which it might not merely control the production, but the price, at its pleasure." [24]

These earlier findings were reaffirmed by new investigations undertaken at the beginning of the twentieth century. In 1902, the United States Industrial Commission reported that Standard, through its control of pipe lines, had been able practically to fix the price of crude oil; and in 1907, the commissioner of corporations supported and amplified this conclusion. While admitting that the company might fall short of an absolute monopoly, the commissioner pointed out that its intentions were nonetheless monopolistic: "There has been apparent throughout their operations a definite, persistent policy of exclusive domination of the petroleum industry." [25] In 1911, the United States Supreme Court confirmed this allegation, observing that "no disinterested mind" could survey the history of the Standard Oil combination from 1870 onward "without being irresistibly driven to the conclusion that the very genius for commercial development and organization . . . soon begot an intent and purpose . . . to drive others from the field and to exclude them from their right to trade and thus accomplish the mastery which was the end in view." [26]

Far from regarding the intricate system of business combination that he had developed as a monster to be curbed or destroyed, a big businessman such as Rockefeller looked proudly upon his creation as a marvel of beneficence, an extraordinary and distinctive expression of American genius. And Carnegie contended "not evil, but good" had come from the phenomenal development of the corporation; he and others pointed out that the world of his day obtained goods and commodities of excellent quality at prices which earlier generations would have considered incredibly cheap. Now, maintained Carnegie, the poor enjoyed what the richest could never before have afforded. Therefore, he said, "Objections to the foundations upon which society is based are not in order because the condition of the race is better with these than with any other which has been tried." [27]

In defending himself against the charge of subverting American values and institutions, the big businessman supported his actions as being entirely in keeping with the business requisites of the day.

Rather than engaging in a conscious conspiracy to undermine equal opportunity, he had sought only the immediate and practical rewards of successful enterprise, rationalizing his business conduct on the pragmatic level of profit and loss.

Instead of deliberately blocking free competition, big businessmen maintained that their actions were only natural responses to that immutable law. Charles E. Perkins, president of the Chicago, Burlington and Quincy Railroad Company, denied the deliberate misuses of power by the railroads in the matter of establishing rates. The truth was, said Perkins, that the price of railroad transportation, like all other prices, adjusted itself. Discriminatory practices were viewed as part of an inevitable conflict between buyer and seller and as a necessary result of competition.[28] Likewise, the payment of rebates and drawbacks was regarded as simply one method of meeting the market. In answer to the accusation that the railroads had made "important discriminations" in favor of Standard Oil, an executive of that company replied, "It may be frankly stated at the outset that the Standard Oil Company has at all times within the limits of fairness and with due regard for the law sought to secure the most advantageous freight rates and routes possible." [29] Rockefeller went on record as saying that although Standard had received rebates from the railroads prior to 1880, the reason was that it was simply the railroads' way of doing business. Each shipper made the best bargain he could, hoping to outdo his competitor. Furthermore, said Rockefeller, this traffic was more profitable to the railroads than to the Standard Oil Company. He claimed that whatever advantage the oil company gained in its constant efforts to reduce freight rates was passed on in lower costs to the consumer. Just as his company later justified certain alleged misdemeanors as being typical of the sharp practices prevailing in the oil fields in the early days, so Rockefeller exonerated the whole system of rebates and drawbacks on the grounds that everybody was doing it, concluding cynically that those who objected on principle did so only because they were not benefiting from it.[30]

Yet despite his public rationalizations, the big businessman's attitude toward competition was ambivalent. On the one hand he lauded it as economic theory, but on the other he sought to deny it by his practical actions. From the first viewpoint, there was no such thing as an absolute monopoly; there was always the threat of latent competition. Whenever a trust exacted too much, competitors would automatically appear, regardless of the perils that might threaten them.[31] Theoretically, competition as a natural law would survive the trusts. "It is here; we cannot evade it," declaimed Carnegie. "And while the law may be sometimes hard for the individual, it is best for the race, because it insures the survival of the fittest in every department." [32]

In practical matters, however, the big businessman conducted himself as if the law had long since become outmoded, if not extinct. Progressive opinion in the business world heralded the growing monopolistic trend as a sign of economic maturity. Increased concentration in capital and industry was defended not only as necessary but as inevitable.[33] Monopolistic practices in general were upheld in business circles on the grounds that they prevented disastrous competition and in the long run benefited, rather than plundered, the public by maintaining reasonable rates and prices.[34] "There seems to be a great readiness in the public mind to take alarm at these phenomena of growth, there might rather seem to be reason for public congratulation," announced Professor William Graham Sumner of Yale. "We want to be provided with things abundantly and cheaply; that means that we want increased economic power. All these enterprises are efforts to satisfy that want, and they promise to do it." [35] As did Sumner, so many big businessmen believed that, practically at least, the rise of the trust in industry and commerce had proved the superiority of combination over competition.

Though the claim was not always true, the business virtues of economy and efficiency were stated to be the chief advantages of the trust. Because the combination was spared the folly and wastefulness of unrestrained competition, there were alleged to be huge savings in cross freight, advertising, sales, and executive expenses. Similarly, the survival of only the most productive forms of business resulted in greater efficiency and cheapened production which in turn meant higher wages and lower prices.[36] In this respect, Standard Oil was represented as a model trust. According to its supporters, it had been formed to curb speculation, waste, and overproduction; and, as Standard took pains to inform stockholders, the company owed its success not to illegal or reprehensible methods but to efficient organization.[37]

In his account of the birth of America's first great trust, Rockefeller advanced a generalization common to big businessmen of his day—that combination arose in response to economic necessity. Like all such generalizations, it was accurate up to a point, but was not universally applicable. Nevertheless, Rockefeller's description of the founding of Standard Oil is an interesting description of the genesis of monopoly from the big businessman's viewpoint. In the beginning, Rockefeller related, because refining crude petroleum was a simple and easy process and because at first the profits were very large, all sorts of people went into it—"the butcher, the baker, and the candlestick maker began to refine oil." And it was only a short time before the market was glutted and the price fell until the trade was threatened with ruin. At that moment, said Rockefeller, "It seemed absolutely necessary to extend the market for oil . . . and also greatly improve the processes of refining so that oil could be made and sold cheaply, yet with a profit." So, Rockefeller concluded with easy logic, "We proceeded to buy the largest and best refining concerns and centralize the administration of them with a view to securing greater economy and efficiency." [38] Though the birth pangs of Standard Oil obviously have been softened and somewhat simplified in the telling, it was on essentially this same basis that Carnegie explained the genesis of trusts in manufactured articles.[39]

Clearly the operative point of view that consolidation of capital and industry was indispensable to the successful execution of the tasks which had devolved upon modern business was the one embraced by big businessmen. In principle most of them agreed with the blunt statement of America's leading financier: "I like a little competition," J. P. Morgan was quoted as saying, "but I like combination better." [40] To the big businessman the choice was not between competition and monopoly, but between fighting to secure a monopoly by driving out competition in a bitter, destructive war and trying to obtain price control through industry-wide agreement.

Many, nevertheless, still paid lip service to the abstraction, though most had already rejected competition in practice. That this ideological discrepancy widely prevailed in the business community has been pointed out by Edward Kirkland: "Obviously there was an awkward contradiction between the belief in competition and the fact of consolidation, between natural laws which men could no more direct than 'they could make water run up hill' and the willed alterations in business organization brought about by trust and holding company, between law as immutable and law as growth and evolution." [41]

This glaring incongruity between business behavior and business theory ridiculed the notion that such economic generalizations as free competition were natural "laws," timeless and placeless, and entitled to sanctity. Rather than a competent expression of fact, the hedonistic theory of a perfect competitive system had turned out to be simply an expedient of abstract reasoning.

What in earlier and more halcyon days had been attributed to the benign operation of the law of competition had been, in most instances, an absence of competition. Before the Civil War, competition was virtually dormant in many parts of the United States largely because of intervening geographical factors, and where it did exist, it usually operated on a local rather than a national scale, cushioning a large portion of the economy from the hardships of rigorous competition. The limitation of the nation's transportation system, for example, often allowed local businessmen a certain amount of monopoly power; and, as Hans Thorelli has pointed out, backward communications, particularly a lack of reliable market information, also had a similar effect.[42] The trouble in many localities was that there was not always enough competition. These imperfections of competition in the ante-bellum period, however, tended to be eliminated by tremendous postwar advances in transportation and communication. Business rivalry also was intensified by the application of new technology to industry and nationalized by the substitution of the big interstate corporation for smaller local individual and partnership enterprises. The immediate outcome was competition with a vengeance and the inauguration of a species of commercial warfare of a magnitude and violence unheralded in economic history. In the long run, the brutal realities of this cutthroat struggle turned out to be unpalatable to the public and big businessmen alike, but while the latter sought to shield themselves by erecting monopolistic barriers, the American people continued to extol the virtues of free competition and to look back fancifully toward an earlier, more ideal state of economic affairs which, if anything, had been distinguished by a notable lack of competition.

That faith in the mythical virtues of competition prevailed widely during most of this period there can be no doubt. The majority of the American people took it for granted that competition was the normal way of life in business.[43] Henry Demarest Lloyd, an outstanding critic of big business, found it highly paradoxical that the American people who were so inalterably opposed to anarchy in politics should have led in advocating it in business; and what was worse in his opinion was that Americans had accepted industrial anarchy as their ideal of economic conduct.[44] Free competition was the shibboleth of practically all reform movements except the Socialists. It spurred the Grange, motivated the Single-Taxers and the Populists, and dominated the economic thought of the Progressives. Most of them desired or, more importantly, thought they desired, free competition. On this matter there existed no clear partisan line. Members of Congress proclaimed "the norm of a free competition too self-evident to be debated, too obvious to be asserted." [45]

The belief in competition was essentially an assertion of economic egalitarianism which took its stand midway between the Gospel of Wealth and the Social Gospel, adopting neither the doctrine of stewardship by the chosen few nor the sweeping substitution of cooperation for competition.[46] In origin, it was a subtle interweaving of the Anglo-Saxon belief that the common law, as well as natural law, always favored competition over monopoly and native American opposition to privilege.[47] Some of the basic materials in this complex were clearly derived from classical economic theory. The economists whose works were most widely read in the United States in the nineteenth century were Adam Smith, John Stuart Mill, and David Ricardo, and their laissez faire attitude toward monopoly dominated the teaching of economics in this country. "All our education and our habit of mind make us believe in competition," said the president of Yale. "We have been taught to regard it as a natural if not a necessary condition of all healthful business life. We look with satisfaction on whatever favors it, and with distrust on whatever hinders it." [48] The Darwinian theory of biological evolution was also generally interpreted as supporting popular notions about competition and individual initiative, although the accord between classical economics and evolutionism was more apparent than real.[49] Without doubt this ingrained habit of economic reasoning retarded public understanding of the new financial and industrial order, but, regardless, it was the belief that proved more important than its actual relevance; for it was sentiment, not fact, that prompted American action against big business.[50]

On the question whether the corporation had to be made to conform to American institutions and principles, or those institutions and principles had to be changed to accommodate the corporation, the American people almost unanimously declared for the first. If economic despotism was the outcome of unchecked corporate growth, then the corporate monster must be brought under control. For most, the way out was the way back. The American economy must be restored to a former golden time of competitive capitalism when the older individualistic values held sway, and the common man was free from the monopolistic pressures of the behemoth corporation.

The way backward, however, was not to be all the way. Completely breaking the trusts was rejected by the more realistic who urged instead that the trusts be permitted but regulated. Somewhat paradoxically, they proposed to liberate competition by imposing new restrictions in the name of freedom, suggesting thereby that they were not too sure that unrestrained competition would prove to be the economic panacea they sought. Practically, however, they justified the theoretical incongruity of their stand on the moral grounds that such restrictions were to be imposed only to prevent *unfair* competition. Apparently it never seriously occurred to them that to acknowledge the defective working of natural law against the forces of corporate immorality was, in reality, an ingenuous admission that the sacrosanct principle of competition was in the long run invalid. Wilfully blind to the logical inconsistencies of their position, the majority clamored for government regulation in the interests of equal opportunity, agreeing almost to a man with the stern dictum: "We must either regulate . . . or destroy." [51]

Responding to popular demand, Congress in 1890 passed the
Sherman Act "to protect trade and commerce against unlawful restraints and monopolies," thus converting an economic myth into
public policy. According to the ideology behind this law, there
existed a direct cause and effect relationship between competition
and monopoly. If the monopolistic obstacles in business were removed, the trend would immediately reverse itself, and full and free
competition would automatically reinstate itself. Despite the stark
realities of the growing trust and combination movement of the late
1880's, it was the public's overwhelming confidence in the efficacy
of this self-regulating mechanism that set the tone of all subsequent
federal action, whether conceived in terms of regulation or trust-
busting.[52] Facts, however, proved otherwise. The Sherman Act,
even when bolstered by later legislation, failed utterly to halt the
combination movement or reverse its trend, making evident the in-
eptitude of any legislation that regards competition as a self-per-
petuating and natural guarantor of economic justice rather than an
intellectual hypothesis without institutional support.

Instead of arresting monopoly as intended, the principal effect
of legalizing the myth of competition was to encourage the growth
of large combinations by deflecting the attack upon them into
purely ideological channels. Since 1890, federal antitrust laws have
stood as a symbol of the American democratic belief that "the only
proper type of society is composed of unorganized competitive
individuals," and all attempts to curb big business by government
action have represented nothing more than a ritual clash between
an anachronistic ideal and a modern need. "In this atmosphere,"
wrote Thurman Arnold, "the antitrust laws were the answer of a
society which unconsciously felt the need of great organizations,
and at the same time had to deny them a place in the moral and
logical ideology of the social structure." [53]

Though seemingly the corporation had been made to conform
to American institutions and principles by means of antitrust laws,
in actuality those institutions and principles had been changed to
accommodate the giant corporation. By declaring the corporation
to be an individual like any other and to have natural rights of life,
liberty, and property, the Supreme Court in 1886 had seriously in-

validated that basic concept of American society, the free individual.[54] Although this doctrine could be logically applied only to the individual as proprietor, partner, or even operating owner of a small company, the jurists ignored the intrinsic conflict between the individualistic myth and the corporate reality, thus evoking the strained future efforts of the Supreme Court to dress "huge corporations in the clothes of simple farmers and merchants." [55] In establishing the legal fiction that the large corporation was a person before the law and therefore entitled to the rights and privileges of a citizen, the court not only undermined the ideal of the morally responsible individual by extending the individualistic ethic to the amoral impersonality of the modern corporation, but in the long run subordinated that ideal to the right of property. For to accord a legal robot equal rights with a living person in the holding and protection of property under the Constitution was to exalt corporate property above the individual person and to pervert the traditional faith in individualism into a juridical sophism. And as the course of American legal history from 1886 to the 1930's amply discloses, such was the ultimate effect of the personification of the corporation.

Thus, in condemning the trusts as "dangerous to Republican institutions" and in branding corporate leaders as Robber Barons "opposed to free institutions and free commerce between the states as were the feudal barons of the middle ages," aroused Americans of the Gilded Age had clearly seized upon the major issue.[56] Whether they thoroughly understood or not, they had somehow recognized that American society with its individualistic traditions was engaged in a life-and-death struggle with the organized forces of dissolution. The business and industrial concentration once welcomed as implementing the promise of America had become a juggernaut threatening the very foundations of the nation. There was more individual power than ever, but those who wielded it were few and formidable. "These modern potentates" were scathingly denounced by Charles Francis Adams, Jr., great grandson of President John Adams, for the autocratic misuse of that power in complete defiance of both government and individuals. Writing in 1871, he foresaw ominous developments for the future:

The system of corporate life and corporate power, as applied
to industrial development, is yet in its infancy. . . . It is a
new power, for which our language contains no name. We
know what aristocracy, autocracy, democracy are; but we
have no word to express government by monied corporations.
. . . It remains to be seen what the next phase in this process of
gradual development will be. History never quite repeats itself, and . . . the old familiar enemies may even now con-
front us, though arrayed in such a modern garb that no sus-
picion is excited. . . . As the Erie ring represents the combination of the corporation and the hired proletariat of a great
city; as Vanderbilt embodies the autocratic power of Caesarism introduced into corporate life, and as neither alone can
obtain complete control of the government of the State, it,
perhaps, only remains for the coming man to carry the combination of elements one step in advance, and put Caesarism
at once in control of the corporation and of the proletariat, to
bring our vaunted institutions within the rule of all historic
precedent.[57]

Yet the public already sensed that something had gone wrong
with American institutions and values. Instinctively, with less understanding than Adams, they felt that somewhere, somehow, the
old rules had been broken. Behind their growing animosity to the
big businessman was the feeling that in some way he was cheating
his countrymen, and the belief was becoming fairly common that
the attainment of extreme wealth was incompatible with honesty.
"The great cities," Walt Whitman wrote in 1871, "reek with respectable as much as non-respectable robbery and scoundrelism." [58]
There were no doubt moral men of wealth, but in the Gilded Age
many Americans were increasingly inclined to agree with Thomas
A. Bland who in *How to Grow Rich* suggested, "In all history,
ancient and modern, the examples of men of honest lives and generous hearts who have become rich . . . is so rare as to be exceedingly exceptional, and even these have invariably profited largely
. . . by the labor of others." [59]
Very revealing in this regard was the portrayal of the big businessman in contemporary fiction. It was to be expected that the

socialist writers would depict him as a "criminal of greed" or an "economic monster" who with other "business animals" preyed upon the life of the nation. Oddly enough, however, in an age when the corporation made unprecedented achievements in production and organization to the enrichment of countless Americans, when big business was the acknowledged power in national affairs, when monetary success was widely favored as a legitimate goal, scarcely a single major novelist of the period presented the big businessman as a hero or even in a favorable or flattering light. Except for a very few hack writers of the Horatio Alger stamp, the business or industrial leader was consistently portrayed as powerful and capable, but invariably as an enemy of American society.[60] To a limited extent this may have reflected the bias of the aesthetic or creative temperament against the pragmatic money-maker, but the big businessman was in disfavor with a much larger section of American society than a mere handful of literary cranks and social theorists. Obviously there must have been some reason for this enmity.

In the popular mind, the vices of lying and stealing were legendarily associated with Wall Street. The big businessmen who dominated "the street" were regarded by some as the ethical counterparts of the pirate and buccaneer. By the simple devices of "stockwatering" or the issuance of fictitious securities not backed by capital assets, big businessmen were generally believed to have stolen millions of dollars from the American people. In characterizing this type of fraudulent stock issue, it was alleged: "Magnificent bubbles were blown into prismatic and profitable radiance with nothing more substantial than borrowed phials of oil and deeds of property, whose only value consisted in the durable nature of the parchment and the abundant stamps wherewith they were adorned." [61] Among the more jaundiced, it became something of a habit to speak of the men of Wall Street as though they had barely skirted prison bars. "If the details of the great reorganization and trustification deals put through since 1885 could be laid bare," contended Thomas W. Lawson, a financier turned critic, "eight out of ten of our most successful stock-jobbing financiers would be in a fair way to get into State or federal prisons." [62]

The truth was that the iniquity of Wall Street was not merely legendary, but had firm basis in fact. Though not all speculators were swindlers nor all speculation gambling, only a small number of the stock exchange transactions during this period could be termed unquestionably of an investment character. The vast majority were virtually gambling.[63] Many corporations, although offering huge blocks of stock to the public, issued only the vaguest and most ambiguous summary of assets and liabilities. While this was not iniquitous in itself, such secrecy too often cloaked fraud. Such business conduct certainly was not calculated to give the lie to Henry Demarest Lloyd's embittered charge, "Wall Street robs us, waters and capitalizes the plunder, and sells back to us at high prices what it took from us for nothing, and then we fondle the quotations as evidence of our wonderful prosperity." [64]

The men at the top who had used the corporate device to make millions did not see it this way at all. They justified their millions on the ground that they had fairly earned it.[65] Cornelius Vanderbilt at the age of eighty-one boasted that he had made a million dollars for every year of his life, but added that it had been worth "three times that to the people of the United States." [66] Apparently some others shared his belief, for in his book *The Railroad and the Farmer*, Edward Atkinson made practically the same statement, asserting that the gigantic fortune of the older Vanderbilt was but a small fraction of what the country gained from the development of the railway system under his genius.[67] The Reverend Julian M. Sturtevant of Illinois College also envisioned the Vanderbilts and Astors of the world as "laborers of gigantic strength, and they must have their reward and compensation for the use of their capital." [68] Carnegie, a multimillionaire himself, maintained that great riches were no crime, insisting, "Under our present conditions the millionaire who toils on is the cheapest article which the community secures at the price it pays for him, namely, his shelter, clothing, and food." [69]

Most Americans, however, did not so readily accept the big businessman's evaluation of himself. Though some recognized that the big businessman in pursuing private ends had served national prosperity, the majority felt that he had taken extravagant profits entirely out of proportion to the economic services he had rendered. Rockefeller's millions were thought to be typical of the fortunes made by the Robber Barons, representing "the relentless, aggressive, irresistible seizure of a particular opportunity, the magnitude of which . . . was due simply to the magnitude of the country and the immensity of the stream of its prosperous industrial life." [70] The feeling was general that the great fortunes of all the railroad magnates, Vanderbilt, Gould, Harriman, Stanford, and the rest, of Carnegie, Morgan, and other big businessmen owed their vastness not so much to the remarkable personal qualities of the men involved as to special privilege which had enabled them to turn the abundant natural resources and all the multitudinous advantages offered by a growing nation into a private preserve for their own profit.

The public at large was not clearly aware of it, but the chief instrument of special privilege was the corporation. Though public franchises and political favoritism played a large part in the aggrandizement of the Robber Barons, in the money-making world of late nineteenth-century America special privilege invariably meant corporate privilege. It was the corporation that enabled Vanderbilt to unify his railroads while making large speculative profits on the side, and it was the same device which made it possible for men like Rockefeller to create and combine private enterprises embodying new technological and financial techniques while diverting enormous profits to themselves. The corporation may have been the constructive power behind the building of the cross-country railroads, but it was also the destructive instrument used by Jay Gould, Tom Scott, Collis P. Huntington and others to convert them into quick money-making machines with no regard for their obligations as public carriers. [71]

If corporate power was a dominant factor in the climb of these big businessmen to riches and notoriety, the problem remains of establishing the relationship of these individuals to the corporation. Judging by their business conduct, either they were not fully cognizant of the tremendous power placed in their hands by the corporation with single men controlling "thousands of men, tens of millions of revenue, and hundreds of millions of capital"; or they chose wilfully to exert this prodigious force for their own private benefit regardless of the consequence to the nation or its ideals. Unhappily most of those labeled Robber Baron by their contemporaries fell into the latter category. [72] Cornelius Vanderbilt, for example, held the law in contempt and, except where his own interests were involved, had little regard for the consequences of his actions, manipulating and remorselessly watering every corporate property he got his hands upon. One year after he took over the New York Central railroad, he increased the capitalization by $23,000,000, almost every cent of which represented inside profits for himself and friends. When admonished that some of his transactions were forbidden by law, he supposedly roared, "Law! What do I care about the law? Hain't I got the power?" [73] That this was clearly his point of view was confirmed by his testimony before the committee on railroads of the New York State Assembly in 1869.[74] But Vanderbilt's methods were in no way exceptional. Practically all of the biggest businessmen of the time made their millions in similar fashion. Of twenty-four who because of notoriety and conspicuous power might be regarded as "typical" Robber Barons, all to a greater or lesser degree combined the role of promoter with that of entrepreneur. Stock manipulation along with corporate consolidation was probably the easiest way to wealth that ever existed in the United States, and the exuberance with which the promoters of the Gilded Age threw themselves into it proved that they were well aware of its golden possibilities.

As a consequence of these reckless corporate maneuverings, however, public opinion turned against the big businessman. While from a corporate point of view the conduct of the money-makers was often legal although ethically dubious, the American public did not see it this way, and they often felt cheated. Puzzled and disenchanted by the way things had turned out, the American people not only questioned the way every millionaire got his money, but were quite ready to believe that behind every great fortune there was a crime. While the exact nature of the crime, its legality or illegality, escaped them, they knew when they had been robbed, and the classic statement of this feeling of outrage was written into the Populist platform of 1892: "The fruits of the toil of millions are boldly stolen to build up colossal fortunes for a few, unprecedented in the history of mankind; and the possessors of these, in turn, despise the Republic and endanger liberty." [75]

Inchoate as were these charges, they were nonetheless accurate. The wealth created by millions was being selfishly appropriated by a few, and the Robber Barons by their irresponsible use of the corporation, essentially a supralegal abstraction above the traditional laws of the land, were undermining American institutions and individualistic values by rendering them impotent in face of their hot pursuit of wealth. If big businessmen like John D. Rockefeller were attacked as Robber Barons, it was because they were correctly identified as destroyers, the insurgent vanguard of the corporate revolution.

3

The Worker's Search for Power
Labor in the Gilded Age
HERBERT G. GUTMAN

U_{NTIL} very recent times, the worker has never seemed quite so glamorous or important as his counterpart, the entrepreneur. This is especially true of the Gilded Age, where attention focuses more readily and with greater delight upon Jim Fisk or Commodore Vanderbilt or John D. Rockefeller than on the men whose labor built their fortunes to dizzying heights. Furthermore, those studies devoted to labor in this period have devoted too much attention to too little. Excessive interest in the Haymarket riot, the "Molly Maguires," the great strikes of 1877, the Homestead lockout, the Pullman strike, and close attention to the violence and disorder attending them has obscured the deeper and more important currents of which these things were only symptoms. Close attention has also focused on the small craft unions, the Knights of Labor, and the early Socialists, thus excluding the great mass of workers who belonged to none of these groups, and creating an uneven picture of labor in the Gilded Age.[1] Surely it is time to broaden the approach into a study of labor in the society of the time as a whole.

Labor history in the Gilded Age had little to do with those matters traditionally and excessively emphasized by scholars. Too few workers belonged to trade unions to make them that important; it is that simple. There is a fundamental distinction between the wage-earners as a social class and the small minority of the working population that belonged to labor organizations. The full story of the wage-earner in that era is much more than the tale of struggling craft unions and the exhortations of committed trade-unionists and assorted reformers and radicals. The dramatic events that rise up out of that generation's labor history mask significant underlying developments. Finally, the national perspective emphasized by so many labor historians often blurs and misrepresents those issues important to large segments of the post-bellum working population and to other economic and social groups who had contact with the wage-earner.[2] Most of the available literature about labor in the Gilded Age is excessively thin and suffers from serious and fundamental deficiencies. There are huge gaps in our knowledge of the entire period.[3] Little of the secondary literature is concerned with the workers themselves, their communities, and the day-to-day occurrences that shaped their outlook. The narrow institutional development of trade unions has been emphasized more than the way the social and economic structure and the ideology of a rapidly industrializing society affected workers and employers. Excessive concern with craft workers has meant the serious neglect of the impact of a new way of life, industrial capitalism, upon large segments of the population.

A rather stereotyped conception of labor and of industrial relations in the Gilded Age has gained widespread credence. Final and conclusive generalizations about labor abound. A labor economist describes industrial conflict in the 1870's in an authoritative fashion:

> During the depression from 1873 to 1879, employers sought to eliminate trade unions by a *systematic* policy of lock outs, blacklists, labor espionage, and legal prosecution. The *widespread* use of blacklists and Pinkerton labor spies caused labor to organize *more or less* secretly, and *undoubtedly* helped bring on the violence that *characterized* labor strife during this period. [Emphasis added.] [4]

A labor historian asserts, "Employers *everywhere* seemed determined to rid themselves of 'restrictions upon free enterprise' by smashing unions." [5] The "*typical* [labor] organization during the seventies," writes another scholar, "was secret for protection against intrusion by outsiders." [6] Such seemingly final judgments are very questionable. How *systematic* were lockouts, blacklists, and legal prosecutions? How *widespread* was the use of labor spies and private detectives? Was the secret union the *typical* form of labor organization? Did violence *characterize* industrial relations?

It is widely believed that the industrialist exercised a great deal of power and had almost unlimited freedom of choice when dealing with his workers after the Civil War. Part of this belief reflects the weakness or absence of trade unions. Another justification for this interpretation, however, is somewhat more shaky. It is the assumption that industrialism generated new kinds of economic power which, in turn, *immediately* affected the social structure and the ideology of that time. The supposition that "interests" rapidly reshaped "ideas" is entirely too simple and therefore misleading. "The social pyramid," Joseph Schumpeter pointed out, "is never made of a single substance, is never seamless." There is no single *Zeitgeist*, except in the sense of a construct. The economic interpretation of history "would at once become untenable and unrealistic . . . if its formulation failed to consider that the manner in which production shapes social life is essentially influenced by the fact that human protagonists have always been shaped by past situations." [7] Too often, the study of industrial development and industrial relations in the Gilded Age has neglected these pertinent strictures.

Careful study of a number of small industrial communities in this era suggests that the relationships between "interest" and "ideology" was very complex and subtle. In this period, industrial capitalism was relatively new as a total way of life and therefore was not fully institutionalized. Much of the history of industrialism at that time is the story of the painful process by which an old way of life was discarded for a new one. The central issue was the rejection or modification of an old set of "rules" and "commands" which no longer fit the new industrial context. Since so much was new, traditional stereotypes about the popular sanctioning of the rules and values of industrial society either demand severe qualification or entirely fall by the wayside. Among questionable commonly held generalizations are those that insist that the worker was isolated from the rest of society; that the employer had an easy time and a relatively free hand in imposing the new disciplines; that the spirit of the times, the ethic of the Gilded Age, worked to the advantage of the owner of industrial property; that workers found little if any sympathy from nonworkers; that the quest for wealth obliterated nonpecuniary values; and that industrialists swept aside countless obstacles with great ease. The usual picture of these years portrays the absolute power of the employer over his workers and emphasizes his ability to manipulate a sympathetic public opinion as well as various political, legal, and social institutions to his advantage.

The story is not so simple, however, as intensive examination of numerous strikes and lockouts shows. The new way of life was more popular and more quickly sanctioned in large cities than in small towns dominated by one or two industries. Put another way, the social environment in the large American city after the Civil War was more often hostile toward workers than was that in the smaller industrial towns. Employers in large cities had more freedom of choice than their counterparts in small towns where local conditions of one kind or another often hampered the employer's decision-making power. The ideology of many nonworkers in these small towns was not entirely hospitable toward industrial, as opposed to traditional, business enterprise. Strikes and lockouts in large cities seldom lasted as long as similar disputes outside of these urban centers. In the large city, there was almost no sympathy for the city worker from the middle and upper classes. At the same time, a good deal of pro-labor and anti-industrial sentiment (the two are not necessarily the same) flowed from similar occupational groups in the small towns. It is a commonplace that the small-town employer of factory labor often reached out of his local environment for aid of one kind or another in solving industrial disputes, but insufficient attention has been given to those elements in the contemporary social structure and ideology which shaped such decisions.

Though the direct economic relationships in large cities and in small towns and outlying industrial regions were essentially similar, the social structure in each of these areas was profoundly different. Here is the crucial clue to these distinct patterns of thought and behavior. Private enterprise was central to the economy of the small industrial town as well as to that of the large metropolitan city, but it functioned in a different social environment. The social structure and ideology of a given time are not derived only from economic institutions.[8] In the Gilded Age, a time of rapid economic and social transformation and a time when industrial capitalism was still young and relatively new to the United States, parts of an ideology that were alien to the new industrialism retained a powerful hold on the minds of many who lived outside the large cities.

Men and their thoughts were different in the large cities. "The modern town," John Hobson wrote of the large nineteenth-century cities, "is a result of the desire to produce and distribute most economically the largest aggregate of material goods: economy of work, not convenience of life, is the object." In such an environment, "anti-social feelings" were exhibited "at every point by the competition of workers with one another, the antagonism between employers and employed, between sellers and buyers, factory and factory, shop and shop." [9] Persons dealt with each other less as human beings and more as "things." The *Chicago Times*, for example, argued that "political economy" was "in reality the autocrat of the age" and occupied "the position once held by the Caesars and the Popes." [10] According to the *New York Times*, the "antagonistic . . . position between employers and the employed on the subject of work and wages" was "unavoidable. . . . The object of trade is to get as much as you may and give as little as you can." [11] The *Chicago Tribune* celebrated the coming of the centennial in 1876 by observing, "Suddenly acquired wealth, decked in all the colors of the rainbow, flaunts its robe before the eyes of Labor, and laughs with contempt at honest poverty." The country, "great in all the material powers of a vast empire," was entering "upon the second century weak and poor in social morality as compared with one hundred years ago." [12]

More than economic considerations shaped the status of the working population in large cities after the Civil War, for the social structure there unavoidably widened the distance between the various social and economic classes. Home and job often were far apart. A man's fellow workers often differed from his friends and neighbors. Face-to-face relationships became less meaningful as the city grew larger and as production became more diverse and more specialized. "It has always been difficult for well-to-do people of the upper and middle classes," wrote Samuel Lane Loomis, a Protestant minister, in the 1880's, "to sympathize and to understand the needs of their poorer neighbors." The large city, both impersonal and confining, made it even harder. Loomis was convinced that "a great and growing gulf" lay "between the working-class and those above them." [13] A Massachusetts clergyman saw a similar void between the social classes and complained: "I once knew a wealthy manufacturer who personally visited and looked after the comforts of his invalid operatives. I know of no such case now." [14] All in all, the fabric of human relationships was cloaked in a kind of shadowed anonymity that became more and more characteristic of urban life.[15]

Social contact was more direct in the smaller post-Civil War industrial towns and regions. The *Cooper's New Monthly*, a reform trade-union journal, insisted that while "money" was the "sole measure of gentility and respectability" in large cities "a more democratic feeling" prevailed in small towns.[16] "The most happy and contented workingmen in the country," wrote the *Iron Molder's Journal*, "are those residing in small towns and villages. . . . We want more towns and villages and less cities." [17] Except for certain parts of New England the mid-Atlantic states, the post-Civil War industrial towns and regions were relatively new to that kind of enterprise. The men and women who lived and worked in these areas in the Gilded Age usually had known another way of life and doggedly contrasted the present with the past. They grasped the realities of the new industrialism for a simple reason: the nineteenth-century notion of enterprise came quickly to these regions after the Civil War, but the social distance between the various economic classes that characterized the large city came much more slowly and hardly paralleled industrial developments. In the midst of the new industrial enterprise with its new set of commands, therefore, men often clung to an older ("agrarian") set of values. They often judged the economic and social behavior of local industrialists by these older and more humane values. The social structure of the large city differed from that of the small industrial town because of the more direct human relationships among the residents of the smaller towns. Although many of these persons were not personally involved in the industrial process, they always felt its presence. Life may have been more difficult and less cosmopolitan in these small towns, but it was also less complicated. This life was not romantic, for it frequently meant company-owned houses and stores as well as conflicts between workers and employers over rights that were taken for granted in agricultural communities and large cities.[18] Yet, the nonurban industrial environment had in it a kind of compelling simplicity. Its inhabitants lived and worked together, and a certain sense of community threaded their everyday lives. Men knew each other well, and the anonymity that veiled so much of urban life was not nearly so severe. There was of course more than enough economic hardship and plain despair in these towns, but the impersonal social environment of the large city in the Gilded Age was almost entirely lacking.

The first year of the 1873 depression suggests sharply the differences between the large urban center and the small industrial town. There is no question about the severity of the economic crisis. Its consequences were felt throughout the entire industrial sector, and production, employment, and income fell sharply everywhere.[19] The dollar value of business failures in 1873 was greater than in any other single year between 1857 and 1893.[20] The deflation in the iron and steel industry was especially severe: 266 of the nation's 666 iron furnaces were out of blast by January 1, 1874, and more than 50 per cent of the rail mills were silent.[21] A New York philanthropic organization figured that 25 per cent of the city's workers, nearly 100,000 persons, were unemployed in the winter months of 1873–74.[22] "The simple fact is that a great many laboring men are out of work," wrote the *New York Graphic*. "It is not the fault of merchants and manufacturers that they refuse to employ four men when they can but one, and decline to pay four dollars for work which they can buy for two and a half."[23] Gloom and pessimism settled over the entire country, and the most optimistic predicted only that the panic would end in the late spring months of 1874.[24] James Swank, the secretary of the American Iron and Steel Association, found the country suffering "from a calamity which may be likened to a famine or a flood." "The nation," he sourly observed, "is to have a period of enforced rest from industrial development. Let the causes be what they may, the fact that we *are* resting is patent to all men." [25]

A number of serious labor difficulties occurred in small industrial towns and outlying industrial regions during the first year of the depression, revealing much about the social structure of these areas. Although each of these incidents had its own unique character, a common set of problems shaped all of them. The depression generated difficulties for employers everywhere. Demand fell away and industrialists necessarily cut production as well as costs in order to sell off accumulated inventory and retain a hold on shrinking markets. This general contraction caused harsh industrial conflict in many parts of the country. "No sooner does a depression in trade set in," observed David A. Harris, the conservative head of the Sons of Vulcan, a national craft union for puddlers and boilermen, "than all expressions of friendship to the toiler are forgotten." [26] The *New York Times* insisted that the depression would "bring wages down for all time," and it advised employers to dismiss workers who struck against wage reductions. This was not the time for the "insane imitations of the miserable class warfare and jealousy of Europe." [27] The *Chicago Times* found that strikers were "idiots" and "criminals," while its sister newspaper, the *Chicago Evening Journal*, said the economic crisis was not "an unmixed evil" because labor would finally learn "the folly and danger of trade organizations, strikes, and combinations . . . against capital." [28] *Iron Age* was similarly sanguine. "We are sorry for those who suffer," it explained, "but if the power of the trade unions for mischief is weakened . . . the country will have gained far more than it loses from the partial depression of industry." After employers withdrew "every concession" made to the unions and "forced wages down to the lowest rates, . . . simple workingmen" would learn they were misled by "demagogues and unprincipled agitators." Trade unions "crippled the productive power of capital" and retarded the operation of "beneficent natural laws of progress and development." [29] James Swank was somewhat more generous. Prices had fallen, and it was "neither right nor practicable for all the loss to be borne by the employers." "Some of it," he explained, "must be shared by the workingmen. . . . We must hereafter be contented with lower wages for our labor and be more thankful for the opportunity to labor at all." [30]

In cutting costs in 1873 and 1874, many employers faced difficult problems, but a central trouble emerged when they found that certain aspects of the social structure and ideology in small industrial towns hindered their freedom of action. It proved relatively easy for them to announce a wage cut or to refuse publicly to negotiate with a local trade union, but it often proved quite difficult to enforce such decisions easily and quickly. In instance after instance, and for reasons that varied from region to region, employers reached outside of their local environment to help assert their local authority.

Industrialists used various methods to strengthen their local positions with their workers. The state militia brought order to a town or region swept by industrial conflict. Troops were used in railroad strikes in Indiana, Ohio, and Pennsylvania; in a dispute involving iron heaters and rollers in Newport, Kentucky; in a strike of Colorado ore diggers; in two strikes of Illinois coal miners; and in a strike of Michigan ore workers.[31] At the same time, other employers aggravated racial and nationality problems among workers by introducing new ethnic groups in their towns as a way of ending strikes, forcing men to work under new contracts, and destroying local trade unions. Negroes were used in coal disputes.[32] Danish, Norwegian, and Swedish immigrants were brought into mines in Illinois, and into the Shenango Valley and the northern anthracite region of Pennsylvania. Germans went to coal mines in northern Ohio along with Italian workers. Some Italians also were used in western Pennsylvania as coal miners and in western and northern New York as railroad workers.[33] A number of employers imposed their authority in other ways. Regional not local blacklists were tried in the Illinois coal fields, on certain railroads, in the Ohio Valley iron towns, and in the iron mills of eastern Pennsylvania.[34] Mine operators in Pennsylvania's Shenango Valley and Tioga coal region used state laws that allowed them to evict discontented workers from company-owned houses in mid-winter.[35]

In good part, the social structure in these small towns and the ideology of many of their residents, who were neither workers nor employers, shaped the behavior of those employers who reached outside their local environments in order to win industrial disputes. The story is different for every town, but has certain similarities. The strikes and lockouts had little meaning in and of themselves, and it is of passing interest to learn whether the employers or the workers gained a victory. The incidents assume broader significance as they shed light on the distribution of power in these towns and on those important social and economic relationships which shaped the attitudes and actions of workers and employers.

One neglected aspect of the small industrial town after the

Civil War is its political structure. Because workers made up a large proportion of the electorate and often participated actively in local politics, they were able at times to influence local and regional affairs in a manner not open to wage-earners in the larger cities. There is no evidence in 1874 that workers held elected or appointed offices in large cities. In that year, nevertheless, the postmaster of Whistler, Alabama, was a member of the Iron Molder's International Union.[36] George Kinghorn, a leading trade-unionist in the southern Illinois coal fields, was postmaster of West Belleville, Illinois.[37] A local labor party swept an election in Evansville, Indiana.[38] Joliet, Illinois, had three workers on its city council.[39] A prominent official of the local union of iron heaters and rollers sat on the city council in Newport, Kentucky.[40] Coal and ore miners ran for the state legislature in Carthage, Missouri, in Clay County, Indiana, and in Belleville, Illinois.[41] The residents of Virginia City, a town famous to western mythology, sent the president of the local union of miners to the national Congress.[42] In other instances, town officials and other officeholders who were not wage-earners sympathized with the problems and difficulties of local workers or displayed an unusual degree of objectivity during local industrial disputes.

It was the same with many local newspapers in these towns, for they often stood apart from the industrial entrepreneur and subjected his behavior to searching criticisms. Editorials in these journals defended *local* workers and demanded redress for their grievances. Certain of these newspapers were entirely independent in their outlook, and others warmly endorsed local trade-union activities.

The small businessmen and shopkeepers, the lawyers and professional people, and the other nonindustrial members of the middle class were a small but vital element in these industrial towns. Unlike the urban middle class they had direct and everyday contact with the new industrialism and with the problems and the outlook of workers and employers. Many had risen from a lower station in life and intimately knew the meaning of hardship and toil. They could judge the troubles and complaints of both workers and employers by personal experience and by what happened around them and did not have to rely on secondary accounts. While they invariably accepted the concepts of private property and free entrepreneurship, their judgments about the *social* behavior of industrialists often drew upon noneconomic considerations and values. They saw no necessary contradiction between private enterprise and gain on the one hand, and decent, humane social relations between workers and employers on the other. In a number of industrial conflicts, segments of the local middle class sided with the workers in their communities. A Maryland weekly newspaper complained in 1876, "In the changes of the last thirty years not the least unfortunate is the separation of personal relations between employers and employees." [43] At the same time that most metropolitan newspapers sang paeans of joy for the industrial entrepreneur and the new way of life, the *Youngstown Miner and Manufacturer* thought it completely wrong that the "Vanderbilts, Stewarts, and Astors bear, in proportion to their resources, infinitely less of the burden incident to society than the poorest worker." [44] The *Ironton Register* defended dismissed iron strikers as "upright and esteemed . . . citizens" who had been sacrificed "to the cold demands on business." [45] The *Portsmouth Times* boasted, "We have very little of the codfish aristocracy, and industrious laborers are looked upon here with as much respect as any class of people." [46]

Detailed illustrations of the difficulties certain employers faced when they sought to enforce crucial economic decisions in small towns reveal a great deal about the social structure of these areas and the outlook of many residents. These illustrations also tell something of the obstacles industrialists often encountered in their efforts to deal with workers.

In 1873 when the depression called a temporary halt to the expansion of the Illinois mining industry, Braidwood, Illinois, was less than a dozen years old.[47] Coal mining and Braidwood had grown together, and by 1873, 6,000 persons lived in the town. Except for the supervisors and the small businessmen and shopkeepers, most of the residents were coal miners and their families. Braidwood had no "agricultural neighborhood to give it support" and "without its coal-shafts" it would have had "no reasonable apology for existing." The town had three coal companies, but the Chicago, Wilmington and Vermillion Coal Company was by far the largest, and its president, James Monroe Walker, also headed the Chicago,

Burlington, and Quincy Railroad. This firm operated five shafts and employed 900 men, more than half the resident miners. Most of the owners did not live in the town: Walker, for example, resided in Chicago. The miners were a mixed lot, and unlike most other small industrial towns in this era Braidwood had an ethnically diverse population. About half the miners came from Ireland. Another 25 per cent were English, Welsh, and Scotch. A smaller number were Swedes, Italians, and Germans, and still others came from France and Belgium and even from Poland and Russia. There were also native-born miners. "The town of Braidwood," a contemporary noted, "is . . . nearly akin to Babel as regards the confusion of tongues."

Although they came from diverse backgrounds, the miners were a surprisingly cohesive social community. A trade union started in 1872 was strong enough to extract a reasonable wage agreement from the three coal firms. A hostile observer complained that nearly all the voters were miners and that a majority of the aldermen and justices of the peace "are or have been miners."

The depression cut the demand for coal and created serious problems for the operators. By March, 1874, at least 25 per cent of the miners were unemployed, and the town was "dull beyond all precedent." In late May the operators, led by the Chicago, Wilmington, and Vermillion firm, cut the rate for digging coal from $1.25 to $1.10 a ton and reduced the price for "pushing" coal from the work wall to the shaft nearly in half. They announced that the mines would close on June 1 unless the men accepted the new contract for a full year. The miners' efforts at compromise and suggestions of arbitration were summarily rejected, and the mines closed. The general superintendent of the largest company displayed "a haughty indifference as to whether the mines 'run' or not" and would not listen to the miners' bitter complaints that they could not have received "worse treatment in the old country" and that the "Wilmington fellows" were "right up and down monopolists." Instead, the Chicago, Wilmington, and Vermillion company contacted private labor contracting agencies in Chicago and recruited a large number of unskilled laborers, most of whom were Scandinavian immigrants and were not miners. Three days after the strike began, 65 Chicago workers arrived. More came two weeks later, and from then on a small number arrived daily until the end of July when the number increased sharply. At the same time, anticipating trouble in putting the new men to work, the operators brought special armed Chicago Pinkerton police to the town.

Difficulties plagued the operators from the start. The miners realized they had to check the owners' strategy in order to gain a victory. As soon as new workers arrived, committees of miners explained the difficulty to them. "We ask the skilled miners not to work," the leader of the strikers explained. "As to green hands, we are glad to see them go to work for we know they are . . . a positive detriment to the company." All but three of the first 65 new workers agreed to return to Chicago, and since they lacked funds the miners and other local residents paid their rail fare and cheered them as they boarded a Chicago-bound train. By mid-July one shaft that usually employed 200 men had no more than ten workers. At the end of July, only 102 men worked in the mines, and not one of them was a resident miner. The disaffected miners also met the challenge of the Pinkerton men. The miners appointed a 72-man committee to prevent violence and to protect company property. The mayor and the sheriff swore in twelve of these men as special deputies, and, with one exception (when the wives of certain miners chased and struck Allan Pinkerton), the miners behaved in a quiet and orderly manner.

Time and again, Braidwood's tiny middle class—the businessmen, the storekeepers, and the public officials—strengthened the striking miners. According to one reporter, they "all back[ed] the miners." They denied complaints by the owners that the miners were irresponsible and violent. One citizen condemned the coal companies for creating "excitement so as to crush the miners" and declared that "public sympathy" was "entirely" with the workers. The *Chicago Tribune* reporter found that "Braidwood is with the strikers root and branch." The attitude of the local publicly elected officials, for example, is of great interest. The operators wanted Pinkerton and his men appointed "special deputies" and made "merchant police" with power to arrest persons trespassing on company properties, but the mayor and the sheriff turned them down and deputized the strikers. Mayor Goodrich forbade parading in the streets by the Pinkerton men, and the sheriff ordered them to surrender their rifles and muskets. The sheriff did not want "a lot of strangers dragooning a quiet town with deadly weapons in their hands," and he said he feared the miners "a good deal less than . . . the Chicago watchmen."

The operators faced other troubles. Local judges and police officials enforced the law more rigorously against them and their men than against the resident miners. In one instance, two new workers who got into a fight one Sunday were arrested for violating the Sabbath law and fined $50 and court costs. Unable to pay the fine, they were put to work on the town streets. One of them, jailed for hitting an elderly woman with a club, was fined $100 and court costs. A company watchman was arrested four times, twice for "insulting townspeople." Frustrated in these and other ways by the miners and the townspeople, the operators finally turned for help to the state government, and E. L. Higgins, the adjutant general and head of the state militia, went to Braidwood to see if troops were needed. Higgins openly supported the mine owners. He tried to prevent union men from talking with new workers, and although he asked the mayor to meet him in the office of the Chicago, Wilmington, and Vermillion firm, he "never went to see the officers of the city . . . to gain an unprejudiced account of the strike." "If this is what the military forces and officers are kept for," one miner observed, "it is high time . . . such men [were] struck off the State Government payroll and placed where they belong." Mayor Goodrich reminded Higgins that neither the Braidwood nor the Will County authorities had asked for state interference. In a bitter letter to the *Chicago Times*, Goodrich wondered whether Higgins had come "in his official capacity or as an agent of the coal company," and firmly insisted that "the citizens of this city were not aware that martial law had been proclaimed or an embargo placed upon their speech."

Unable fully to exercise their authority in the town and worried about the possibility of losing the fall trade, the operators confessed their failure and surrendered to the strikers fourteen weeks after the conflict had started. The final agreement pleased the miners, and they were especially amused when the Chicago, Wilmington, and Vermillion company agreed to send all the new workers back to Chicago. A spokesman for the operators, however, bitterly assailed the Braidwood mayor and other public officials for their failure to understand the meaning of "peace, order, and freedom." Surely the operators had further cause for complaint in 1877 when Daniel McLaughlin, the president of the miners' union, was elected mayor of Braidwood, other miners were chosen aldermen, and one was chosen police magistrate.

Manufacturers in the small industrial iron towns of the Ohio Valley such as Ironton and Portsmouth, Ohio, and Newport and Covington, Kentucky, had troubles similar to those of the Braidwood coal operators in 1873 and 1874.[48] Several thousand men and fifteen iron mills were involved in a dispute over wages that lasted for several months. The mill owners who belonged to the Ohio Valley Iron Association cut the wages of skilled iron heaters and roller men 20 per cent on December 1, 1873. After the workers complained that the manufacturers were taking "undue advantage" of them "owing to the present financial trouble," their wages were cut another 10 per cent. The valley mill owners worked out a common policy; they decided to close all the mills for a month or so in December and then reopen them under the new scale. Hard times would bring them new workers.

Although the mill owners in large cities such as St. Louis, Indianapolis, and Cincinnati found it easy to bring in new workers from the outside, it was another story in the small towns. They could hire new hands in Pittsburgh, Philadelphia, and other eastern cities, but the social environment in Covington, Portsmouth, Newport, and Ironton made it difficult for them to hold on to these men. The locked-out workers found sympathy from other townspeople. In such an environment they were a relatively homogeneous group and made up a large part of the total population of the town. When workers agitated in small towns, paraded the streets, or engaged in one or another kind of collective activity, their behavior hardly went unnoticed.

The difficulties faced by the small-town iron manufacturers beset especially Alexander Swift, owner of the Swift Iron and Steel Works in Newport, Kentucky. Although his workers suffered from almost indescribable poverty after the factory closed, they would not surrender. When Swift reopened his mill, he had it guarded by armed "special policemen." Some of the new workers left the town after they learned of the conflict, and the "police" accompanied the rest to and from their work. The old workers made Newport uncomfortable for the new hands. There was no violence at first, but many strikers and their wives, especially the English and Welsh workers, gathered near the mill and in the streets where they howled at the "black sheep" as they went to and from work. The Newport workers exerted pressure on them in "the hundred ways peculiar to workingmen's demonstrations." Swift was embittered, for at the end of January only a few men worked in his mill.

Swift was not alone in his troubles; mill owners in Covington, Ironton, and Portsmouth were in similar difficulty. Early in February, therefore, the Ohio Valley Iron Association announced that unless the men returned to work on or before February 20 they would lose their jobs and never again be hired in the valley iron mills. When most of the workers refused to return, they were fired. New workers were quickly brought to the towns, and Swift demanded special police protection for them from the Newport City Council, but it assigned only regular police to guard them. Crowds jeered the new men, and there were several fights. A large number of new workers again left Newport. Swift appealed to the police to ban street demonstrations by the workers and their families, but his plea was rejected. "We never went any further with those fellows," a striker explained, "than calling them 'black sheep' and 'little lambs.' . . . When they'd be going to work in the morning with the policemen on each side of them, we'd cry 'Ba-a-a-a.' " Swift armed his new workers with pistols. When the strikers and their supporters gathered to jeer these men, one of the new workers shot wildly into the crowd and killed a young butcher's helper. The enraged crowd chased Swift's men out of the city, and Swift, after blaming the shooting on the failure of the Newport authorities to guard his men properly, closed the mill.

These events did not go unnoticed in the Ohio Valley. The *Portsmouth Times* leveled a barrage of criticism at Swift and the other manufacturers. It asked whether or not they had a "right" to circulate the names of strikers in the same manner as "the name of a thief is sent from one police station to another." Such action was "cowardly . . . intimidation," and the *Times* asked: "Does not continued and faithful service deserve better treatment at the hands of men whose fortunes have been made by these workmen they would brand with the mark of CAIN? . . . Is this to be the reward for men who have grown gray in the service of these velvet-lined aristocrats? . . . Out on such hypocrisy!" After the shooting in Newport, the *Times* turned on Swift and called him a "blood-letter." Violence was wrong, the *Times* admitted, "wrong in theory and practice," but it nevertheless advised the striking iron workers: "If the gathered up assassins from the slums and alleys of the corrupt cities of the East are brought here to do deeds of lawlessness and violence, the stronger the opposition at the beginning the sooner they will be taught that the city of Portsmouth has no need of them."

Immune from such criticism, Swift continued to try to break down the strength of the Newport workers. In the end he succeeded. He realized that the only way to weaken the strikers was to suppress their power of public demonstration and therefore urged the Newport mayor to enforce local ordinances against dangerous and "riotous" crowds, asked the Kentucky governor to send state militia, and even demanded federal troops. Although the mayor banned "all unusual and unnecessary assemblages" in the streets, Swift still asked for state troops, and on March 5, the Kentucky governor ordered twenty-five members of the Lexington division of the state militia to Newport. The arrival of the militia weakened the strikers and created a favorable environment for Swift and his plans. Street demonstrations were banned. The police were ordered to arrest "all persons using threatening or provoking language." When a number of unskilled strikers offered to return at the lower wage, Swift turned them away. He also rejected efforts by a member of the city council to effect a compromise with the old workers. A week after the troops arrived and three and a half months after the start of the lockout, Swift fully controlled the local situation. New men worked in his factory, and the strikers admitted defeat.

The use of troops, however, was bitterly condemned in the Ohio Valley. A reporter for the *Cincinnati Enquirer* found that the "general opinion" in Newport was that Swift's maneuver was "little else than a clever piece of acting intended to kindle public sentiment against the strikers and . . . gain the assistance of the law in breaking up a strike." A Newport judge assailed the Kentucky governor, and a local poet sang of the abuse of state power:

> Sing a song of sixpence
> Stomachs full of rye,
> Five-and-twenty volunteers,
> With fingers in one pie;
> When the pie is opened
> For money they will sing,
> Isn't that a pretty dish
> For the City Council Ring?

There was less drama in the other Ohio Valley iron towns than in Newport, but the manufacturers in Portsmouth, Ironton, and Covington faced similar trouble. The old workers persuaded many new hands to leave the region. "A few men who try to work," wrote an Ironton observer, "are 'bah-d' at from the cross streets as they go to and from the shops. To have a lot of boys follow one up with cries of 'bah, black sheep' is a torment few workmen can endure." When fourteen Philadelphia workers arrived in Ironton and learned of the troubles for the first time, they left the city. Strikers paid their return rail fare. In Portsmouth, the same happened, and the departing workers publicly declared, "A nobler, truer, better class of men never lived than the Portsmouth boys . . . standing out for their rights." Nonstrikers in these towns also acted contrary to the manufacturers' interests. Each week the *Portsmouth Times* attacked the mill owners. "We are not living under a monarchy," the *Times* insisted, and the "arbitrary actions" of the employers were not as "unalterable as the edicts of the Medes and Persians." A Covington justice of the peace illustrated something of the hostility felt toward the companies. Three strikers were arrested for molesting new hands, but he freed one of them and fined the other men a dollar each and court costs. A new worker, however, was fined twenty dollars for disorderly conduct and for carrying a deadly weapon. He also had to post a $500 bond as a guarantee that he would keep the peace.

In the end, except in Newport where Swift had successfully neutralized the power of the workers, a compromise wage settlement was finally worked out. Certain of the mills succeeded in bringing in new men, but some manufacturers withdrew the blacklist and rehired their striking workers. Commenting on the entire dispute, a friend of the Ohio Valley iron manufacturers bitterly complained: "Things of this sort make one ask whether we are really as free a people as we pretend to be." Convinced that the workers had too much power and that the manufacturers were not fully free entrepreneurs, this devotee of classical laissez faire doctrine sadly concluded: "If any individual cannot dispose of his labor when and at what price he pleases, he is living under a despotism, no matter what form the government assumes."

Although hardly any Negroes worked in coal mines before 1873, soon after the depression started mine operators in the Ohio Hocking Valley recruited hundreds of Negroes from border and southern cities. Some Negroes had been sparingly employed in certain Indiana and Ohio mines, but they attracted little attention. It was different in the Hocking Valley in 1874. A large number of white miners struck and showed an unusual degree of unanimity and staying power. They found support from members of the local middle classes, and the operators, unable to wear down the strikers, brought in Negroes. Although the miners were defeated, the problems they raised for their employers indicated much the same social environment as in Braidwood and in the Ohio Valley iron towns.

The railroad revolutionized the Hocking Valley economy after the Civil War, for it opened new markets for bituminous coal, and the years between 1869 and 1873 were a time of great prosperity and economic development. Production figures shot up spectacularly: in 1870, 105,000 tons left the valley and in 1873 just over one million tons were shipped. Two years later, more than 20 per cent of the coal mined in Ohio came from the Hocking Valley. Although entry costs were low, the ten largest firms in 1874 employed nearly two-thirds of the valley's miners.[49]

The miners fell into two social groupings. Those born in and near the valley had spent most of their lives in the mines and often held local positions of public trust and esteem. A Cincinnati reporter found that miners held "a good position in society . . . as a class" and filled "a fair number of municipal, church, and school offices." These men had watched the region develop and had seen their status depersonalized as they quickly became part of a much larger labor force dependent on the vicissitudes of a distant and uncontrollable market. They unavailingly complained when operators brought in many more miners than needed for full-time work. A perceptive observer found that many of the older miners "have worked in these mines since they were boys and feel they have an actual property right to their places." Most of the new men who flocked to the valley after 1869 came from distant areas, and a good number were from England, Wales, and Ireland. The rapid growth of the industry made it difficult to support trade unions in the valley.[50]

Economic crisis in 1873 suddenly punctured the prosperity of the entire region. At best, miners found only part-time employment, and cash wages were less common than usual, for working miners received mostly 90-day notes and store credit. The operators complained that labor costs were too high and made the selling price of coal in a competitive but depressed market prohibitive. Talk of wage cuts, however, turned the miners toward trade-unionism, and in December, 1873, they founded several branches of the newly established Miners' National Association. The operators responded by forming a region-wide trade association, and each of them posted a $5,000 bond as proof he would follow its directives. They also announced a sharp wage cut effective April 1, 1874, and entirely proscribed the new union. Prominent union leaders lost their jobs. One operator closed his supply store "for repairs," and another locked his men in a room and insisted that they sign the new wage agreement. But the union thrived. Only nine "regular" miners favored the new contract, and no more than twenty-five or thirty regulars refused to join the union. The union men agreed to the lower wage but refused to abandon their organization. The operators remained adamant and insisted that the "progress or decay" of the region hinged on the destruction of the new union—"a hydra too dangerous to be warmed at our hearth." A strike over the right of labor organization started on April 1.[51]

The strike brought trouble for the operators. Except for the *Logan Republican*, the weekly valley newspapers either supported the strikers or stood between them and the operators. The *Nelson-*

ville Miner time and again antagonized the powerful operators. The *Hocking Sentinel* and the *New Lexington Democratic Herald* defended the miners and criticized reporters from Columbus and Cincinnati who uniformly wrote in support of the operators. Unions were essential, insisted the *Athens Journal,* when capitalists made "extortionate" demands of their workers.[52]

The operators had other troubles. No more than thirty regular miners accepted the new contract on April 1 and only seventy men entered the mines that day. Local public officials declined to do the bidding of prominent operators. The New Straitsville police deputized strikers, and after Governor William Allen sent the state inspector of mines to investigate reported miner violence, county and town officials assured him there was no trouble and a committee of merchants and "other property owners" visited Allen "to give him the facts." New Straitsville town officials joined the miners to check the effort of operator W. B. McClung to bring in from Columbus "a posse" of nine special police armed with Colt revolvers and Spencer rifles. The miners felt it "unnecessary" for armed police to come to "their quiet town," and men, women, and children paraded the streets in protest. They made it uncomfortable for McClung's police, and he promised to close his mine and return the men to Columbus. But the mayor on the complaint of a miner issued a warrant for their arrest for entering the town armed, for "disorderly conduct," and for "disturbing the peace and quiet." Ordered to stand trial, the nine left town after McClung's superintendent posted their bond. "At the depot, there was a large crowd of miners, and one of their leaders wanted to give the Columbus party three cheers on their departure," but the much abused men "declined the honor." Except for the Nelsonville operators, the other mine owners closed their mines on April 1 for two months and just waited out the strikers. Toward the end of May, the operators divided among themselves. A few settled with strikers, but the largest operators rejected suggestions of arbitration and rebuked the union.[53]

Compromise was out of the question, insisted the more powerful operators. They attacked the governor for not sending militia to aid them and to protect private property. The triumph of the union would soon lead to the "overthrow" of "our Government and bring upon us anarchy and bloodshed that would approach, if not equal, the Communism of Paris." [54]

Unable to exert their authority from within, the operators brought in between 400 and 500 Negroes in mid-June. Most of the Negroes came from cities such as Memphis, Louisville, and Richmond; few, if any, had had experience as coal miners. They were told nothing of the dispute and were generally misinformed about conditions in the valley. They also were offered high wages. One operator admitted that "the motive for introducing the negro was to break down the white miners' strike." Another boasted of his "great triumph over Trades-Unions" and called the use of Negroes "the greatest revolution ever attempted by operators to take over their own property." Gathered together in Columbus, the Negroes then were sped by rail to one of the mines which was turned into a military camp. The county sheriff, twenty-five deputies, and the governor's private secretary were there, too. Apparently with the approval of these officials, the operators armed the Negroes with "Government muskets," bayonets, and revolvers, and placed them on "military duty" around the property. No one could enter the area unless endorsed "by the operators or police." In the meantime, state militia were mobilized in nearby Athens, in Chillicothe, and in Cincinnati.[55]

Anger swept the Hocking Valley when the strikers learned of the coming of the Negroes. The first day 1,000 miners and their families stood or paraded near the Negro encampment. No violence occurred, but the miners made their displeasure known by calling across the "picket lines" of armed Negroes and urging them to desert the operators. The second day even more miners paraded near the encampment and urged the Negroes to leave. Small numbers of Negroes left the operators. The miners succeeded in "raiding" the operators with an "artillery of words." In all, around 120 Negroes went back on the operators. Two of the Negro defectors addressed the miners and admitted they had been "led by misrepresentations to come North" and "wouldn't interfere with white folks' work." They defended unions as "a good thing" and advocated "plenty of good things" for everyone. The strikers housed the Negroes in their union lodge rooms, and with the help of some local citizens raised about $500 to help them return South. But this

was just a small victory for the union miners. Enough Negroes remained to strengthen the hand of the operators and to demoralize
the union men. Negroes went to other mines even though strikers
begged them not to work and "mothers held their children in their
arms pointing out the negroes to them as those who came to rob
them of their bread." [56]

Outside of the Hocking Valley, the press applauded the operators. The *Cleveland Leader* found the strikers were "aliens" who
would not understand their rights and duties as Americans for another fifty or sixty years. The leading correspondent for the *Cincinnati Commercial* called the strikers drunkards, thieves, and assassins. In the Hocking Valley, however, some residents complained
of the "mercenary newspaper men and their hired pimps." The
valley newspapers especially criticized the operators for using
Negroes. Some merchants and other business folk also attacked the
operators. Certain Nelsonville businessmen offered aid to the strikers and unsuccessfully pleaded with the operators to rehire all the
miners. They even talked of starting a new company to "give employment to miners who are citizens and who have lost their
places." The Nelsonville police also were friendly to the miners,
and the New Straitsville mayor prevented the sending of militia to
his town.[57]

Destruction of the union and the introduction of Negro workers did not bring industrial harmony to the Hocking Valley. There
were strikes over wage cuts in 1875 and 1877, and there also was
conflict between the Negro and white miners. In 1875, when the
miners resisted a wage cut, the operators tacitly admitted that their
power in the valley still was inadequate. Two of them, W. F.
Brooks and T. Longstreth, visited Governor Allen and pleaded
that he "restore order" in the valley towns. The governor was
cautious, however, and would not be used as a tool by the owners.
Allen sent no troops and the operators returned empty-handed to
Nelsonville. But their plea revealed the employers' anxieties, and
their need for outside power to control their men as well as their
businesses.[58]

Nothing better illustrates the differences between the small
town and large city in this period than attitudes toward public works
for the unemployed. Urban newspapers frowned upon the idea,

and relief and welfare agents often felt that the unemployed were "looking for a handout." The unemployed, one official insisted, belonged to "the degraded class . . . who have the vague idea that 'the world owes them a living.'" Unemployed workers were lazy, many said, and trifling.[59]

Native-born radicals and reformers, a few welfare officers, ambitious politicians, responsible theorists, socialists, and relics from the pre-Civil War era all agitated for public works during the great economic crisis of 1873–74. Protest meetings boasted craft-unionists, agitators of all hues, and responsible citizens as well as the unemployed workers themselves as they aired their demands for remedial public works. The earliest advocates urged construction of city streets, parks and playgrounds, rapid transit systems, and other projects to relieve unemployment. These schemes, in most cases, depended on borrowed money or fiat currency, or issuance of low interest rate bonds on both local and national levels. Public assistance was necessary because the job was too big for private enterprise, which could not deal with the "present gigantic difficulty." The government had aided the wealthy classes in the past, and now it was time to "legislate for the good of all not the few." Street demonstrations and meetings by the unemployed occurred in November and December of 1873 in Boston, Cincinnati, Chicago, Detroit, Indianapolis, Louisville, Newark, New York, Paterson, Pittsburgh, and Philadelphia. In December, Chicago and Cincinnati workers paraded the streets with placards that read: "Work or Bread" and "Death to Starvation." The *Chicago Tribune* found the city "entirely unprepared for anything of the kind." The plea of aid struck "like lightning from a clear, blue sky." More than 4,000 persons jammed into Cooper Institute on December 11, and despite a heavy rainfall, thousands milled outside. Indianapolis witnessed the largest labor meeting in its history, and on December 21 an overflow crowd of between 5,000 and 7,000 packed into Chicago's Turner Hall. The dominant theme at all these gatherings was the same: unemployment was widespread, countless persons were without means, charity and philanthropy were poor substitutes for work, and public aid and employment were necessary and just.[60]

The reaction to the demand for public works contained elements of surprise, ridicule, contempt, and genuine fear. The Board

of Aldermen refused to meet with committees of unemployed Philadelphia workers. Irate Paterson taxpayers forced an end to a limited
program of street repairs that the city government had started.
"When the question of economy comes before the citizens," explained the *Cincinnati Gazette* of the rejection of public works
programs by the Board of City Improvements, "the plea of love
for the laborer will not be received." Chicago public officials and
charity leaders told the unemployed to join them "in God's work"
and "rescue the poor and suffering" through philanthropy not
public employment.[61]

The urban press rejected the plea for public works and responsibility for the unemployed. Public employment was "sheer un-
adulterated bosh," and men demanding such aid were "disgusting,"
"crazy," "loud-mouthed gasometers," "impudent vagabonds," and
even "ineffable asses." They were ready "to chop off the heads of
every man addicted to clean linen." They wanted to make "Government an institution to pillage the individual for the benefit of the
mass." Hopefully, "yellow fever, cholera, or any other blessing"
would sweep these persons from the earth. Depressions, after all,
were normal and necessary adjustments and workers should only
"quietly bide their time till the natural laws of trade" brought renewed prosperity. Private charity and alms as well as "free land"
were adequate answers to unemployment. "The United States,"
said the *New York Times*, "is the only 'socialistic,' or more correctly 'agrarian,' government in the world in that it offers good
land at nominal prices to every settler" and thereby takes "the
sting from Communism." If the unemployed "prefer to cling to the
great cities to oversupply labor," added the *Chicago Times*, "the
fault is theirs." [62]

None of the proposals of the jobless workers met with favor,
but the demand by New York workers that personal wealth be
limited to $100,000 was criticized the most severely of all. To re-
strict the "ambition of building up colossal fortunes" meant an end
to all "progress," wrote the *Chicago Times*. The *New York Tribune*
insisted that any limitation on personal wealth was really an effort
"to have employment without employers" and that was "almost as
impossible . . . as to get into the world without ancestors." [63]

Another argument against public responsibility for the unemployed identified this notion with immigrants, socialists, and "alien" doctrine. The agitation by the socialists compounded the anxieties of the more comfortable classes. Remembering that force had put down the Paris Communards, the *Chicago Times* asked: "Are we to be required to face a like alternative?" New York's police superintendent urged his men to spy on labor meetings and warned that German and French revolutionaries were "doing their utmost to inflame the workingman's mind." The *Chicago Tribune* menacingly concluded, "The coalition of foreign nationalities must be for a foreign, non-American object. The principles of these men are wild and subversive of society itself." [64]

Hemmed in by such ideological blinders, devoted to "natural laws" of economics, and committed to a conspiracy theory of social change so often attributed only to the lower classes, the literate non-industrial residents of large cities did not identify meaningfully with the urban poor and the unemployed. A Chicago Unitarian minister warned his congregation: "There are thousands who . . . are ready to become the writhing body of any monster mob that can find a head, like the *sans-culotte* of the French Revolution." And Thurlow Weed, the aged but wise Republican politician, saw only danger from the unemployed. He urged an enlarged program of private relief and charity. "It is not a question of duty, of sympathy, or of interest but one of *safety*," Weed warned New Yorkers. The matter concerned "the rich far more deeply than the poor," but he feared that the wealthy class would "draw its purse strings too tightly." Most well-to-do residents of large cities in 1873 and 1874 believed that men rose or fell solely through individual effort. They viewed the worker as little more than a factor of production. They were sufficiently alienated from the urban poor to join the *New York Graphic* in jubilantly celebrating a country in which republican equality, free public schools, and cheap western lands allowed "intelligent working people" to "have anything they all want." [65]

The extreme reaction against the concept of public responsibility for the unemployed by the residents of large cities was not just a response to the radical character of that demand. The attitude displayed toward the unemployed reflected a broader and more encompassing attitude toward labor. Unlike similar groups in small towns, the urban middle and upper income groups generally frowned upon labor disputes and automatically sided with employers. Contact between these persons and the worker was casual and at best indirect. Trade unions, moreover, were abstractions. Labor unions, therefore, did little more than violate certain immutable "natural and moral laws" and deter economic development and capital accumulation.[66] The *Chicago Times* put it another way in its discussion of workers who challenged the status quo: "The man who lays up not for the morrow, perishes on the morrow. It is the inexorable law of God, which neither legislatures nor communistic blatherskites can repeal. The fittest alone survive, and those are fittest, as the result always proves, who provide for their own survival." [67]

Unions and all forms of labor protest, particularly strikes, were condemned. The *New York Times* described the strike as "a combination against long-established laws" especially "the law of supply and demand." The *New York Tribune* wrote of "the general viciousness of the trades-union system," and the *Cleveland Leader* called "the labor union kings . . . the most absolute tyrants of our day." Strikes, insisted the *Chicago Tribune*, "implant in many men habits of indolence that are fatal to their efficiency thereafter." Cleveland sailors who protested conditions on the Great Lakes ships were "a motley throng and a wicked one," and when Cuban cigar makers struck in New York, the *New York Herald* insisted that "madness rules the hour." City officials joined in attacking and weakening trade unions. The mayor forbade the leader of striking Philadelphia weavers from speaking in the streets. New York police barred striking German cigar workers from gathering in front of a factory whose owners had discharged six trade-unionists including four women. Plain-clothes detectives trailed striking Brooklyn plasterers. When Peter Smith, a nonunion barrel maker, shot and wounded four union men, killing one of them, during a bitter lockout, a New York judge freed him on $1,000 bail supplied by his employers and said his employers did "perfectly right in giving Smith a revolver to defend himself from strikers." [68]

A brief review of three important labor crises in Pittsburgh, Cleveland, and New York points out different aspects of the underlying attitude toward labor in the large cities. The owners of Pittsburgh's five daily newspapers cut printers' wages in November,

1873, and formed an association to break the printers' union. After the printers rejected the wage cut and agreed to strike if nonunion men were taken on, two newspapers fired the union printers. The others quit in protest. The *Pittsburgh Dispatch* said the strikers "owe no allegiance to society," and the other publishers condemned the union as an "unreasoning tyranny." Three publishers started a court suit against more than seventy union members charging them with "conspiracy." The printers were held in $700 bail, and the strike was lost. Soon, Pittsburgh was "swarming with 'rats' from all parts of the country," and the union went under. Though the cases were not pressed after the union collapsed, the indictments were not dropped. In 1876, the *Pittsburgh National Labor Tribune* charged, "All of these men are kept under bail *to this day* to intimidate them from forming a Union, or asking for just wages." The weekly organ of the anthracite miners' union attacked the indictment and complained that it reiterated "the prejudice against workingmen's unions that seems to exist universally among office-holders." [69]

In May, 1874, Cleveland coal dealers cut the wages of their coal heavers more than 25 per cent, and between 400 and 500 men struck. Some new hands were hired. A foreman drew a pistol on the strikers and was beaten by them. The foremen and several strikers were arrested, and the coal docks remained quiet as the strikers, who had started a union, paraded up and down the docks and neither spoke nor gestured to the new men. Police guarded the docks, and a light artillery battery of the Ohio National Guard was mobilized. Lumber heavers joined the striking workers, and the two groups paraded quietly on May 8. Nearly one hundred police led by the mayor patrolled the docks, and the light artillery battery waited in the armory with seventy-five rounds of cannister. Although the strikers were orderly, the police jailed several of their ring-leaders. The strikers did not resist and dispersed when so ordered by the law. In their complaint to the public, the strikers captured the flavor of much of urban industrial conflict:

> The whole thing is a calumny, based upon the assumption that if a man be poor he must necessarily be a blackguard. Honest poverty can have no merit here, as the rich, together with all

their other monopolies, must also monopolize all the virtues. We say now . . . we entertain a much more devout respect and reverence for our public law than the men who are thus seeking to degrade it into a tool of grinding oppression. We ask from the generosity of our fellow citizens . . . to depute [*sic*] a commission of honest men to come and examine our claims. . . . We feel confident they will be convinced that the authorities of Cleveland, its police force, and particularly the formidable artillery are all made partisans to a very dirty and mean transaction.

The impartial inquiry proved unnecessary; a few days later several firms rescinded the wage cut, and the strikers thanked these employers.[70]

Italian laborers were used on a large scale in the New York building trades for the first time in the spring of 1874. They were cheap, unskilled labor and were used to break strikes. They lived "piled together like sardines in a box" and worked mainly as rag pickers and street cleaners. They were men of "passionate dispositions" and, "as a rule, filthy beyond the power of one to imagine." "Their mental condition," a doctor insisted, "somewhat corresponds to their physical condition." Irish street laborers and unskilled workers were especially hard on the Italians, and numerous scuffles between the two groups occurred in the spring of 1874. In spite of the revulsion toward the Italians as a people, the *New York Tribune* advised employers that their "mode of life" allowed them to work for low wages.[71]

Two non-Italians, civil engineers and contractors, founded the New York Italian Labor Company in April, 1874. It claimed 2,700 members, and its superintendent, an Italian named Frederick Guscetti, announced: "As peaceable and industrious men, we claim the right to put such price upon our labor as may seem to us best." The firm held power of attorney over its members, contracted particular jobs, provided transportation, supplied the "gangs" with "simple food," and retained a commission of a day's wages from each monthly pay check. Guscetti said the company was started to protect the Italians from their Irish "adversaries," and he said the men were ready and willing to undertake work "at panic prices." The non-Italian managers announced the men would work for 20 per cent less in the building trades. Employers were urged to hire them "and do away with strikes." [72]

Protected by the city police and encouraged by the most powerful newspapers, the New York Italian Labor Company first attracted attention when it broke a strike of union hod carriers. Irish workers hooted and stoned the Italians, but the police provided them with ample protection. The *Cooper's New Monthly* complained that "poor strangers, unacquainted with the laws and customs and language of the country," had been made "the dupes of unprincipled money sharks" and were being "used as tools to victimize and oppress other workingmen." This was just the start. The firm advertised its services in *Iron Age*. By the end of July, 1874, it had branched out with work gangs in New York, Massachusetts, and Pennsylvania.[73]

There is much to say about the attitude toward labor that existed in large cities, but over all opinion lay a popular belief that iron laws governed not only the economy but life itself, and that he who tampered with them through social experiments or reforms imperiled the whole structure. The *Chicago Times* was honest if perhaps callous in saying: "Whatever cheapens production, whatever will lessen the cost of growing wheat, digging gold, washing dishes, building steam engines, is of value. . . . The age is not one which enquires when looking at a piece of lace whether the woman who wove it is a saint or a courtesan." It came at last almost to a kind of inhumanity, as one manufacturer who used dogs as well as men in his operation discovered. The employer liked the dogs better than the men. "They never go on strike for higher wages, have no labor unions, never get intoxicated and disorderly, never absent themselves from work without good cause, obey orders without growling, and are very reliable." [74]

The contrast between urban and rural views of labor and its fullest role in society and life is clear.[75] In recent years, many have stressed "entrepreneurship" in nineteenth-century America [76] without distinguishing between entrepreneurs in commerce and trade and entrepreneurs in industrial manufacturing. Reflecting the stresses and strains in the thought and social attitudes of a generation passing from the old agricultural way of life to the new industrial America, many men could justify the business ethic in its own sphere without sustaining it in operation in society at large or in human relationships. It was one thing to apply brute force in the market place, and quite another to talk blithely of "iron laws" in operation when men's lives and well-being were at stake.

Not all men had such second thoughts about the social fabric which industrialism and commercialism were weaving, but in the older areas of the country, still susceptible to the cries of an ancient conscience, the spirits of free enterprise and free action were neither dead nor mutually exclusive. As the story shows clearly, many elements of labor kept their freedom of action and bargaining even during strikes. And the worker was not without shrewdness in his appeal to public opinion. There is a certain irony in realizing that rural, or at least small-town America, supposedly alien and antagonistic toward the city and its ways, remained in this period a stronghold of freedom for the worker seeking his economic and social rights.

But perhaps this is not so strange after all, for rural America, whatever its narrowness and faults, had always preached individualism and personal freedom. It was the city, whose very impersonality would one day make it a kind of frontier of anonymity, which often preached personal restriction and the law of the economic and social jungle. As industrialism triumphed, the businessman's powers increased, yet it is significant that in this generation of genuine freedom of action, he was often hindered and always suspect in vast areas of the nation which cheered his efforts toward wealth even while often frustrating his methods.[77]

Facile generalizations are easy to make and not always sound, but surely the evidence warrants a new view of labor in the Gilded Age. The standard stereotypes and textbook clichés about its impotence and division before the iron hand of oppressive capitalism do not fit the facts. Its story is far different when surveyed in depth, carrying in it overtones of great complexity. And it is not without haunting and instructive reminders that even in an age often dominated by lusts for power, men did not forget or abandon old and honored concepts of human dignity and worth.

4

Spoilsmen and Reformers
Civil Service Reform and Public Morality

ARI HOOGENBOOM

THE REACTION of an American historian to the phrase "Gilded Age" is nearly as predictable as that of a Pavlov dog to a bell. Thoroughly conditioned, the historian thinks of corruption. He will condemn (often while enjoying) Senator Roscoe Conkling's affair with Kate Chase Sprague that Senator Sprague abruptly terminated by running Conkling off his property with a shotgun; Reverend Henry Ward Beecher's success at seducing his lady parishioners that resulted in the most spectacular trial of the nineteenth century; or capitalist Jim Fisk's insane infatuation for Josie Mansfield that led to his murder on the steps of the Fifth Avenue Hotel. A notorious libertine, ravisher of railroads, and corrupter of governments, Fisk achieved immortality thanks largely to two reformers, Charles Francis Adams, Jr., and his brother Henry, who described in intimate detail Fisk's sordid relations with both the Erie Railroad and public officials.[1]

Ever since the Adams brothers wrote their essays the immorality, especially the political immorality, of the Gilded Age has attracted historians. Using Fisk as an example, they insist that public and business morals matched private ones. On the municipal level there was New York's spectacularly corrupt Tweed ring, overshadowing the more modest activities of Philadelphia's gas ring and Washington's Boss Shepherd. State governments were also corrupt. The *Nation* reported in the spring of 1867 that votes of New York legislators were bought and sold like "meat in the market."[2] And corruption was not limited to the Northeast. Southern governments, badly tainted during Reconstruction, found the Bourbon restoration only a slight improvement. In the West, United States Senator Samuel Clarke Pomeroy of Kansas failed of re-election in 1873 after allegedly attempting to buy a state senator's vote for $7,000.[3] And in the federal government itself, Oakes Ames bribed fellow congressmen with Credit Mobilier stock, the whisky ring of internal revenue agents and distillers defrauded the country of millions, and the Star Route frauds cost the Post Office Department millions. In textbooks and lectures the Gilded Age consistently outscandalizes any other age in our history.

These familiar misdoings, and others, account for the free association of corruption with the Gilded Age. But should the association be so free? Were these scandals typical? Are Jim Fisk and the Tweed ring full-blown symbols of an age or are they symptoms, traces of a disorder that was by no means general?[4] Was this age as corrupt as historians have implied, or was it a prim age whose scandals have been exaggerated by contrast? More basically, what is meant by corruption?

If political corruption is the violation of duty for a consideration, usually monetary, many frequently cited examples of Gilded Age corruption are of questionable validity. President Ulysses S. Grant's participation in Jay Gould's and Jim Fisk's scheme to corner the gold market, for instance was naïve, not corrupt; ignorant, not immoral. The Salary Grab Act of 1873, while perhaps greedy, was not illegal. Indeed, salaries of high federal officials needed to be increased. John D. Sanborn's contract to collect delinquent taxes for a 50 per cent fee was not an invention of Secretary of the Treasury William A. Richardson but a new application of the ancient moiety system. Far more significant than the collection of moieties during this period was the public reaction resulting in their elimination in 1874. The resentment aroused by the Sanborn contract should be cited as an example of growing administrative efficiency.

And if, like George Washington Plunkitt, one differentiates between honest and dishonest graft, he further reduces the ranks of the corrupt. Honest graft, that estimable Tammany Hall politician said, was the profit that flowed from advance inside information on future government action. Why not make a little money on real estate, paving blocks, or what the occasion called for, if one could?

Who was hurt by it? [5] And while one usually does not speak of George Washington Plunkitt, Andrew W. Mellon, and George C. Humphrey in one breath, they are perhaps spiritual brothers, with Plunkitt exceeding the other two in candor if not in profits. Before rejecting Plunkitt's distinction between honest and dishonest graft, one should observe that twentieth-century conflicts of interest more than match nineteenth-century honest graft. The Gilded Age has lost some of its dubious distinction.

The typical historian has been too loose in applying the term "corruption." Specifically, he labels a politically partisan civil service corrupt rather than inefficient; he equates the spoils system with corruption when honest spoilsmen far outnumber dishonest ones; he pronounces Gilded Age politicians guilty of corruption for associating with corruptionists even while attacking guilt by association in his own day.

One apparent reason why the historian has exaggerated the corruption of the Gilded Age is his desire to enliven lectures and writings. All the world loves a scandal, and the historian is loathe to abandon the pleasure of dispensing "vicarious sin." More basically, the historian dislikes the dominant forces in the Gilded Age. The historian is usually liberal, more often than not a Democrat. He is, typically, hostile to big business, an advocate of government regulation, of strong executive leadership, and of a civil service staffed by experts. The post-Civil War era stands for all the historian opposes. It was an era of Republicanism, of big business domination, of few and ineffectual attempts at government regulation, of weak executives, and of an essentially nonprofessional civil service. The historian naturally dwells upon the shortcomings of the period, particularly on the failures of Ulysses S. Grant, whose political career both personifies all the historian abhors and symbolizes Gilded Age politics.

Another reason the historian has exaggerated corruption in this period is the bias of his sources. The most articulate individuals in this age were its severest critics. Their enforced inactivity (foolishly imposed by business and political opponents) gave them both a cause and the time for writing, while their enemies managed conventions and built railroads. Reformers' letters and writings, their journals and newspapers dominate footnotes with good reason.

Take, for example, the *Nation* under the editorship of reformer
Edwin Lawrence Godkin. Outstanding contributors and particularly Godkin, hard-working, hardheaded, a trifle hardhearted, and
very hard-hitting, made the *Nation*, to quote James Bryce, "the
best weekly not only in America but in the world." [6] When not
quoting the *Nation*, the historian turns to George William Curtis'
graceful editorials in *Harper's Weekly*, America's leading illustrated paper. For a quarter of a century Curtis was the most conspicuous civil service reformer in America. Among monthly magazines, both *Harper's* and the *Atlantic* reflect reformism, while the
venerable old quarterly the *North American Review* could at times
be considered a reform organ. Reformers dominated newspaper
sources such as the *New York Evening Post* and the younger *New
York Times*—in fact opposition to civil service reform by distinguished papers was almost limited to Whitelaw Reid's *New York
Tribune*.

Finally, the reformers are the most quotable men in the period.
Even though Jim Fisk could coin a beautiful phrase, the area of his
interests and the level of his perception limits application of his
words. Contrast his broad humor with the acid wit of Henry
Adams' superb and readily available letters and his autobiography,
The Education. Readers enraptured with Adams' prose also become
enraptured with Adams' prejudices.

Reformers exaggerated the inefficiency and corruption of the
Gilded Age. A typical instance was the estimate in January, 1866,
by President Johnson's Revenue Commission that $12,000,000 to
$25,000,000 were lost annually in the New York Customhouse. Six
years later the Grant Civil Service Commission under the leadership
of George William Curtis projected the earlier figures and estimated
that one-fourth of the annual federal revenue was lost in collection.
In the ensuing presidential campaign, liberal Republican Senator
Lyman Trumbull, citing the commission's report, calculated that
the corrupt Grant regime annually lost $95,830,986.22 of the na-
tion's revenue. When an enraged Grant supporter protested and
demanded to know the origin of these figures, the commission explained that its estimate was designed to provide the "most force-
able illustration of the mischief of the system" and actually dated
from "the administration of Andrew Johnson when the evils of the

'spoils' system culminated." The loss was not money collected and then stolen but money due the government and never collected. The commission also claimed that during Grant's administration deficiencies and defalcations under the internal revenue law had been reduced to one-seventh of those suffered during Johnson's term of office. "We regret," the commissioners concluded, "that in our desire to divest our report of any partisan character whatever and to make it as concise as possible, we failed to explain this statement, more in detail, & to show how ingenious and successful were the efforts of the administration to prevent the loss to which we alluded." [7] Quite obviously the commission had wished to paint the bleakest picture possible to demonstrate the need for reform. To accomplish this purpose the commission knowingly used an obsolete estimate since it testified that the internal revenue system was seven times more honest under Grant than under Johnson. The commission could hardly afford to have the spoils system reformed by spoilsmen.

Along with exaggerating corruption in the civil service, reformers embraced a devil theory respecting their enemies. Grossly overrating the organization of satanic spoilsmen, reformers' writings abound with reference to conspiracies and rings. In November, 1871, Charles Eliot Norton wrote Godkin from Dresden, Germany, "The whole country is, like New York, in the hands of the 'Ring,' —willing to let things go, till they get so bad that it is a question whether they can be bettered without complete upturning of the very foundations of law & civil order." So great was Norton's revulsion against rapacious capitalists that he questioned the further validity of the "systems of individualism & competition. We have erected selfishness into a rule of conduct, & we applaud the man who 'gets on' no matter at what cost to other men." Norton even approved the recent attempt of the Paris Commune to redress its grievances by force, and although he shared the typical reformer's aversion to violence, especially violence that would overturn social order, he advocated "occasional violent revolutionary action to remove deepseated evils." Norton's radicalism, though a temporary romantic aberration rather than a permanent view, reveals nevertheless a man deeply distressed, or more accurately frustrated, by repulsive politicians and capitalists. Norton was so frustrated that he advocated violent revolution to make men "more conscious of their duties to society." [8]

Norton revealed a good deal more of himself than of his homeland. The whole country was not in the hands of the "Ring," Tweed, whisky, or otherwise. All capitalists were not buccaneers like Jim Fisk, and there was no revolution. American reformers, with Norton among them, were content to espouse civil service reform, revenue reform, and hard money, a program they hoped would recreate the golden age of the past. But men with a program to reform society are hardly unbiased observers of that society. Obviously reform is achieved through "knocking" not "boosting" which explains the hypercritical bent of civil service reformers. The historian, however, faithfully reflects the reformers' dim view of the Gilded Age.

The cause of the reformers' dim view and their espousal of civil service reform can be found in their careers. Their morality, their heritage of Puritan virtue cannot be denied, but reformers recognized the evils of the spoils system only after it thwarted their ambitions. The career of the temporary revolutionary, Charles Eliot Norton, serves as an example. Son of Andrews Norton, Harvard Divinity School professor, and cousin of Charles W. Eliot, future president of Harvard University, Charles Eliot Norton was born into the "best" Cambridge circles. After graduating from Harvard, he attempted a career in business but was not successful. Literature and the arts enthralled him; account books did not. Norton traveled widely abroad where he met George William Curtis, his life-long friend, and hobnobbed with the Brownings, Thackeray, Ruskin, Carlyle, and the Pre-Raphaelites. Before the Civil War Norton contributed to the *Atlantic,* sympathized with the antislavery cause although he personally did not care for abolitionists ("the most self righteous set of radicals"), and supported the Republican party. During the war he edited the Loyal Publication Society broadsides, which for three years helped shape northern public opinion by supplying editorials to local newspapers. With James Russell Lowell, Norton became co-editor of the *North American Review* in 1864, and in 1865 he joined with Godkin and others to found the *Nation.* [9]

The postwar world disenchanted Norton. He was suspicious of democracy, observing that it contributed to the unfortunate national "decline of manners." Norton had no use for Andrew Johnson but even less for radical Republican politicos. He opposed the impeachment of Johnson reasoning that "three months of Ben Wade are worse than two years of A. J." Johnson's acquittal encouraged Norton only because it enhanced reformers' opportunity to capture the Republican party. "I think," he wrote Godkin, "we have a better chance now than we had any right to expect so soon for reforming the party & freeing it from the burden of the sins of the extremists who have tried to usurp the leadership." As the election of 1868 drew near, Norton, like everyone else, fell under Grant's spell. " 'Honesty & Grant,' 'good-faith & Grant' must succeed," he wrote from Manchester, England. "Grant grows daily in my respect & confidence," Norton wrote Curtis after the election and rapturously described the president-elect as "so simple, so sensible, so strong & so magnanimous." Assuming Grant would be especially generous to the reform element, Norton added, "If you see a perfectly fit and easy opportunity, I should be glad to have you use it to suggest my name as that of a suitable person for the mission to Holland or Belgium." Although Curtis wrote to the newly appointed Secretary of State Hamilton Fish in Norton's behalf, nothing happened. The reformers' hope to re-establish themselves in their old stronghold, the diplomatic service, proved futile. A few months later, bitterly disillusioned after his season of hope, Norton wrote Curtis: "Grant's surrender, partial though it may be, to the politicians was an unexpected disappointment, but a very instructive one. His other mistakes were what might have been expected,—what indeed we ought to have been prepared for. But some of his appointments are disgraceful,—personally discreditable to him. . . . The question seems to be now whether the politicians,—'the men inside politics,'—will ruin the country, or the country take summary vengeance, by means of Jenckes's [civil service reform] bill, upon them." [10]

Norton's disappointments paralleled those of his friends, particularly those of George William Curtis. Exposed early to transcendentalism at Concord and Brook Farm, Curtis never escaped its influence. After the grand tour abroad, he embarked on a literary career, becoming one of the most popular writers of the 1850's and associate editor of *Putnam's Monthly*. When this magazine collapsed, Curtis assumed a debt he was not legally responsible for and paid it by lecturing on the lyceum circuit. An ardent Republican, Curtis supported the Lincoln administration from his editor's post on *Harper's Weekly*. He soon became a power in the New York Republican party, unsuccessfully ran for Congress in 1864, attempted to influence patronage distribution during Lincoln's administration, and was offered a diplomatic post in Egypt. Curtis was not opposed to the spoils system until it ceased to function satisfactorily for him and for his friends.[11]

Not only Johnson but politicians in general snubbed Curtis and his peers. In the fall of 1866 Charles Eliot Norton launched a campaign to elect Curtis United States senator. Although Curtis' sensitive nature was not a political asset, the *Nation* and several other journals strongly supported him. Success, however, did not follow. "Conkling is undoubtedly to be the man," Curtis wrote Norton in January, "but his friends and [Noah] Davis's and [Ira] Harris's— the three real contestants—have each declared for me as their second choice. Still even that would not bring it because I am not enough of a politician for the purposes of the men who make Senators." As if to prove his point, Curtis "declined absolutely" to unite with the weakest candidate against Roscoe Conkling, who was elected. A few weeks later Curtis, in answer either to public opinion or to personal frustration with politics, wrote in *Harper's Weekly* favoring the passage of the Jenckes civil service bill by the expiring 39th Congress. Although tardy, Curtis' espousal of civil service reform lasted until his death twenty-five years later. In this period he became its most conspicuous leader.[12]

Politicians continued to snub Curtis and each snub made him more of a reformer. In September, 1870, he played a prominent role in Conkling's behalf at the New York State Republican Convention. To give convention proceedings an air of respectability, Conkling men elected Curtis temporary chairman. Having won by a wide margin, Curtis delivered an impressive address, which he hoped would stampede the convention into nominating him for governor. When William Orton, head of Western Union and one of Conkling's chief allies, approached him about the nomination, Curtis, feigning disinterest, replied: "If it is evidently the wish of the Convention I will not decline. But I don't want the office and I entrust my name to your honorable care." Professional politicians made short work of the Curtis candidacy. He was nominated by an efficient Conkling lieutenant, Charles Spencer, who effectively confused Curtis supporters by later voting for another candidate. "In one word, my dear boy," Curtis wrote Norton, "I was the undoubted choice of the Convention and I had been disgracefully 'slaughtered' by my friends!" Curtis attempted to convince himself he was "glad" that he would not have to run. "The only real harm the affair can do me," he confided to Norton, "is that my influence will decline with those who think I want office!!" [13]

Politics held further disappointments for Curtis who remained loyal to the Republican party, headed Grant's Civil Service Commission, and supported Grant in the campaign of 1872. The president, however, snubbed Curtis after 1872. When the New York surveyor vacated his position, reformers considered the nomination of his successor a test case. Grant hesitated but, prodded by Curtis, nominated the deputy surveyor in accordance with the new civil service commission rules. Although reformers tasted victory, they again grew apprehensive when members of the Conkling machine bragged that Grant would withdraw the nomination. Two weeks later the nomination was indeed withdrawn with the assurance that reform methods would be used in selecting the new surveyor. A committee of three, including Curtis and Collector Chester A. Arthur, was named to select the customhouse employee best fitted for the post. Once more reformers' suspicions were allayed. But spoilsmen were to be the final victors. Curtis' serious illness kept the committee from holding an examination or making a report. In mid-March, George H. Sharpe, an active politician and the local United States marshal, was appointed without the committee's knowledge. Sharpe's appointment goaded an ill and testy Curtis into action. Three days after it was announced, he published a letter in the *New York Tribune* emphasizing that Sharpe's appointment was made without his knowledge or consent and ominously adding that "men do not willingly consent to be thus publicly snubbed." On March 18, 1873, Curtis resigned as chairman of Grant's Civil Service Commission.[14]

Curtis was more aggressive when he returned to his editorial work after his illness and resignation. Ignored by the administration and unable to realize his political ambitions, he attacked Grant's civil service policy with special vigor. Curtis relished his new independence and was proud when the anti-administration *Springfield Republican* called one of his articles "another Bomb Shell." He acknowledged in an editorial that "public disbelief of the reality and thoroughness of the reform" was not surprising. "The President forbids political assessments upon subordinates, and issues an executive order virtually reproving the political officiousness of officers of the service. But, in total contempt of his orders, they levy assessments, desert their posts of duty, assume the management of all party assemblies, and continue to use patronage as a party lever." Grant could have inspired confidence in his administration, Curtis contended, if he had fired his corrupt brother-in-law who was collector of New Orleans, dismissed the postmaster at St. Louis for levying political assessments, filled New York Customhouse posts according to the rules, and required civil servants to attend to their duties instead of their party's needs. "Unless these things are done, constantly and consistently done," Curtis concluded, "the work of the Commission, faithful, able, and devoted as we know it to be, will be in vain, and the Republican party will have no right to claim that it has really reformed the civil service." [15]

Unlike Curtis, Henry Adams expected little from Grant and very quickly learned to expect nothing. "We here look," Adams wrote from Washington in February, 1869, "for a reign of western mediocrity, but one appreciates least the success of the steamer, when one lives in the engine-room." Two months later, Adams wrote with the satisfaction his family always seemed to feel when it had just suffered defeat: "My hopes of the new Administration have all been disappointed; it is far inferior to the last. My friends have almost all lost ground instead of gaining it as I hoped. My family is buried politically beyond recovery for years. I am becoming more and more isolated so far as allies go. I even doubt whether I can find an independent organ to publish my articles, so strong is the current against us." And a few days later Henry wrote his brother Charles Francis, Jr., the treasurer of the Social Science Association, which was agitating for civil service reform, "I can't get you an office. The only members of this Government that I have met are mere acquaintances, not friends, and I fancy no request of mine would be likely to call out a gush of sympathy." Nor could Henry obtain anything for himself. The administration was presumptuous enough to ignore the Adams family.[16]

With their ambitions thwarted, the Adams brothers forsook the conventional methods of political advancement and espoused civil service reform. In February Henry had recognized that the struggle against "*political* corruption" was more basic than free trade and its eradication would be more difficult than the antislavery crusade. By June he was writing an article called "Civil Service Reform," which he described as "very bitter and abusive of the Administration." Although Adams expected it to get him into "hot water," he believed he had "nothing to lose." Henry and his brothers, Charles Francis, Jr., and John Quincy, were "up to the ears in politics and public affairs, and in time," Henry hoped, "we shall perhaps make our little mark." [17]

The *North American Review* published and the *Nation* applauded Adams' article. In it Adams revealed reformers' disdain for the new men of politics and their concern over the passing of a more compatible political age. Two members of Grant's Cabinet, Ebenezer Rockwood Hoar and George S. Boutwell, epitomized the change. Boutwell, Adams stated, was "the product of caucuses and party promotion," but Hoar was "by birth and by training a representative of the best New England school, holding his moral rules on the sole authority of his own conscience, indifferent to opposition whether in or out of his party, obstinate to excess, and keenly alive to the weaknesses in which he did not share. Judge Hoar belonged in fact to a class of men who had been gradually driven from politics, but whom it is the hope of reformers to restore. Mr. Boutwell belonged to the class which has excluded its rival, but which has failed to fill with equal dignity the place it has usurped." [18]

The careers of Norton, Curtis, and Henry Adams demonstrate that the civil service reform movement fits into a pattern of those out of power versus those in power.[19] Reformers invariably wished to curtail the appointing power after they thought it had been abused, and to them abuse occurred when men of their own social station or political faction were not appointed to office. The post-Civil War political world was not what the "outs" expected it to be. In their disappointment they turned to reform.

The civil service reformer's political impotence accurately reflected his loss of social and economic power. He was out of step with the rest of society. The main tenet of his philosophy, laissez faire, was rendered obsolete by the post-Civil War industrial transformation of the United States. His ideas were largely ignored. He favored free trade in an age of growing protectionism. He demanded hard money when cries for currency expansion grew louder. He hated monopoly and rapacious capitalism when big business swept all before it. He disliked unions, strikes, and radicals, but these all became more common. He was engulfed in the city of his fathers by an increasing flood of immigrants from eastern and southern Europe. He opposed imperialism but in the twilight of his career witnessed America's most hypernationalistic war. The reformer stood for little government in a period when the civil service proportionately grew faster than the population. The reformer was an outsider, philosophically as well as politically.

Like its proponents, the civil service reform movement was essentially conservative. Its leaders were not interested in revolutionizing anything or even in recognizing the fundamental alteration industrialism had made in the pattern of American society. They were prosperous and to some extent were leaders of society, but their anticipations were much higher than their achievements. Without sacrificing the material gains of the present, civil service reformers wished to return to the attitudes of the good old days before Jacksonian democracy and the industrial revolution, when men with their background, status, and education were the unquestioned leaders of society. In their frustration, reformers attacked the hated spoilsmen's conspicuous source of strength, the civil service.

If zealous reformers exaggerated the corruption of government in the Gilded Age, what was the actual condition of the civil service? In 1865 it was at its nadir thanks to the Civil War which swelled its ranks abnormally and provided Republicans with an excuse, that of disloyalty, for firing more officeholders than ever before. There is more than rhetoric in Julius Bing's complaint, "At present there is no organization save that of partisanship; no test of qualification save that of intrigue." [20] Like most reformers, Bing, the clerk of the Joint Select Committee on Retrenchment who helped Thomas A. Jenckes lay the groundwork for the civil service reform movement, took a dim view of the civil service. Actually, the government would not have functioned at all if corruption and incompetence were as universal as reformers alleged. Nevertheless, professionalism was almost nonexistent in the civil service, and politics permeated it to the core.

At the end of the Civil War the bureaucracy was subdivided into seven departments employing 53,000 workers whose annual compensation amounted to about $30,000,000. Uncle Sam was then, as he is now, the largest employer in the United States. The Post Office Department, with an office in nearly every village, employed more than half of all civil servants. Next in size and in political importance was the Treasury Department with a large office in Washington, sizable customhouses in major port cities, and internal revenue agents dispersed throughout the country. The somewhat smaller Interior Department was also politically significant because of the Land, Patent, Indian, and Pension bureaus. The remaining War, Navy, State, and Justice departments controlled less patronage.[21]

The civil service lacked system. Uniformity in personnel policy outside of Washington was by accident rather than by design, and only a loose personnel system existed even in Washington where clerks were divided into four grades, compensated accordingly, and examined for competence upon appointment. Other evidences of a personnel system were the formal provision for supervision of clerks, the fixing of hours by Congress, the experimentation with efficiency ratings, and the tendency to reward the proficient with promotion. In practice, however, the personnel system was primitive. Examinations were farcical, nepotism was common, no real promotion policy existed, and there was neither a training program for new recruits nor provision for retirement.[22] In these respects the American bureaucracy was not unique. British personnel practices, despite progress toward reform, were also primitive, and those of private business were even more backward.

Tenure of civil servants was short and uncertain in the 1860's. Although every department could point to civil servants who had been in office for many years, these workers were the exception. They formed the working core of the civil service, provided continuity and consistency in administration, and trained new recruits. An example frequently cited is that of William Hunter, the second assistant secretary of state, who in 1868 had been employed in the

State Department for thirty-nine years. Unlike Hunter, most civil
servants held their positions only a short time and anticipated early
dismissal. Tenure varied, with offices requiring a high degree of
technical knowledge retaining their employees the longest. In 1868
twenty-seven of the fifty-five officers in the New York assay office
had been employed more than ten years and forty-five of them had
worked there more than six years. The office of the United States
treasurer, however, is more representative. A tally taken in December, 1867, found that 219 of the 282 employees had been appointed
within the preceding four years. Only five individuals had been employed over ten years.[23]

The training and backgrounds of civil servants differed widely.
For positions requiring technical competence, such as jobs in assay
offices and in the Patent Office, men of ability were secured and
retained. In other offices, standards were less exacting. The 282 employees in the treasurer's office, for example, were a motley group.
They numbered in previous occupations "7 accountants, 13 bankers, 18 bookkeepers, 27 clerks, 1 detective, 2 druggists, 1 editor, 5
farmers, 1 hackdriver, 1 housekeeper, 1 hotel steward, 16 laborers,
1 lawyer, 1 machinist, 1 manufacturer, 8 mechanics, 14 merchants, 2
messengers, 1 minister, 1 page, 1 porter, 1 postman, 2 salesmen, 1
sculptor, 12 students, 1 surveyor, 24 teachers, 2 telegraphists, 1
county treasurer, 1 waiter, 1 washerwoman, 1 watchman, and of no
particular occupation, 112." [24] These appointments were not the result of haphazard policy. They were the fruit of the spoils system.

The spoils system, though hoary in some aspects, had grown
with democracy; it was no accident that the two developed side
by side. With frequent elections decided by large numbers, democracy forced politicians to build elaborate organizations to influence
voters. The best assets in building a "machine" were local, state, and
federal employees whose jobs depended upon politicians. With the
application of pressure these civil servants would contribute both
time and money to their patron's political wars. Frequent elections,
however, meant frequent changes, for winning politicians would
force their enemies out of office. By 1865 the spoils system (like
democracy) was well established and rested on three major principles: appointment primarily for political considerations, congressional dictation of most appointments, and rotation of officeholders.

Although the spoils system controlled more offices more completely than ever before, the stress of war exposed its deficiencies and stimulated interest in reform. In this way, the Civil War contributed both to the rise and to the fall of the spoils system. The needs of the public service itself and the prodding of obstreperous reformers like Norton, Curtis, and Adams, resulted in slow but steady improvement dating from the immediate postwar years. Public service under Grant was actually more efficient than under Lincoln and Johnson. During the Grant regime the internal revenue service improved and Congress abolished moieties. Although Grant earned the dubious distinction of abandoning civil service reform, no previous president had even experimented with it. Grant was not a civil service reformer, but he was decidedly more interested in reform than his predecessors just as his successors were far more committed to reform than he.

In Grant's cabinet the most maligned administrator was George S. Boutwell, the secretary of the treasury whom Henry Adams singled out as the personification of the spoils system. Yet from 1870 to 1872 Boutwell administered stringent tests in his department. He also appointed E. B. Elliott, a friend of reform who later became a civil service commissioner, to the treasury board of examiners. Elliott helped prepare a guide for treasury clerkship examinations designed to aid in hiring competent workers. These examinations especially stressed arithmetic, but also included a knowledge of weights, measures, bookkeeping, grammar, spelling, geography, history, and law. According to Elliott, admission to the Treasury Department under Boutwell was "invariably" at the lowest level and written examinations were "invariably" required for promotion. Elliott testified that enforcement of these rules was "steady & regular & firm, the standard moderate but persistently enforced examination in no case merely formal." He also stated that Boutwell's system, unlike competitive examinations, "took cognizance of special qualifications derived from experience in previous employment and of other special attainments." The first competitive examination in the United States civil service was held in Boutwell's department in 1870, when six third-class clerks were examined for vacancies in the next class. Although competitive, this examination was not open to all applicants.[25]

Inherent demands of the civil service necessitated reform in Boutwell's department. His connection with competitive and stringent examinations seems strange considering his opposition to civil service reformers and their intense dislike of him, but it was Boutwell's job to administer a large office. As a responsible official, he recognized the need for skilled employees, a need which increased as government functions multiplied and became more complex. Boutwell, like reformers, desired efficient workers and was prepared to use examinations to obtain them, but unlike reformers, he wished to continue making political appointments. Historians, relying mainly on such partisan sources as the *Nation*, have overlooked Boutwell's reform activities. What was actually an enlightened regime from the standpoint of personnel administration has been renowned as a blatant example of the spoils system.

The most important, the most publicized, and consequently the most maligned office in the country was the New York Customhouse. There, as in government service elsewhere, conditions gradually improved during the Gilded Age. In January, 1866, the New York Customhouse was the scene of frauds, waste, and incompetence; during the next five years removals numbered 1,678, the equivalent of twice the entire force or more than one removal per secular day. Daily collections of $480,000 (the chief source of federal revenue) and the intricacies of tariff legislation required a sensitive business organization, which the customhouse did not have. The cost of collecting revenue in the United States in 1874 was three, four, and five times that of France, Germany, and Great Britain respectively.[26]

The administration of the New York Customhouse improved steadily after Chester A. Arthur replaced Thomas Murphy as collector in 1871. Since Murphy and Arthur both belonged to the Roscoe Conkling faction of the New York Republican party, Arthur's political dirty work had already been accomplished. The change of collector brought no change in faction; tenure became more secure. Kept on his mettle by a series of investigations, Arthur was an able administrator who brought a measure of efficiency to the New York Customhouse.[27]

While hostility to the Conkling machine usually motivated these New York Customhouse investigations, they helped reform long-standing abuses such as the general-order warehouse system. This system required merchants to pay duty on their goods and to take possession of them within forty-eight hours after a ship entered port. Goods remaining beyond this inadequate period were discharged from the vessel under a general order by the collector. Once in the custody of customhouse officials, general-order goods were sent to a specially designated warehouse where, besides cartage, a month's storage was charged even if the goods were removed immediately.[28] Congressional hearings in January and February, 1872, completely aired the general-order business and acquainted the public with the activities of two shadowy figures, George Leet and Wilbur T. Stocking. Leet, a one-time chief clerk in a Chicago freight depot, enlisted as a Union private in 1862 and emerged from the Civil War a colonel attached to Grant's staff. While still holding his army commission, he secured a War Department clerkship in 1868. When Leet informed President-elect Grant that he wished to settle in New York, Grant wrote a letter of recommendation to Moses Grinnell, a prominent New York merchant. Leet knew that Grant intended to appoint Grinnell New York collector and informed Grinnell of that fact when he presented his letter. Overwhelmed by his good fortune and by the coincidence that Leet brought both news of his appointment and a letter from Grant, Grinnell asked Leet what he wanted. Leet promptly demanded the general-order business, from which he expected to clear $60,000 annually. Somewhat intimidated by this demanding friend of Grant, Grinnell gave Leet supervision over the general-order business which Cunard and North German Lloyds had formerly handled themselves. After farming out his newly acquired general-order business for $5,000 a year and half of all profits over $10,000, Leet returned to Washington and kept his transaction under cover by using a New York agent. During the years 1869 and 1870, Leet resided in Washington, roomed and boarded with Grant's private secretaries, generals Horace Porter and Orville Babcock, maintained an army commission, and retained his War Department post, where he filed Grant's army papers. Even while drawing three salaries, Leet used his intimacy with Grant's official household to threaten Grinnell with dismissal unless he received a larger share of the general-order business. Grinnell's successor, Tom Murphy, gave

Leet and his friend William T. Stocking, former army sutler, the whole North River general-order business. At this point, Leet moved to New York and openly took charge of his customhouse interests.

Revelation of the circumstances under which Leet gained his "sinecure" compounded New York merchants' dissatisfaction with the general-order business. Their earlier complaints about the rise in rates accompanying Leet's monopoly had not been answered. Even when Grant told Murphy in May, 1871, to sever Leet's connection with the customhouse because of hostile criticism, Murphy successfully defended him by saying that the attack was engineered by the steamship companies. Publicity from the investigation in early 1872, however, proved too much for Leet. He testified that in twenty months he and Stocking had netted only $55,000, but refused to corroborate his statement with his firm's books. The value of his plum will never be known, but a recent investigator, William Hartman, accepts as reasonably accurate the $172,000 estimate by the Democratic minority of the investigating committee. Even before the committee presented its report, public opinion forced Grant to instruct Murphy's successor, Arthur, to reform the general-order business. Storage rates were lowered by 35 to 40 per cent, and the public careers of Leet and Stocking ended.[29]

The January, 1872, customhouse investigation also exposed the moiety system, and the issuance of general search warrants. Merchants, however, were plagued with these abuses for two more years. Designed to provide incentive, the moiety system was used in the customs service to uncover fraud. When a shipment was confiscated one-half went to the government, one-quarter to the informer, and the remaining quarter was divided equally among the collector, naval officer, and surveyor of the port. Although the moiety system had been under periodic attack for twenty years, it did not come under heavy fire until the exposure and publication of the Phelps-Dodge case in early 1873. A disgruntled clerk, who had been fired for dishonesty, accused Phelps, Dodge and Company of undervaluing certain shipments. A special treasury agent investigated this charge (aided by broad powers enabling him to search the company's books) and concluded—or at least alleged—that it was true. According to law, the whole shipment had to be forfeited. The undervaluations were made on items in shipments totaling $1,750,000. The value of the property on the invoices was $271,017. The undervaluation itself came to $6,000, and the duties the company avoided paying came to about $2,000. Phelps, Dodge and Company settled out of court for $271,017. Merchants and reformers thought "knavish politicians" searching for personal and party funds were responsible for the Phelps-Dodge predicament. They complained that seizures of books and papers were outrageous and that the moiety system drove treasury agents to excess. When attempts were made in Boston and in New York to repeat the Phelps-Dodge success, so great was the reaction that in January, 1874, even Ben Butler, who probably shared in the moieties from Phelps, Dodge and Company, introduced a bill to end the moiety system.[30]

By June, 1874, a bill abolishing the moiety system and placing restrictions on the right of search became law. Although the bill raised the official salaries of collectors, their incomes sharply decreased. New York Collector Chester A. Arthur's salary dropped from approximately $56,000 to $12,000 a year. The office of collector was no longer the political plum it had been. Merchant reformers were largely responsible for the ending of the moiety system, a significant step toward civil service reform. This important group of reformers had practical reasons for supporting reform. It would enable their businesses to function more smoothly during their constant contacts with customhouse employees.[31]

Under President Hayes the administration of the New York Customhouse further improved. Hayes attacked the Conkling machine by attempting to remove Arthur and naval officer Alonzo Cornell. After a long battle, Hayes prevailed. The original objective of displacing Conkling appears not to have been reform but the building of an administration party from the remains of the old Reuben Fenton machine. The administration stood to gain doubly by attacking Conkling—not only would reformers be pleased, but also a hostile faction that failed to deliver the New York vote in 1876 would be eliminated. Yet whatever Hayes originally intended, the struggle continued so long and its publicity was so great that he could do nothing but make the customhouse a showcase for reform. "My desire," he wrote Arthur's successor Edwin A. Merritt, "is that your office shall be conducted on strictly business principles, and according to the rules which were adopted on the recommendation of the civil service commission by the administration of General Grant. In making appointments and removals of subordinates you should be perfectly independent of mere influence. Neither my recommendation, nor Secretary Sherman's, nor that of any member of Congress, or other influential persons should be specially regarded. . . . Let no man be put out merely because he is Mr. Arthur's friend, and no man put in merely because he is our friend." [32]

Publication of Hayes's letter to Merritt brought praise from reformers, and this praise grew louder with publication of the new rules. These rules applied to all New York Customhouse and subtreasury appointees except a few officers of special trust. Appointments were to be made from the three candidates ranking highest on a competitive examination to be administered by one of three examining boards and observed by "well-known citizens." New appointees were to enter only at the lowest grade; other vacancies were to be filled by promotion within the customhouse.

Naval officer Silas W. Burt, an early and ardent civil service reformer, was the dynamic force behind the new customhouse rules. Although not opposed to competitive examinations, Collector Merritt believed the experiment would be short-lived and asked Burt to enforce the rules. "If you can revive this corpse you are entitled to all the glory," Merritt assured Burt. It was Burt's idea to invite prominent citizens, particularly editors, to observe examinations, an idea that George William Curtis enthusiastically approved. Twelve citizens were invited to each examination, and Curtis attended them all to explain the proceedings. "The editors who attended," Burt later recalled, "were specially interested and their impressions, always favorable, were reflected in their papers." Editors favoring the spoils system, however, invariably declined invitations. [33]

Despite his lukewarm attitude toward the competitive system, Merritt pleased reformers. Even the *New York Times* (highly critical of Hayes) admitted in July that "after four months' experience, it is simple justice to say that the reform has been applied there [the New York Customhouse] in good faith, and with a degree of pertinacity, a patient attempt to make it successful, and an enlightened appreciation of its nature and its scope, which have been an agreeable disappointment to the doubters." An energetic civil service reform leader, Dorman B. Eaton, later reported to Hayes that Merritt's administration of open-competitive examinations was highly successful. Never before, according to Eaton, had so much time been given to proper work and so little to partisan politics. Economy, efficiency, promptness, and high morale characterized the service. Even though political activity had not been entirely eliminated, Eaton was encouraged by its decline. Reformers rightly thought that Burt was responsible for the success of the president's pilot program.[34]

The New York Customhouse was not the only federal office in the nation showing improvement. Under Thomas L. James, a Conkling Republican, reform in the New York Post Office was in certain respects even more advanced than in the customhouse. When James was appointed in March, 1873, "incompetency, neglect, confusion, and drunkenness" that staggered "credulity" prevailed in the post office. James found 400 to 600 neglected bags of mail scattered throughout the building, and on one occasion a book clearly addressed to Vice President Schuyler Colfax was delayed for months. James replaced this chaos with system. He dismissed drunkards and incompetents but conducted no partisan proscription. He set up examinations and despite political pressure refused to hire unworthy applicants. By May, 1879, he decided that noncompetitive examinations were not adequate and instituted open-competitive examinations a few weeks after they were established in the New York Customhouse. Eaton and New York businessmen were proud of their post office. In 1880, the volume of mail had increased one-third over 1875, yet the mails were delivered for $20,000 less, and collections and deliveries had been increased.[35]

Despite improvement of government service and a growing awareness even among spoilsmen that further improvement was necessary, the civil service in the Gilded Age was not yet reformed. Until 1883 it was basically nonprofessional and was characterized by lack of training, insecure tenure, and low morale. Politicians whose interests were local dominated the civil service, and the government worker, frequently owing his position to the turn of events in a congressional district, was understandably provincial in outlook. A civil service reform law requiring that appointments be made on the basis of open-competitive examinations could not pass Congress. The charges of corruption leveled by the reform press usually failed to convince most Americans. Rising industrialists, urban laborers, and rural farmers did not support civil service reform. Only after President Garfield's assassination by an insane office seeker did reformers have a simple, emotion-packed illustration which the previously uninterested masses could easily understand. The spoils system equaled murder. Goaded by an aroused public opinion, Congress approved the Pendleton Act in 1883.

Under the Pendleton Act the trend toward improvement accelerated. The power of the Civil Service Commission grew with the steady increase of classified positions. An unprofessional civil service became more professionalized. Better educated civil servants were recruited and society accorded them a higher place. Thanks to secure tenure local political considerations gave way in civil servants' minds to the national concerns of a federal office. Business influence and ideals replaced those of the politician.[36]

Although these changes outlined the future development of the American bureaucracy it is well to recall that the roots of change were in the Gilded Age. Curiously the reformers, the assiduous cultivators of those roots of change, frequently refused to recognize that improvements in the public service had resulted indirectly from their labor. In fact, prior to the Pendleton Act the more improved the public service became the more shrill were reformers' protests over public immorality. Their noise not only obscured improvements but also gave the profession of politics a disreputable name it does not deserve, a reputation that even now discourages the reform-type from entering politics. It is indeed ironic that the Gilded Age is indebted to the reformers for its tarnished reputation as well as for its improvement in public morals.

5

The Republican Party Revisited,
1877-1897

VINCENT P. DE SANTIS

LORD BRYCE discovered that describing the American party system in *The American Commonwealth* was more difficult than explaining our Constitution and government. "Hitherto we have been on comparatively firm ground, for we have had definite data to rely upon, and the facts set forth have been mostly patent facts which can be established from books and documents," he wrote. "But now we come to phenomena for a knowledge of which one must trust to a variety of flying and floating sources, to newspaper paragraphs, to the conversation of American acquaintances, to impressions found on the spot from seeing incidents and hearing stories and anecdotes, the authority for which, though it seemed sufficient at the time cannot always be remembered. Nor have I the advantage of being able to cite any previous treatises on the subject," continued Bryce, "for though the books and articles dealing with the public life of the United States may be counted by hundreds, I know of no author who has set himself to describe impartially the actual daily working of that part of the vast and intricate political machine which lies outside the Constitution." [1]

Yet for all his apologies and obstacles Bryce left a classic commentary on the parties of the Gilded Age that has influenced every historian's thinking about them. He believed that the two major parties of these years were in danger of losing their functional usefulness because they failed to offer the electorate an opportunity to vote on issues and because they used public office to reward party workers. According to Bryce, "Neither party has any principles, any distinctive tenets. Both have traditions. Both claim to have tendencies. Both have certainly war cries, organizations, interests enlisted in their support. But these interests are in the main the in-

terests of getting or keeping the patronage of the government. . . .
All has been lost except office or the hope of it." The two major
parties in this period "were like two bottles. Each bore a label de-
noting the kind of liquor it contained, but each was empty." [2]

Other thoughtful observers of the political life of the Gilded
Age agreed with Bryce. "One might search the whole list of Congress, Judiciary, and Executive during the twenty-five years 1870–
1895 and find little but damaged reputations," wrote Henry Adams.
"The period was poor in purpose and barren in results." [3] The impulse to spring to the aid of the underdog has brought forth champions of the cultural, literary, and technological achievements of the
Gilded Age, but none to defend its political record. "Even among
the most powerful men of that generation," said Adams, speaking of
the politicians, there were "none who had a good word for it." [4]
While present-day historians have had the benefit of more sources
and perspective than either Bryce or Adams, they have usually sub-
scribed to their conclusions. They have vied with each other to
censure the political life of the Gilded Age for its barrenness, dreari-
ness, and monotony. They have felt that at no other period in
American history was the moral and intellectual tone of political
life so uniformly low or were political conflicts so concerned with
patronage rather than with principles. Charles Beard has called it
the "age of negation," and Morison and Commager have described
it as the dreariest chapter in American politics in which the titular
leaders "contributed nothing of lasting importance to American
politics or American life." [5]

Because the Republican party occupied the presidency for most
of these years, it has received the bulk of the criticism. It has become
an historical convention to represent it as being conservative and to
condemn it for evading issues, for dodging the responsibility of
enacting major legislation, for not reflecting the mood and purposes
of the American people, for deteriorating into a group of spoilsmen,
for ignoring the needs of the farmer, the laborer, and the consumer
in the industrial age, and for best serving the ends of business as it
was itself best served by business collaboration. It is no wonder then
that historians have pictured the eras of President Wilson and the
two Roosevelts as times when America struggled out of the darkness
into the light.

In the post-Civil War generation the Republican party possessed tremendous moral assets from which it profited immensely. It appeared as the savior of the Union and this allowed it to equate party loyalty with national patriotism and to charge the Democrats with having fought under the Confederate flag. The Republicans also offered the voters a surplus of Civil War veterans. With the exception of James G. Blaine, all Republican nominees for the presidency from Rutherford B. Hayes to William McKinley had an enviable Union war record, in sharp contrast to the only one the Democrats could produce in the person of General Winfield Scott Hancock in 1880. There was also the magic tradition of Lincoln. Americans hailed him as the Great Emancipator, and Republicans capitalized on their role as the party of liberation. They were so successful in emphasizing this point that the Democrats were unable to show that the Republicans had spurned the question of emancipation in 1860 and had accepted it only as a war measure.

If the Republican party had assets it also had liabilities. Probably the most important of these was a severe limitation upon its power. Contrary to popular belief the post-Reconstruction period was not one of Republican supremacy. It was an era of party stalemate and equilibrium in which a bitter fight developed between the two major parties for control of the government. And while the Republicans prevented the Democrats from having charge of it, except for a few years, they could not direct it themselves. In the five presidential elections from 1876 to 1892 the Republicans, while winning three of them, failed to carry a majority of the popular vote in any one of them, and in only one, that of 1880, did they receive a plurality—but even that plurality was less than one-tenth of one per cent. In three of these elections the difference between the popular votes for the two major party candidates was less than one per cent, although in the electoral college votes, majorities ranged from 1 in 1876 to 132 in 1892. Throughout much of this period the Republicans depended for victory upon the very small majorities they received in such key states as Indiana and New York, and they never once won a plurality of the counties in the nation as a whole.

Added to the struggle to win the presidency was that to gain command of Congress. Between 1877 and 1897 the Republicans controlled the presidency and Congress at the same time for only four years, in 1881–83 and again in 1889–91. Only in the latter instance did they have a working majority. On the first occasion they had a margin of but one in the House, and only the cooperation of William Mahone, the readjuster from Virginia, enabled them to organize the Senate. In contrast the Democrats held the presidency and Congress at the same time for only two years, 1893–95.

The Republican party of the Gilded Age has invariably been described as conservative, and the Republican presidents from Hayes to McKinley have generally been characterized as respectable mediocrities who in their social and political thinking were convinced that their party's support of American individualism was in accord with some prearranged plan. Many of these judgments have resulted from treating the period in terms of present-day concepts about liberals and conservatives. In retrospect the achievements of the political leaders of the Gilded Age often seem few and meaningless. But though they lacked the boldness and imagination of Wilson and the two Roosevelts, they were clearly wholly different personalities; and there was an entirely different political situation and set of circumstances in the seventies and eighties than there has been in the twentieth century. A more fruitful study would measure the standards and ideas that prevailed in the Gilded Age and try to discover how the period actually looked to contemporaries who took part in its events.

The men who served in the presidency and Congress in the post-Reconstruction years knew little, if anything, about the major problem of their time—the adjustment of American politics to the great economic and social changes that came to the United States with the rise of industrial capitalism and urbanism. They were not educated for reform as were their successors in the Progressive era by muckrakers. In terms of prevailing ideas today about the relationship of government to the economy, the Republican leaders of the Gilded Age were conservatives. They believed governmental interference with economic natural laws impeded progress; thus government regulation should be limited to the barest minimum. To them, taxation hurt the economy and must be kept at a minimum. But in their own minds and in those of many contemporaries, they were not conservatives. They were not committed to lessening federal power. They did not oppose spending public money for special interests, as their support of national subsidy programs shows, especially the protective tariff. In this the Republican leaders differed markedly from the conservative Democrats, sometimes called Bourbons, who believed that the protective tariff and subsidies to special interest groups violated natural law.

Political studies of the last quarter of the nineteenth century emphasize the corrupt alliance between the Republican party and the business interests and the dominant role of the latter in shaping party policy. From this view, the party leaders were business hirelings. If this be true, how does one explain voter acquiescence in the arrangement? It is interesting to note not so much that this supposed combination was corrupt, but that it lasted so long without interference from the voters. E. L. Godkin in the *Nation* of May, 1873, put his finger on the situation when he wrote, "All being corrupt together what is the use of investigating each other." While writers have noted that the Republican party of the Gilded Age differed from that of Fremont and Lincoln, they overlook the shift in the character of political thought and democracy that followed the Civil War. Professor Robert McCloskey has set forth the idea that American politics of the post-Civil War generation was a product of perversion of democracy. A general deterioration of standards and ideals took place in these decades under the impact of an expanding capitalism, and it would be strange if this widespread debasement were not reflected in the age's political attitudes, and if it had not changed some of the assumptions of American democracy. Democracy became perverted when capitalism was welded to the democratic creed and when aims of democracy and business became indistinguishable. With democracy identified with property rights, it was harder to secure social reforms. For while the reformers called for some curtailment of economic freedom, they were also troubled by their attacks upon the democratic faith. If this bothered reformers it likewise disturbed politicians.[6]

It is true that business dominated, but the bulk of Americans were sympathetic to business. The ideas of Social Darwinism and laissez faire prevailed, and most Americans regarded government intervention as unnecessary, unjust, and even immoral. Even reformers confined government regulation of business to those cases where it was clearly necessary and where a careful study had been made. Private enterprise and free competition without government interference, except to maintain law and order and to protect property rights, was held as an ultimate truth by a great majority of Americans. The Republican leaders of the Gilded Age were nothing more than the products of their time, and if we indict them for their conservatism and for their subservience to the business interests, then we must indict an overwhelming portion of effective and vociferous public opinion. Above all we must not read into this period of American politics the ideas about conservatism and liberalism and the relationship of the government to the economy that have grown up since the Progressive movement.

One of the most serious charges leveled against the Republican party of the Gilded Age is its failure to deal with the problems created by the industrial expansion of the post-Civil War years. It is customary to say that politics in these years became the fine art of avoiding issues. Not that there was any lack of important issues, for the problems arising out of the recurrent industrial crises and depressions of the period demanded vigorous government action. But the Republicans, and the Democrats too, so runs the charge, preferred to shun these new issues and to revive the old ones. The problems of the new economic order thus failed to get a hearing in the political arena except through the third parties, and the political battles of these years appear to have been fought over superficial issues.

The customary explanation for this shortcoming is that no important differences existed between the two major parties on the vital issues. The Democrats differed in no significant respect from the Republicans in outlook and achievement. Neither one of the old parties wished to disturb the status quo, and neither one believed that there was anything fundamentally wrong with American life. This is why Beard calls this period the "age of negation." But the critics have neglected to take into account the fact that the government in the post-Reconstruction years rarely concerned itself with economic and social matters as it has done in the twentieth century. The predominant feeling among Americans in the closing decades of the nineteenth century was simply that the government should not handle them.

But a number of other factors help to explain the legislative inactivity of the Republican party. Perhaps the most important of these was the sharp contest for power between the parties and the failure of either one to dominate the national government for any length of time. The struggle between a Republican president and a Democratic Congress, or vice versa, affected legislative achievement in the post-Reconstruction years as it did in any period in American history when political power has been thus divided. The case of President Hayes illustrates how these liabilities hampered the development of effective party leadership. He worked under severe handicaps that have not been fully appreciated. He held office with a disputed title, and Republicans and Democrats alike referred to him as "the de facto President," "His Fraudulency," and "Old Eight to Seven." His program for the South and for civil service reform along with his show of independence caused such a deep split to develop within his own party that at one time he had but three supporters in the Senate, and one of them, Stanley Matthews of Ohio, was a lifelong friend and relative. Moreover, the Democrats controlled the House throughout the whole of Hayes's administration and the Senate for the last two years of his term. Under these circumstances it is amazing that Hayes could accomplish anything.

Further crippling effective Republican leadership were the great factional feuds that plagued the party throughout the Gilded Age. Stalwart, Half-Breed, and Mugwump were pitted against each other in a naked grab for control of the party. The real leaders of the party like Blaine, Roscoe Conkling, John Logan, William E. Chandler, and others wasted their talents and energies in bitter personal rivalries rather than using them in the solution of the period's most pressing problems. The achievements of these men are few and insignificant. Their names are not associated with any major legislation.

The seat of national political power for most of these years was in Congress and not in the presidency. By 1877 a group of arrogant Republican leaders, who had dominated the federal government for nearly a decade, sat in the Senate. They had largely made the Republican party, and in a sense they were the party. They had over-thrown President Andrew Johnson, had gained nearly complete possession of Grant, and they strove to put the succeeding presidents from Grant to McKinley at their mercy. The bitter struggle between the executive and legislative branches that had begun with Johnson and Congress, especially over the Tenure of Office Act, instead of dying down, continued to harass most of the presidents in this period. Added to this was the fact that the office of president in these years was at low ebb in power and prestige. Senator John Sherman, Republican leader of Ohio, himself a perpetual aspirant to the office, wrote, "The executive department of a republic like ours should be subordinate to the legislative department. The President should obey and enforce the laws, leaving to the people the duty of correcting any errors committed by their representatives in Congress." Republican leaders acted on these principles. "The most eminent Senators," wrote George F. Hoar of Massachusetts, "would have received as a personal affront a private message from the White House expressing a desire that they should adopt any course in the discharge of their legislative duties that they did not approve. If they visited the White House, it was to give, not to receive advice." Henry Adams agreed with this when he commented, "So far as the President's initiative was concerned, the President and his Cabinet might equally well have departed separately or together to distant lands." [7]

Sectionalism also accounted for much of the legislative inactivity of the period. An analysis of the voting and debates in Congress clearly reveals the sectionalism of the country on issues of national importance and the fact that both major parties were split into sectional wings. The sectionalism of the seventies and eighties resulted from two movements, expansion of the West, particularly in the trans-Mississippi West, and the growth of industrialism in the Northeast.

Sectional alliances in this period proved to be flexible and shifted with changing economic conditions. For example the East North Central states (Ohio, Indiana, Illinois) which usually voted with the West North Central (Michigan, Wisconsin, Minnesota, Iowa) and southern states in the 1870's, by 1890 had joined hands with the Northeast. This change probably resulted from the growth of industry in the East North Central areas which affiliated them economically with the East.

Political personalities in the post-Reconstruction years played a subordinate role to an adjustment between the interests of the sections and party allegiance in determining the outcome of the vote on national policies. The leading issues of the country as indicated by the party platforms and congressional action were currency and banking, tariff, public lands, internal improvements, railroad and trust regulation, and immigration. While all these produced strong sectional feeling, they manifested one common feature—opposition of the agricultural regions to the industrial centers of the country.

More sectional voting occurred in the periods of depression and more party voting in the years of prosperity. Those sections hardest hit during a depression broke party ranks and combined with other hard-hit sections to redress their grievances. The vagueness of party platforms until 1888 also stimulated sectional divisions, since it allowed discontented sections to interpret the planks to suit their own interests without being accused of party disloyalty.

Much of the Republican voting in Congress on the leading issues of the seventies and eighties followed sectional lines. During the depression of the seventies, 70 per cent of the Republican vote was sectional. The New England wing, which remained consistently conservative on economic matters, opposed the North Central faction. In 15 per cent of the votes a majority of Republicans in all parts of the country sided with the radical minority located primarily in the North Central regions. In 15 per cent of the votes the party acted as a unit. In the years of prosperity, 1879–82, the Republican sectional voting fell to 41 per cent. Again New England and the West were on opposite sides. In 23 per cent of the votes the party acted almost as a unit, although a small radical minority existed in the West Central states, and 36 per cent was a purely party one. But in the slump of the mid-eighties the Republican sectional voting rose to 60 per cent only to drop to 33 per cent in the more prosperous years of the later eighties.[8] In the seventies men like James A. Garfield, William McKinley, and Joseph Cannon, who later became influential Republican leaders, voted for radical financial legislation because their sections demanded it. McKinley's record on this matter was a source of embarrassment to the Republican party in 1896 when he campaigned on the gold standard plank.

Sectional voting was also more pronounced in Congress when both houses were divided between the two parties than when one party was in control. This was equally true for both depression and prosperity years in the seventies and eighties. Thus not only did Republican presidents have to deal with Democratic congresses for most of the time in the post-Reconstruction years but with congresses in which their own party members did more sectional than party voting.

Much has been made also of the meaninglessness and futility of the platforms upon which the Republican party campaigned in these years. But those who wag their heads about this matter fail to take into consideration certain factors. Theoretically, political parties offer to voters a distinctive set of principles or programs, and theoretically the public rewards the party whose principles it approves by voting for it. From this reasoning it follows that the necessity of competing for votes will cause the parties to vie with one another in giving the electorate a program it wants.

This is theory: practice is another matter. The major parties have had, or have at least professed principles, but the principles have appeared to be the same. Each generation has had its Bryce commenting on the empty bottles of American politics. Party contests cannot settle matters of vital importance, because a minority will not submit to an adverse majority vote on a question which it regards as essential to its security. Those who hold to this view point to the refusal of the South to acquiesce in the election of Lincoln. The point has also been made that party competition works best when parties have reached an implicit agreement on general principles.

The theory of party competition apparently breaks down in the Gilded Age if one accepts Edmund Burke's definition of party as a body of men united for promoting by their joint endeavor the national interest upon some particular principle on which they agree. But students of American politics believe that the only groups in this country that would come close to meeting this description have been those third parties fatally dedicated to forwarding limited interests or specific panaceas.

Perhaps the significance of our political system is not the alignment of voters pro and con in purely intellectual terms but rather in the maintenance of institutions which keeps key political power contingent and provides alternative sets of rulers. In practice our major parties have not been primarily concerned about drafting a distinctive program with a distinctive set of issues, but rather they have tried to find some way of bringing together into a reasonably harmonious relationship as large a proportion of the voters as possible. The methods used to achieve this end have been dictated by the times, the circumstances, and the kind of men in control of the party. Principles and issues have generally remained relative and subordinate to these conditions.[9]

The Republicans faced the necessity of holding together the various elements that made up the party—businessmen, farmers, Negroes, federal officeholders, Union war veterans, and labor. They also had to combat the Democrats in the very closely contested elections of the period. Because of this the Republicans found it inexpedient and unwise to commit themselves in advance to a definite program. They could not in all probability have secured agreement among their ranks for it, nor could they have won general support for it. Yet the very lack of agreement allowed a degree of personal freedom for individual candidates that would have been impossible under other conditions. The Republican leadership labored to achieve the goal of any party, a working combination of sections, interests, and of liberals and conservatives. For this effort the Republicans must be credited with some degree of group diplomacy in politics. Professor H. Wayne Morgan has described the Republican party of the post-Civil War era as a classic coalition in American politics. It offered lands to the West, tariff protection to the East, some sort of controlled inflation to the Midwest, pensions to veterans, "and the moral rhetoric of the original anti-slavery crusade. The party built its success on a program rather than on corruption."

Even though the Republican party was labeled as conservative and the protector of the business interests, it enjoyed a highly diversified group and broad geographical support. True, the Republican party remained sectional in a sense, for it had little visible support in the South, but outside this section a number of different elements voted for it. In these years the Republicans were strong in the small northern cities and in the rural districts. They were strong in the

New England mill towns, the mining districts of Pennsylvania, everywhere on the farms and especially in the Old Northwest, among the small farmers and "poor whites" in the mountain districts of West Virginia, eastern Kentucky and Tennessee, and western Virginia and North Carolina, and the mining camps of the mountain and Pacific coast states. In spite of their reputation as the champions of the corporations and as having their special preserve in the East, the Republicans had their strongest congressional districts in the North Central and Central states. The Republicans were able to confine Democratic strength largely to the South, New York City and vicinity, and to parts of the Central states which had been settled by southerners.

The matter of spoils and patronage remains. If Bryce's view is accepted that the use of public office to reward party workers is wrong then it would certainly follow that the Republican party in the Gilded Age had degenerated into a group of spoilsmen and had failed in some of the functions for which it had come into existence. But it must also be remembered that the spoils system served a necessary purpose. Parties must be financed. Under the spoils system the government financed them in large measure. Sometimes incompetent persons received office, and at times, there were no duties to perform, for the usual requirement for obtaining the appointment was not fitness for office but partisanship. All this aroused at the time, and ever since, considerable protest. But the spoils system did provide a method for financing political parties. Unless men became suddenly virtuous and altruistic so that they were prepared to do party service at their own expense, some legal method of furnishing the party organization with funds had to be found. The spoils system was open and subject to much publicity and was in sharp contrast to the secret system, whereby large corporations, with special interests, supplied the money in exchange for favors. If for no other reason than that it was public, the spoils system was to be preferred.[10]

While the Republicans dominated the presidency in the last quarter of the nineteenth century and appeared to have political supremacy, both in the national government and the country at large, their party, as we have seen, suffered from a sectional and minority status that seemed impossible to overcome. The loss of the

South by 1877, the presence of a large bloc of doubtful voters in some of the Eastern and Central states,[11] and the insecure hold of the Republicans upon the North are fundamental to the explanation of their failure to keep a complete and uninterrupted grip upon the national government after their great victory of 1872 in which they gathered 57 per cent of the popular vote in the North and West while in the South and the nation as a whole they polled 55.8 per cent. These developments along with the sharply contested elections of the post-Reconstruction years produced a series of major efforts by Republican strategists to find more recruits for the party. In their attempt to gain a more secure footing in the North they intensified their waving of the bloody shirt, twisted the tail of the British lion to please the Irish-Americans, and ingratiated themselves with the northeastern business community through favorable legislation. To win votes in the doubtful states the Republicans made concessions in the form of taking their presidential and vice-presidential nominees from these areas and by naming congressmen from these districts to important committee assignments. The Democrats matched them in their strategy in the doubtful states and among the businessmen.

But how to appeal to the South remained a major problem for the Republicans. They had not been able to maintain the Republican state governments set up in the South during Reconstruction. One by one they had fallen to the Democrats in spite of Force Bills and President Grant's efforts to uphold them with the use of the military. Even the most vigorous wavers of the bloody shirt realized this fact. "Gen. Grant held up the Southern Republican administration by main force for more than four years, and they got no stronger on their legs, but rather weaker and weaker," observed the *New York Tribune*. "We cannot continue that policy after experience has so fully demonstrated its futility." [12] The *National Republican* pointed out, "The Republican party in the South has heretofore tried to rule by force of arms and Federal bayonets, and it failed." [13]

The loss of the South was a bitter disappointment to the Republicans, for they were painfully aware of the severe handicap they had in the struggle to win control of the federal government when the Democrats had most of the 90 representatives and all of the 22 senators and 112 electoral votes in the South. Not only was it nearly impossible to make sufficient gains elsewhere to compensate for this loss, but it was illogical and poor strategy to allow the situation to continue without an attempt to remedy it. With their vote concentrated in the northern and western states, Republicans could expect to maintain their majority in the Senate. They could hope to battle for the presidency with the Democrats on fairly even terms, but without success in the South their prospects for gaining complete control of the national government were slim.

Because the South has been overwhelmingly Democratic since the Compromise of 1877 it has generally been assumed that the Republicans, apart from Reconstruction, have never really been seriously interested or active in building a strong party in this section. Furthermore, the belief has prevailed that with the removal of the troops, the Republicans gave up the fight in the South as hopeless and unprofitable and wrote off this part of the country as a possible area to contend for. All this has helped to foster one of the great myths of American politics, for Republican failure in the South did not come from lack of effort. Republican leaders worked constantly to break up the Democratic South and to rebuild their party in these states on a strong and permanent basis.[14] They had no intention of permitting the South to go Democratic by default. They needed the South, and they needed it badly if they wished to become the majority party in all major sections of the country as they had done in 1872, and if they wanted to retain their grip on the federal government.

To coax southern Democrats out of their party and into the Republican fold involved a changeover from a policy of military interference to one of nonintervention in the South. Such a turnabout was a revolution in Republican policy, and the whole matter was debated privately and publicly toward the end of Reconstruction and was eventually adopted. Above all, Republicans hoped to benefit from Democratic cleavages in the South. They knew that a large number of Democrats in the South were dissatisfied with their party organization and leaders. Republicans also witnessed further Democratic discontent in the South in the rise of agrarian radicals. This led to the formation of independent movements which gathered strength in the late seventies and which reached their zenith in the Populist revolt of the nineties.

The Republicans launched their new policy in the South with the removal of the last of the federal troops from this section. Over the next twenty years they sought in a variety of ways to win over southern Democrats to the Republican party. But the Republican performance in the South in this period was so inept that it led many Republicans outside the South to conclude that their southern party was hopeless, and it caused many contemporaries and later generations to believe that the Republicans had permitted the South to go Democratic by default. Although this was clearly not the case these two notions, largely based upon faulty or erroneous history, grew up about the Republican party and the South and still persist in many quarters in spite of the evidence to the contrary.

The Republicans failed in the South not through any lack of interest or action on their part but because of the almost insuperable obstacles confronting their new venture. Southern white hostility toward the Republican party and fear of Negro supremacy did not give way before Republican blandishments. Republicans could afford to stand up for the rights of their southern brethren, but they could not afford to support their wrongs. The carpetbagger Negro governments had not won the respect of the country. "Carpet bag governments had not been successful," President Hayes told the editor of the New Orleans Times. "The complaints of the southern people were just in this matter." [15] Neither had these radical governments in the South reflected a Republican sentiment based on a political conviction and sympathy growing among southern whites. In the main they had portrayed political shrewdness, skill in manipulating political machinery, and personal greediness. The one fatal defect of Republican policy since the Civil War, said the New York Tribune, was that of giving opportunity for "adventurers, who were utterly without standing or consideration in any Northern community, and who if not propped up by United States bayonets could not have been elected to any office by colored men of the South, to fasten themselves upon the party and the country as the representative Republicans of reconstructed States." "All other blunders put together," continued the Tribune, "have not cost the

Republican party as many votes as the single fact that it was represented and controlled in reconstructed States by unworthy men." [16]

Factional disputes also interfered with the attempted rejuvenation of the Republican party in the South. The problem was to find a formula, to bring together large numbers of whites and Negroes in the same party. But factionalism and splits between "black-and-tan" and "lily-white" groups undermined such attempts. Factionalism turned out to be the bane of southern Republicanism, and every Republican president since Grant has wrestled with it. Finally, the ability of Democrats to keep southern Republicans from the polls or to nullify their vote drastically reduced Republican strength in all the southern states after Reconstruction and nearly eliminated it entirely in some parts. The success of the whites in excluding the Republican vote as an important factor in southern politics contributed significantly to national Democratic victories.

By the end of these two decades the Republicans still had little support in the South. Twenty years of planning, maneuvering, and fusing still left them without electoral votes in this section. They were yet a sectional party without any great appeal for southern whites, and their party in the South faced a greater problem of rejuvenation than it had in 1877. But the Republicans had not allowed the South to go Democratic by default. They had not written it off as hopeless. They had fought for it. They had tried to Republicanize it, and while the fruits of their effort seem small, they prepared themselves for a fresh try in the twentieth century.

One of the most controversial, tragic, and least understood aspects of the history of the Republican party of the Gilded Age is its relationship to the southern Negro. The Republican party emerged from the Civil War as the champion and protector of the southern Negro. It had emancipated and enfranchised him and had provided him with the same political and civil rights as the white man. And by joining hands with the Negro the Republicans were able to gain temporary political control of the South. While this Republican-Negro alliance produced fruitful political results in the beginning it also created a problem that still vexes both sides. In order to understand the nature of this problem it is necessary to recall what each side wanted from the other. The Republicans desired the votes of the Negro, and the freedman sought protection for his newly acquired rights and asked for the enforcement of the Fourteenth and Fifteenth amendments. He also wished to have greater political recognition and a larger share of the patronage for delivering his vote to the party of liberation.

In the last quarter of the nineteenth century the Republican party, through its official statements, gave every appearance of being the best friend that the Negro had. In their platforms from 1876 through 1896 the Republicans solemnly pledged themselves to enforce the Fourteenth and Fifteenth amendments, to secure to "every American citizen of whatever race and color complete liberty and exact equality in the exercise of all civil, political, and public rights," to protect "honest voters" against terrorism, violence, and fraud, and never to relax their efforts "until the integrity of the ballot and purity of elections . . . be fully guaranteed in every state." They demanded that every citizen, white or black, be allowed to cast one free unrestricted ballot and to have it counted and returned. They denounced the "continuous inhuman outrages" perpetrated upon American citizens for political reasons, and the "fraud and violence practiced by the Democracy in the Southern States." [17] In Congress, Republicans moved investigations of fraud and violence in elections in the South, accused southern Democrats of holding their seats illegally and of exercising a disproportionate voting influence, and focused attention upon indiscreet statements by southern leaders and the press such as the editorial of the *Times-Democrat* of New Orleans which exclaimed, "The aim and desire of every white citizen of Louisiana is to eliminate the Negro from politics." [18]

But the Republican party turned out to be among the poorest of friends that the southern Negro had after Reconstruction. For while the Republicans talked much about safeguarding the vote of the colored man and loudly lamented the state of political affairs in the South, they took few steps to remedy the situation or to meet their obligations to the freedmen. Instead of looking after the Negro as the ward of the nation, they deserted him and left him as the ward of the dominant race in the South. On three major occasions over these decades, the Republicans abandoned the Negro ally: when President Hayes removed the troops; when President Chester Arthur chose to work with southern independents; and when President Benjamin Harrison and a Republican Congress backed away from the Force Bill of 1890 to regulate federal elections.

In part this abandonment was beyond the control of the Republicans, for throughout most of this period they lacked the political power to enforce the Fourteenth and Fifteenth amendments. But the abandonment was also part of the new policy that Republicans had inaugurated in the South in 1877. These new plans called for a shift in Republican appeals in the South from Negroes to whites in the hope such strategy would result in the building of a Republican party in the South that could command the respect and support of southern conservative whites. This is not to say that the Republicans had lost interest in the Negro vote. On the contrary they wished to maintain, and even increase, their Negro support, but they also wanted to swell their ranks with white recruits. Thus Hayes forsook the Negro when he recalled the troops because he hoped this would reconcile North and South, conciliate southern whites, and ingratiate the Republican party with them. Arthur cast off the colored man when he joined hands with the white Independents in the South, because he believed that in order to exploit the Democratic cleavages in the South, which he had concluded was the only path to Republican success in this section, it was necessary to subordinate the freedman. In 1890 the Republicans abandoned the Negro when they failed to pass the Force Bill, because they had a greater interest in tariff and silver measures, although there was considerable opposition to the elections scheme in party ranks.

It must also be remembered that the Republican abandonment of the Negro was only a part of the general desertion of the freedman by northerners. By the end of Reconstruction the North had significantly changed its mind about the Negro. The *Nation*, one of his staunch northern champions, following the decision to take the troops out of the South, declared, "The negro will disappear from the field of northern politics. Henceforth the nation, as a nation, will have nothing more to do with him." [19] Except for the Republican party interest in the Negro vote, there was not much concern among northerners for the colored man in the South. After 1877, northerners were, for the most part, in substantial agreement with southerners that the Negro was not prepared for equality and that the South should be allowed to deal with him in its own way. The

North had come to believe that the elimination of the Negro from politics must be recognized to give more meaning to the reunion of North and South. Northerners were coming to regard the Negro as a thorn in their flesh, and as standing in the way of a return to national solidarity and a development of trade relations between the two sections. They were coming to look upon the Negro as the American peasantry, and as being inferior in race stamina, and they were coming to believe that the only hope for good government in the South rested upon the assured political supremacy of the white race.[20]

The Republicans in their drive for new recruits from among southern whites had subordinated and even forsaken their Negro allies. In turn the Negro became suspicious and critical of the Republican party. Yet for all his misgivings and hostility the Negro preferred Republicans to Democrats and was reluctant to adopt the strategy of independent action. During the controversy over the new policy President Hayes had launched in the South, a Negro Republican from Baltimore in an open letter said that the defense of Horace Greeley in 1872 was child's play compared with efforts to defend Hayes among Republicans. This Negro had not met a Republican in weeks who attempted to disguise his disgust with Hayes's policy. Yet in all this he saw nothing to encourage the Negro except the prospect of their vindication by the defeat of the Republican party in 1880. "This would be a questionable satisfaction," wrote the Negro correspondent, "and as a remedy is worse than the disease." At the end of this period, in 1895, just before he died, Frederick Douglass pointed out that although the Republican party had become indifferent toward the Negro, "still we have a chance of getting a better man from the Republicans than from the Democrats." [21] Whether this was a wise decision is surely debatable, for in our own time when the Negro has divided his political loyalty, both major parties have eagerly sought his vote.

The manner in which historians have treated the Republican party of the Gilded Age is reminiscent of a story of the mining country of the old West. In one of the mining camps there was a bully who cheated everyone he knew. He lied, he swore, he killed, and finally he died with his boots on. Now the miners wanted to give him some sort of religious service, but did not know how to do it. So they sent two of their group to a neighboring camp where they heard there was an old-time itinerant preacher prospecting for gold. They found him and asked him to preach a sermon over the dead man's remains. When he asked about the character of the dead man, the two miners replied, "We can say nothing good for him. He is guilty of every crime on the calendar and had no conscience, no sympathy, no honor." When the preacher answered "all right," they asked, "You mean you are going to preach the sermon over his remains in spite of what we said." "Oh, yes." "What will you say?" they asked. "Well, I shall speak of the great times in which he lived."

The point is well made concerning the decades following the Civil War. It is a period in which the United States became the greatest industrial nation of the world. The chief actors on the American scene were businessmen. Americans witnessed a vast change in politics as the country became industrialized. Historians have called it the political triumph of business achieved through a corrupt alliance of business and government. Against such a background American historians have produced a stereotyped picture of a Republican party composed of ever needy and worthless Union veterans, greedy monopolists, and corpulent businessmen who made their corrupt senators and representatives dance to the tunes of enormously high protective tariffs, the gold standard, easy pensions, and extravagant river and harbor bills. This traditional description has been overdone as the authors of general histories and the most commonly used textbooks have competed with each other to find suitable disparaging phrases with which to describe the Republicans of the Gilded Age. Most certainly the Republican party must be judged in late nineteenth-century political terms. Those judgments must fit the situation as it actually was and not as we might like to have it be or suppose it was.

6

Greenbackers, Goldbugs, and Silverites
Currency Reform and Policy, 1860-1897
PAOLO E. COLETTA

THE currency problems of the Gilded Age, posed originally by the financial exigencies of the Civil War, were directly affected by the government's political and fiscal policies, the end of the frontier and the rise of industry and of the city, swings of the business cycle, new discoveries of silver and gold, and learned and popular conceptions of the part the government and the banks should play in providing and regulating the currency.

Unable to finance the stupendous war costs out of taxes, short-term loans, and hard money, Secretary of the Treasury Salmon P. Chase, in his report for December, 1861, suggested a national banking system which would create a uniform currency, provide a market for government bonds, and prevent the overexpansion and depreciation of the currency. The issue of partial legal tender notes acted as a temporary palliative; a constitutional and practical reform was needed to permit the government, like the individual and the corporation, to use the same money the people used, to borrow from banks as the people did, and above all to use fully its exclusive constitutional control over the monetary system.[1] After both the banks and the government suspended specie payments late in December, 1861, Secretary Chase proposed not a new federal bank but a system of banks with national charters, the principles for which had been evolved by Alexander Hamilton in preparing the charter for the first United States bank.

Backed by the Lincoln administration and applauded by public opinion, the act passed on February 20, 1863, and was approved by Lincoln five days later. At the time there were some 1,700 banks established under the laws of twenty-eight states. Each bank issued its own currency, and there was "no common regulator . . . no check or control," as Sherman put it.[2] Before the Civil War the Union had used only hard money under the independent treasury system and had had no contacts with banks for nearly twenty years. The new act combined the interests of the government and the people, made them partners in a system of national banks whose liabilities would provide a government-supervised national currency. Note issues would be convertible into United States notes while the war lasted and afterwards into coin; the currency would be uniform; and the system would furnish a market for government bonds. Chase's difficulties in selling bonds, however, are exemplified by his telling the bankers that unless they took certain loans on his terms he would issue paper money "until it takes $1000 to buy a breakfast." [3]

In 1862, Hugh McCulloch, president of the very successful Bank of the State of Indiana, had gone to Washington to protest the passage of the national banking act. He was convinced by Secretary Chase that the law was necessary, and shortly thereafter he was asked to take charge of organizing and controlling the system as the first comptroller of the currency. McCulloch reluctantly accepted,[4] and his suggestions were incorporated in the drastic revision of the law in the National Banking Act of June 3, 1864. The most pertinent changes forbade state banks to issue national currency, permitted the secretary of the treasury to use the national banks as depositories even though the subtreasuries established in 1846 were retained, and modified the reserve requirements established in the original act by calling for reserves proportional to liabilities and by permitting part of the reserve to be in the form of bank credit.[5] Lincoln's approval of this act, on March 3, 1865, was a bench mark in American financial history. It nationalized the banking and currency system. The 2 per cent tax on state bank issues, raised to a prohibitive 10 per cent by Congress on March 3, 1865, asserted federal sovereignty and deprived the state banks of the note-issuing power they had used for eighty years. It provided a uniform paper currency and enabled the government and the public to use the same money. And the government sold millions in bonds, as required reserves, to the large number of banks that converted to or originated under national charter, most of them after the war. The act posed the heart of the American farmers' dilemma throughout the Gilded Age.

According to the terms of the national banking acts, a banking association could emit circulating notes to the value of 90 per cent of the bonds deposited with the government. But by requiring a minimum capitalization of $50,000 for banks in places under 6,000 population, the acts practically precluded the establishment of banks in rural areas. The older banks, which first received the privilege of note emission, were located mostly in eastern cities.[6] While the national bank currency was a great improvement over the morass of state bank note issues—often spurious ones—of earlier years, it hurt the farmer by proving inflexible: no provision had been made for adjusting circulation according to changes in conditions of population and trade. National bank note issues were limited to $300,-000,000 and were tied to holdings of federal bonds. During periods of stringency, seekers after safe investments drove up their market price and induced the banks to sell them at a profit, thereby reducing the amount of circulation just when inflation was needed. During flush times, they bought them from holders who sold them to invest in something more profitable, thereby contributing to an overabundance of currency which often led to rash speculation. Through its refunding programs, the government gradually withdrew many bonds, and the banks had to compete for them with those who sought them for investment purposes. Thus, whereas in 1865 there was $171,300,000 in the bank note circulation, $291,800-000 in 1870, and $344,500,000 in 1880, there was $318,600,000 in 1885 and only $186,000,000 in 1890, even though the limit on their volume had been repealed in 1875, permitting free banking. The banking system was not geared to the farmer, who needed special long-term credits sufficient to cover a season extending from the planting of a crop to its sale. Since his medium of exchange was cash instead of bank paper, and since the national banking system wiped out the small rural state bank, he was particularly hard hit.

The farmer had other complaints. The national banks could not lend on mortgages. Nor were their note issues acceptable in payment of customs, taxes, and public lands. It irked the farmer that the banker obtained a double profit, the interest on the bonds deposited with the treasury and the interest received from lending his bank notes. Because the older banks were the first to receive the note emission privilege and the newer banks were in the South and West, the farmer charged that he was subjected to sectional discrimination. He saw that the concentration of financial power in the Northeast allowed a few men to enjoy a disproportionate amount of political power, and that the consolidation of economic gains into the hands of creditor interests was enhanced by the repeal of the wartime internal revenue taxes, except on tobacco and alcoholic liquors, by the reduction (1867) and abolition (1872) of the wartime income tax, and by the retention of high tariffs.

The inadequacies of the national banking system's long-term credit facilities drove the farmer to the eastern money market, deepening the gulf of sectional antipathy. To fill the credit vacuum left in the West and South came mortgage loans from eastern sources.[7] If hordes of landless Americans in the generation following the Civil War placed their faith in the future prosperity of the country and invested in farm land, they nevertheless paid a high price for their confidence. Until the mid-eighties land values generally appreciated. When the bubble burst they were squeezed out.

Many measures funding the war debt were enacted between 1865 and 1879, when the debt was reduced to $2,349,600,000, of which $346,681,000 was in greenbacks. Some bonds called for payment in gold or coin; others said nothing about the money to be used in redemption; and Jay Cooke, the treasury's bond sales agent, had promised coin (gold or silver).[8]

Because financial conditions improved and interest rates declined, Congress in the refunding acts of 1870 and 1871 issued, among others, noncallable 4 per cent 30-year bonds, failing to consider that interest rates might go still lower or that the treasury might later be in position to retire them at call. By 1880 the national debt of 1865 had been reduced by 50 per cent, and interest payments by almost 40 per cent. During the 1880's, treasury surpluses became a financial headache because the interest rate went below 3 per cent and after 1887, when the debt redeemable at par was extinguished, noncallable bonds could be retired only by buying them at high cost in the open market. Between 1888 and the middle of 1890 these purchases cut the national debt to a mere $725,000,000, thereby drastically reducing the number of national bank notes and contracting the circulation. Once the national debt was extinguished, a serious problem would be posed by fiscal and currency laws that piled surplus revenues and a high proportion of the circulating medium into the treasury.[9]

By nationalizing the banking system, the Lincoln administration had made banking and currency problems national rather than statewide or sectional in scope. Now the people, as partners with the government in the new arrangement, would have much to say about its operation, but most national fiscal officials favored orthodox banking, currency and debt policies, and regressive tax policies. No legislation relating to the national banks was enacted or even considered from 1883 to 1890, and the American Bankers' Association's "Baltimore Plan" for strengthening and centralizing the national banking system could not even obtain a hearing.[10] For about seventy years this system withstood all challenges. It rebuffed all attempts to remove the tax on state bank notes. The legal tenders, first found to be unconstitutional, later held to be valid, caused trouble to future generations. State banks of deposit persistently challenged the entire system, forty years of wrangling occurred over methods of repaying the government's wartime borrowings, and the farmer's complaints against the system availed him nothing. Not until 1900 were the National Banking acts amended to permit the banks to issue notes to the full par value of bonds deposited instead of 90 per cent and to reduce the capitalization requirement for towns of less than 3,000 population to $25,000 instead of $50,000. Real reform in short-term credits as such awaited the Federal Reserve Act of 1913 and the Agricultural Credits Act of 1923.

The second of the two subcommittees of the Ways and Means Committee appointed in 1861 to study revenue measures and methods of obtaining loans, respectively, recommended the issue of noninterest bearing United States or treasury notes which would be legal tender even though not redeemable in specie. Banker opposition to these "greenbacks" was quick and sharp, and the Legal Tender Act passed, on February 25, 1862, largely because Chase asserted that it was the only way to provide the government with funds. Thus appeared the first real paper money issued by the national United States government.[11]

The first skirmish in the battle of the standards was the "paper war" fought over the legal tenders issued during the Civil War. Many of those who agreed with Secretary Chase on the necessity of their issue, such as John Sherman and Hugh McCulloch, also pointed out the dangers of the experiment; legal tenders would raise prices, increase the cost of prosecuting the war, drive all specie from circulation, cripple labor, throw large wealth into the hands of the rich, and give the party in power the means of perpetuating its control of the government. Others charged that "fiat" paper was immoral, a breach of the public faith. However, there were those who believed paper money perfectly acceptable and justifiable; it would not depreciate because it was based upon the resources of the country and would increase the amount of the currency to fit the needs of an expanding economy.[12] Necessity overcame all opposition, and the $450,000,000 in greenbacks not only helped finance the war but became a symbol of prosperity to the agriculturists of the North and West.[13]

Whether the raising of more taxes and the sale of other bonds would have made the issue of greenbacks unnecessary is irrelevant,[14] for they were an historic fact, and the Congress, which had asserted that their first issue would be the last, authorized more and more of them. Tariff duties, the internal revenues, and the income tax of 1861–65 netted the government only $632,205,000. In contrast, long-and-short-term loans amounted to $2,142,000,000, to which should be added the issue of $450,000,000 in greenbacks and $50,000,000 in fractional currency. The problem of a way of repaying these debts fell first to Secretary McCulloch, 1865–69, who converted all the temporary obligations of the government and began their funding before leaving office and before the legal tender cases were decided. He recommended the sale of bonds for the retirement of the legal-tender notes and said that the only way to pay off the national debt was to raise taxes until government income exceeded expenditures. On December 18, 1865, the House resolved 144 to 6 in favor of the early resumption of specie payments. This resolution availed nothing, for normal peacetime contraction set in shortly thereafter.[15]

The greenbacks provided a constant subject for squabbling during the Gilded Age. They had proved troublesome by depreciating in terms of specie and goods from the moment they were issued.

While speculators and those who needed it bought gold at a premium with depreciated greenbacks, wage-earners paid in paper money suffered severely from inflation; their wages lagged far behind prices, which increased 116 per cent from 1860 to 1865. The government suffered too, for it had heavy expenses yet collected only a portion of its income in the specie required to pay the interest on its debt. The basic causes of the depreciation of the greenbacks were the great increase in demand by government's war spending and the consequent expansion of currency, credit, and income.[16] Inflationists were right in asserting that the Civil War was financed with a 50-cent dollar and paid back with a 100-cent dollar, for in 1864 the greenback went as low as 39 cents.

By 1868 McCulloch had used the Funding Act of April 12, 1866, to convert many short-term notes and certificates into long-term bonds, retire others, and reduce the greenbacks to $356,000,-000.[17] But rather than "monetize" the paper debt by permitting its convertibility into bonds payable in coin, the Congress repealed the Funding Act in 1868, and, in his annual message of December, 1868, President Johnson alienated many by recommending that holders of government bonds be paid not more than the government had received from them in real money. In the three years following the end of the war little progress was actually made toward the resumption of specie payments, and no serious debate on the subject was heard for several additional years, the treasury meantime having raised the amount of greenbacks to $371,400,000.

But the currency question had now entered politics. The Middle West, particularly, protested against hard money redemption, and the Democratic platform of 1868 endorsed the "Ohio Idea" of paying the interest on the national debt in paper money.[18] But the Democratic presidential candidate, the New York banker Horatio Seymour, was "sound" on financial questions and repudiated it. Grant, who knew nothing about finance, took advice from rich sycophants on the subject. One of his first acts was to sign a gold payment bill on May 18, 1869. The inflationists suffered an additional defeat when during the next year the Supreme Court found the legal tender acts of 1862 and 1863 unconstitutional (*Hepburn v. Griswold*, 8 Wallace 603). However, a reconstituted court the following year found that greenbacks could be used to satisfy a debt incurred either before or after the acts had been passed. Eventually, the court liberally interpreted the power of the Congress to "coin money and to borrow" and to issue currency.[19]

The constitutionality of the greenbacks having been settled, their quantity was the next question. Calling for "the same money for the bondholder and the plowholder," low income groups battled high income groups. Debtors, usually agrarians and generally inflationists, opposed creditors, usually those who had purchased bonds in depreciated greenbacks and wanted them paid in coin or in a greenback increased in value. The latter called themselves "sound money" men.

In 1872 the Democrats like the Republicans denounced "repudiation" in every form. If "Black Friday" of 1869 revealed dangers in too close a connection between the treasury and Wall Street, the depression beginning in 1873, which greatly deflated prices, inflamed agrarians against strangling financial measures which they believed emanated from the cities of the East. They opposed any policy that meant contraction of the currency as a "monstrous power" likely to rob them of their daily bread.[20] The attempt of the Republican Congress in April, 1874, to still the popular clamor for relief through the issue of additional "blood stained" greenbacks was vetoed by President Grant. The vote on the bill revealed that economic rather than purely political considerations dictated the casting of the ballots, for the Congress split geographically, with Ohio as the dividing line and the eastern members voting against the bill.[21] Hoping to saddle the Democrats with its enforcement, the lame-duck Republican Congress passed the Specie Resumption Act, "an expression of death-bed repentance," [22] submitted by Senator John Sherman and calling for permanent resumption of specie payments on January 1, 1879. Not a single Democrat voted for it.

This historic act further provided that the volume of greenbacks would be reduced from $382,000,000 to $300,000,000, that fractional paper currency would be replaced by gold coin, and that to resume specie payments the treasury could use any unappropriated surpluses in its coffers and, if necessary, sell bonds for coin. Failure to spell out the meaning of "coin" (though silver had not circulated for forty years) and failure to provide for the retirement of the greenbacks brewed trouble for the future. However, good crops, a favorable balance of trade, an upswing in the business cycle, and his ingenuity in amassing gold from abroad enabled the secretary of the treasury, John Sherman, to put the act into effect on schedule.[23] Meantime a sop had been given the inflationists by an act which made the $346,681,000 in greenbacks then authorized a permanent part of the circulation, and a coalition of eastern Republicans and Democrats foiled an attempt by western Democrats to repeal the Resumption Act before it became effective. In 1879, after seventeen years of agitation, the inflationists had failed to stop the deflation which began in 1861. They had been inconsistent and sporadic in their attack and their success had been meager. They had lost the battle for redemption in paper but won that to declare the greenbacks constitutional. When the resumption of specie payments began on January 2, 1879, the greenbacks were quoted at parity, and their supporters had to rest content with the fact that most of them were now part of the national circulation. Agitation over them had not disappeared, however, before new arguments were heard concerning silver. The "Crime of 1873" had been uncovered in debates on the first free silver bills, introduced in 1876, and the basis had been laid for the battle of the monetary standards fought out through 1896.

Since Hamilton and Jefferson had agreed on the unique experiment of a bimetallic system, the national currency had not been treated as a strict party question. The law of April 2, 1792, established the mint, provided for the free and unlimited coinage of both gold and silver without charge for minting, and adopted the ratio of 15 to 1 by establishing a silver dollar of 371.26 grains and a gold dollar of 24.75 grains. (The ratio is determined by dividing the number of grains in the silver dollar by the number of grains in the gold dollar.)

The first problem encountered in the operation of the law was that of maintaining by legislative fiat a ratio between metals which changed in their relative amounts in the world's commercial markets. Since several European countries valued gold higher than the United States in relation to silver, gold went abroad during the early decades of the nineteenth century and left the United States on what was practically a silver standard. When Congress, in 1834, changed the ratio to 16 to 1, it overvalued silver, which in turn tended to disappear from circulation. In 1837 and 1853 the Congress changed the ratio again, the second time to 14.882 to 1. This ratio allowed silver such a small premium over gold that no profit could be made by shipping it abroad in exchange for gold. The coinage of silver, therefore, was undisturbed, and the mint and coinage values remained practically the same until 1874, when they became equal. The American experience seemed to prove that bimetallism could be maintained by a careful adjustment of ratio so long as the relative amounts of the metals remained fairly constant, though no ratio was sacrosanct.

The problem was endlessly complex, and involved both domestic and foreign considerations. In the domestic sphere the monetary policy of the nation included a determination of the connection between the government, the treasury, and the banks, between gold and silver, and between coin and legal tender. Prosperity or depression, whether industrial or agricultural, provoked demands for raising or lowering the internal revenue taxes and customs duties to effect changes in the public debt and the treasury surplus or deficit. The amounts of gold or silver mined, exported, or imported, the balance of international payments, and the way in which the metals were treated all over the world had to be taken into account. At home, debate over currency policies captured the imagination of political parties, induced dissenters to form parties of their own, and incited class, sectional, and moral schisms. Opposition of debtor to creditor, the popular hatred of the "money power," and idealists seeking panaceas in utopian schemes further confused an already complex problem.

Having lost the war over resumption, inflation advocates burnished their arguments in favor of silver, the production of which had increased annually from $2,000,000 to almost $29,000,000 between 1861 and 1872, and to $45,000,000 in 1878, with the Comstock lode in Nevada yielding almost half of the latter. The bullion value of silver had meantime dropped from $1.03 in 1861 to $0.93 in 1878, and the ratio of silver to gold had dropped from 15.50 to 1 to 17.12 to 1. The silver producers wanted Congress "to do something" for silver. Powerless alone, they saw that they could hide their demand for governmental assistance behind the western and southern farmers' demands for an inflationary measure incited by the depression of 1873. But when they arose to their charge they found that in the congressional recodification of the coinage laws in 1873, begun in 1869 by John Jay Knox under the direction of Secretary Boutwell, the silver dollar had been dropped from the minting list. The Act had dropped from the list of authorized coins the silver dollar of 412½ grains, the standard silver dollar of the coinage, and had authorized in substitution a "trade dollar" of 420 grains.[24] No silver dollars of 412 grains had been coined since 1808, and since 1853 there had been no silver in circulation. To some it appeared that "the act simply made what was fact also law"; to others it constituted the "Crime of 1873."

There is no evidence that the silver dollar had been dropped from the coinage by fraud and collusion.[25] But, coming when it did, it lent credence to the story that the important commercial nations of the world had connived to discredit silver in favor of gold. The international monetary conference held in Paris in 1867 had recommended the gold standard, and in the following decade one nation after another adopted the gold standard and sought dumping grounds for silver. The simultaneous suspension of silver coinage by these nations and the increased production of American silver in large part accounted for the fall in the commercial value of silver following 1873.[26]

No objection was made to the passage of the act of 1873 because only eight million silver dollars had been coined from 1792 to 1873 and the market value of silver was 3 per cent greater than that of gold, with gold favored over silver by those who desired a greater volume of money in circulation. After that date, however, the demands that something be done for silver came from many sides. Free coinage of silver would force the government to buy practically the entire output of the American mines at a price greater than its commercial value. The general public, accustomed since 1834 to silver as an appreciated rather than depreciated metal, seemed favorably disposed to free coinage. Agitation for the free coinage of silver increased as the hope for more greenbacks diminished, and the rift widened between debtor and creditor, between soft and hard money advocates, between the East and the West and South. Debtors had preferred greenbacks to bank money because they were government money and not susceptible to control by domestic or foreign banking interests. Failure to stop coin resumption drove the debtors to their second line of defense, that of a silver coin maintained at parity with gold. They were ably seconded by the American silver mine owners, whose selfish interest cannot be overlooked.

On March 2, 1877, a congressional commission reported in favor of remonetizing silver.[27] The national party platforms had been silent on silver in 1876, but in 1877 western Republican platforms began calling for remonetization. After the failure of several of his free coinage measures, Representative Richard P. "Silver Dick" Bland got one passed on November 5, 1877, by a vote of 167 to 53. Only six votes against it came from west of the Alleghanies and south of Mason and Dixon's line; only nine were cast for it by representatives from the New England and Middle Atlantic states, although the 92 "not voting" meant that many representatives were dodging the issue. The Senate, however, divested it of free coinage at 16 to 1, made silver a legal tender for obligations public and private "except where otherwise expressly stipulated in the contract," and limited the purchase of silver for coinage to not less than $2,000,000 nor more than $4,000,000 per month. It authorized the issuance of notes against coin deposited in the treasury and directed the president to invite the members of the Latin Monetary Union and other European nations to a conference with the United States with a view to agreement upon a ratio between gold and silver. (This second international monetary conference met in Paris in 1878 and failed to reach agreement.)

Extreme silverites castigated Allison's perversion of Bland's measure in the Senate, and Bland threatened to attach riders to appropriation bills if necessary to restore its pristine character. Failing in that, he favored "issuing enough paper money to stuff down the bondholders until they are sick," and voted for his amended bill only under protest. On the other side, men like Senator Sherman took political as well as financial considerations into account: the measure was immensely popular with the rank and file of all parties; it would placate the silver Republicans; it would pass over a presidential veto; and it would not inject enough silver into the currency to endanger either parity or government credit. President Hayes, however, characterized the bill as a "grave breach of the public faith" and as authorization for the "violation of sacred obligations" and vetoed it. Congress promptly passed it over his veto, and the treasury's resumption operations halted.[28] Strangely enough, one month later Hayes approved the act of May 31, 1878, which prohibited further contraction of the "battle scarred and blood stained" greenbacks.

The Bland Allison Act provided a "limping standard," one neither fully monometallic nor fully bimetallic, which pleased neither those who wanted unlimited free silver coinage nor those who granted gold alone. Nor could silver be used in settling international balances. Although western Democrat and Greenback state platforms demanded free coinage, the Senate rebuffed all bills providing for free coinage between 1878 and 1880. In July, 1880, Secretary Sherman privately stated, "The silver law threatens to produce within a year or so a single silver standard. . . . I could at any moment, by issuing silver freely, bring a crisis." [29] Garfield, a "sound money" man, was elected in November, and in his message at the end of the year President Hayes forcefully urged the suspension of silver coinage.

Cleveland began his first term in 1885 with the fear of the suspension of gold payments looming over financial circles. Even before his inauguration he was warned that President Arthur's secretary of the treasury was striving to maintain gold payments until March 4, 1885, so that the inevitable suspension would take place in a Democratic administration.[30] The pessimism of Cleveland's informant was founded on the results of both fiscal and financial policies. Another international monetary conference, held in Paris in April, 1881, "adjourned for politeness' sake," really *sine die*, without reaching agreement. Instead of using treasury surpluses to pay off the national debt, the Arthur administration spent them on pensions and river and harbor works. Protectionists killed its attempt to lower the tariff duties and thereby reduce the revenues, and reductions of the internal revenues coincided with a period of adverse trade balances and, more important, the piling up of silver in the treasury which helped cause the recession of 1884.[31] Under the Bland-Allison Act, although every secretary of the treasury had kept silver purchases to the minimum required, the government had minted 378,166,000 silver dollars and had succeeded in forcing much of this amount into trade channels, only to find silver re-dundant during and after the short business depression beginning in 1883.[32] While the government was paying its creditors in gold, its debtors were paying their obligations in silver. Silver was being exchanged for gold at the treasury by those who needed it to make contractual payments at the same time that the government, with customs dwindling, was expected to maintain both a gold reserve of $100,000,000 and parity between gold and silver.

In 1875 Congress had empowered the secretary of the treasury to sell bonds to establish in the treasury a reserve fund for gold for the redemption of greenbacks. Although no definite sum had been specified, the public had come to regard $100,000,000 as a safe minimum, a minimum which Cleveland respected and eminent financiers held sacred. Such men as Abram S. Hewitt, Manton Marble, Samuel Randall, and Samuel Tilden, suspecting that silver might replace gold as the standard of value, urged Cleveland to ex-press himself in favor of relieving the danger to gold by stopping the coinage of silver. Hewitt and Randall hastily prepared an appropriate bill. The silver men countered with a round robin addressed to Cleveland, February 11, 1885, signed by ninety-five Democratic congressmen, in which they urged him to stand fast against the de-mands of those who would suspend silver coinage. Cleveland was warned that the South and West would not agree to the suspension of silver coinage, that three-fourths of the Democracy opposed sus-pension, and that suspension would kill all his hopes for other de-sirable reforms and weaken his party in many states recently con-verted from Republicanism.[33] Although Cleveland felt it indelicate for a president-elect to appear to meddle in the affairs of Congress, he deemed the danger grave enough to warrant expressing himself. He allowed Tilden and Marble to draft a public letter which he signed reluctantly and addressed to the avid silverite, Representative A. J. Warner. He deemed it "most desirable . . . to maintain and continue in use the mass of our gold coin, as well as the mass of silver already coined. This is possible by a present suspension of the purchase and coinage of silver. I am not aware that by any other method it is possible." [34]

"Your silver letter is absolutely perfect. It is the only silver thing I know that transmutes itself into gold," Tilden wrote Cleveland.[35]

Ex-President Hayes confided to his diary that he was more pleased with Cleveland than was the majority of the Democratic party.[36] As a result of his position, however, the first Democrat elected president in twenty-four years was slapped in the face by his party even before his inauguration. Two days after the publication of his letter Congress overrode Hewitt's suspension bill, with a majority of 118 Democrats and 52 Republicans against 54 Democrats and 64 Republicans. Nevertheless, Cleveland had served notice that he would be deaf to all inflationist schemes.

Cleveland remained obdurate in his demand for the suspension of the compulsory coinage clause of the Bland-Allison Act and equally unyielding toward the barrage of bills providing for the free coinage of silver which marked the first half of his administration.[37] Cleveland repelled all attacks, even if by slim margins. The House in turn refused to carry out the administration's wishes with respect to silver. Ironically enough, the president found his most telling support against silver in the Republican Senate. For the last two and a half years of his administration the deadlock remained unbroken.[38] A fourth international monetary conference failed to reach agreement, and a British royal commission in 1888 evenly divided, half rejecting bimetallism, half recommending it.

The Republicans won the elections of 1888 on a platform which favored both silver and gold. Heretofore scattered elements favoring silver were beginning to organize on a national scale at the instigation of the silver mine owners and under the leadership of both private and public men of the Middle and Far West. The First National Silver Convention, which met in St. Louis late in November, 1889, summarized the feelings of the silverites. It resolved that the demonetization of silver worked a practical violation of every contract, was responsible for a drop of more than 30 per cent in commodity prices,[39] contracted the currency, and made debts practically perpetual by taking from the debtor his ability to pay. It resolved that the 51st Congress should require the secretary of the treasury to coin the maximum of $4,000,000 of silver each month, as provided by the Bland-Allison Act, until it could provide for the free and unlimited coinage of silver. The platform, written by Bland, was adopted enthusiastically by the delegates of thirty states and territories stretching from Ohio to Kansas, with the representatives of the farming areas more impassioned in their pleas for silver than those of the mining states.[40]

In 1889 the president, Senate, and House, for the first time since 1875, were all Republican, but the majority in the Congress consisted of only eight men in each house. The party was pledged to tariff reform, "the use of both gold and silver as money," and increased governmental expenditures because surpluses dogged the treasury. William McKinley, who had favored the larger use of silver since his election to Congress in 1876 and who was now chairman of the Ways and Means Committee, led the House into believing that something must be done for silver in order that the issue of paramount importance to him, tariff reform "upward," should encounter no opposition from the silverites.

There were enough Republicans in the House who, if nothing were done for silver, would vote with the Democrats for free silver coinage. There were also a sufficient number of silver Republicans in the Senate, the eighteen men in the western or silver bloc, to insure the passage of a free coinage bill or to kill a higher tariff law. Secretary of the Treasury William Windom would have had the government buy at the market price all the American and foreign silver offered it and issue against it silver certificates redeemable in silver at its market price. Unable to study this plan thoroughly, President Harrison refused to endorse it.[41] At the time the ratio of silver to gold was 22 to 1 and the silver bullion value was 72 cents. The bill embodying Windom's scheme was defeated in the Senate, after which a free coinage substitute was approved by 42 to 25, the majority including 16 of the 18 in the silver bloc. That same day, June 5, the Senate decided to sit on the McKinley tariff just received from the House. Following a strenuous contest in which Bland led the Democrats and McKinley the almost solid Republican vote, the House disagreed with the Senate (135 to 152) and the bill went into conference. There Senator Sherman, who had had little to do with the matter until it reached the conference committee, acted the part of the great compromiser. Fearing that if he failed a free coinage measure would be passed and that Harrison could not be depended upon to veto it, he remodeled the bill into the shape in which it finally passed. On July 14 the Sherman Silver Purchase law passed the House by 123 to 90, 116 not voting, and the Senate by 39 to

26 by strict party vote,[42] and the McKinley tariff was passed soon thereafter.

The Sherman law was a compromise that simply staved off unlimited silver coinage by allowing a more liberal purchase plan. Western Republicans who cared little for a protective tariff but much for free silver traded votes with eastern Republicans who cared much for protection. Not a Democrat voted for it, not a Republican against it.[43] When Speaker Reed attempted to bury the Senate's free coinage bill in committee, McKinley moved that it be forced into the light.[44] In another compromise, southern senators gave up their plan to filibuster until Lodge's Force Bill was killed in return for allowing a vote to be taken on the McKinley tariff bill. Colorado's Senator Edward O. Wolcott, steered by his colleague, Henry M. Teller, then served notice that the silver men were entitled to as much consideration as the tariff interests and that if something were done for the East as much should be done for the West.[45]

The new law authorized the treasury to purchase monthly four and a half million ounces of silver bullion for coinage into dollars, to be paid for with treasury certificates of full legal tender. These were redeemable in gold or silver at the discretion of the secretary of the treasury. The price paid for 371.25 grains of pure silver was not to exceed $1 (equal to $1.2929 per ounce); after July 1, 1891, standard dollars could be coined only when necessary for the redemption of the notes. The law also reiterated the government's purpose to maintain gold and silver at parity.

Unlike the notes of 1878, the new treasury certificates were full, not partial, legal tender. Since they could be redeemed by the treasury in either gold or silver, silver was on a parity with gold. Under the old law, purchases of silver were made with dollars; under the new law, by ounces. Before, each dollar bought more silver as silver's price fell; now the same number of silver dollars would be added to the circulation even when the price of silver fell.

The Sherman law provided for government purchase of the entire silver output of the American mines. It reassured those who feared that such large purchases of silver would result in depreciation of the standard by promising note redemption in either gold or silver. Although the banks readily accepted the treasury certificates, predictions were made that a crash would follow within eighteen months, and the suspension of silver coinage on July 1, 1891, because note redemption was not being demanded, provoked both vociferous abuse and loud praise. As a result of the Baring panic of 1890, American gold was called abroad. With seven-eighths of its customs duties paid in silver certificates and only one-eighth in gold, the government found itself again short of gold. Those who had predicted a crash pointed to silver as its major cause.

The supply of currency in circulation increased about 50 per cent between 1866 and 1896. The amount of gold added, about $800,000,000, was not only insufficient but unstable, fluctuating with the shifts in the balance of international payments. The reduction of about $126,000,000 in national bank note circulation between 1886 and 1890 confirmed the silverites in their contention that the monetary medium would be insufficient without the use of silver. Since industrial production had increased at a rate even greater than that of the monetary supply, they asserted that the amount of silver injected into the circulation between 1878 and 1890 had not proved excessive; more currency was needed simply to provide the community with the means of carrying on larger trade and business transactions.[46] Finally, by comparing the value of silver and of gold with commodity prices, they concluded that it was more nearly correct to say that the gold dollar of 1873 had become a two-dollar dollar in 1893 than it was to say that the silver dollar of 1873 had become a 50-cent dollar, that gold had appreciated rather than that silver had depreciated.[47] But they overlooked two cogent facts. First, commodity prices had fallen in the United States from 100 in 1873 to 71.5 in 1893; second, by 1890 almost 90 per cent of the total volume of business transactions was made by check, and only 10 per cent in currency. Moreover, silver was being accepted by the banks only because a law of 1882 prohibited the extension of the charter of any national bank that accepted membership in a clearinghouse that refused silver. To those who believed in the quantity theory of money [48] and to the millions who had no checkbooks and hated the banks, these facts made little sense.

Objections to the Sherman law, including Sherman's, were voiced even while the vote was being recorded.[49] President Harrison later admitted that he did not understand the law and that he signed it because Sherman, Aldrich, and Windom assured him that he could do so safely. The East objected to the law's involving the dangerous possibility of silver monometallism; the West complained that it did not provide for the unlimited coinage of silver. The West could not believe that the new law would furnish more money than the nation could absorb. Indeed, it would have been pleased to see the predictions of its eastern critics come true and have silver drive gold out of circulation and force a rise in the price level.[50]

The Sherman law gave the silver miners all the support they could expect from the government; yet in November, 1890, twenty state conventions went on record as favoring unlimited silver coinage and the Republicans lost the House and many governorships in a sweeping political reversal. The balance of trade had turned against the United States in 1888, the Baring failure of 1890 soon ramified to New York and South America; early in 1893 the United States was engulfed in a worldwide depression which stimulated vociferous debate over the efficacy of the Sherman law and worldwide concern with devising improved currency systems. Attempts to organize the American farmer and laborer since the early 1870's apparently stood on the threshold of fruition in the formation of the People's party in 1892. The year following July 1, 1893, witnessed Coxey's army, the Pullman strike, the failure of the Wilson tariff bill, and the first sale of bonds for gold. William H. Harvey's best seller, *Coin's Financial School*, appeared in June, 1894.[51] Cleveland, returning as president in 1893, persisted in favoring gold and thereby enabled the relative newcomer to politics, William Jennings Bryan, to contend with him for the control of the party. In January, 1896, various silver propaganda organizations merged into the American Bimetallic Union, and the nonpartisan National Silver party was also born. Finally, the election of 1896, although very narrowly won by the Republicans, settled the currency issue for the foreseeable future on the gold basis favored by industrial, financial, and urban America.[52]

By 1892 the base of support for the old agrarian-labor parties had widened. Terence V. Powderly of the Knights of Labor and Samuel Gompers of the American Federation of Labor were aided by a host of political friends including John Peter Altgeld, Clarence Darrow, Henry D. Lloyd, and Lyman Trumbull.[53] Political leadership in the agrarian field devolved upon such picturesque personalities as Mary E. Lease, Ignatius Donnelly, "Sockless" Jerry Simpson, the marvelously bewhiskered William A. Peffer, the ubiquitous James B. Weaver, the irascible Tom Watson, and the affable Bryan.[54] Bryan and many Populists believed and convinced millions of others that there existed an international conspiracy of creditors to despoil the poor, "one destined in its consummation to produce more misery than war, pestilence, and famine," as Bryan put it, and that the fall in the price of agricultural products was directly related to the decline in the price of silver.[55]

Statehood came to six western territories in 1889 and 1890—the Dakotas, Wyoming, Washington, Idaho, and Montana. They were all Republican and all silverite.[56] Their seeking special support for their mining and agricultural interests was as natural and understandable as the industrialists' demanding high tariff duties. To the industrial-financial-urban, and to the silver interest, was now added a third, the combination of farmer-laborer groups into state organizations and finally into a third party that sought to span both the agricultural and silver interests.

From the days of Daniel Shays, inflationist sentiment has fascinated the American farmer, so long as he remained a debtor, and the American worker, so long as he was caught by low or fixed wages and rising prices. The early 1890's were particularly aggravating to these groups which had so much in common. The East saw labor violence and radical politics. In the West, the boom times enjoyed during the period of rising land values in the early 1880's, while rain fell, ended when drought hit. Europe's crops were good, and new foreign areas, such as India and Argentina, began to export wheat. Having no crops to tend, thousands and tens of thousands of farmers met in schoolhouses and elsewhere to voice their grievances and demand government action for their relief, to "raise less corn and more Hell," as Mrs. Lease suggested. The organizations they established built directly upon the Granger and Greenback movements, aiming to force the decent treatment of farmers by monopolies. Their lack of success spurred many of them to join political organizations stressing financial reforms.[57]

The National Labor Reform party of 1872 called for the abolition of the national banks, a true national currency, and the repudiation of the government's funding program. Four years later, the Independent National party adopted a platform almost wholly financial in character, demanding the repeal of the Specie Resumption Act of 1875, authority to purchase interest-bearing bonds with paper money, the suppression of national bank notes, and an end to the government's right to sell bonds for foreign gold. The miniscule vote of 30,000 for the National Labor Reform party increased to 81,700 for the Independent National party in 1876. The Independents had only sectional appeal; their votes came only from Illinois, Indiana, Iowa, Kansas, Michigan, and Missouri. When laborers and farmers joined in 1878 into the Greenback Labor party, they received votes from California, Georgia and Maryland, and Pennsylvania, New York, and Maine as well as from the Middle West, and their million votes enabled them to send fourteen representatives to Congress. By 1888 the Party was moribund due to labor's withdrawal. It had received only 175,400 votes in 1884, and many of its members now transferred to state alliances and People's parties.[58] The party nevertheless left behind statewide organizations from Illinois to California which objected to the special privileges extended by the postwar Republican administrations to industrial and financial America. Men who had countered the contractions of the currency implicit in the resumption of specie payments now shifted to silver as a device to cheapen money and provide relief from debt, retained a vision of gathering into one party all the "honest workers" of the nation, and furnished much of the leadership of the national Populist party.[59]

The People's party built upon statewide or sectional farmer-labor organizations, especially upon the Northwest Alliance and the Southern Alliance, and hoped to merge the political power of the western farmer and eastern worker. By the 1890's, however, the urban workers, although unhappy with the increase in real wages since 1865, began to support their employers against the inflation and consequent high food and textile prices demanded by the farmer. Like the Greenbackers, the Populists attacked special legislative privilege to the masters of capital who despoiled America's natural resources, demanded "equality" of treatment for agrarian America, and concentrated upon financial reforms.[60] Their first platform, adopted in 1892, was particularly concerned with the issues of land, finance, and transportation. Following a preamble which dramatically provided a rallying cry for liberals everywhere, they demanded a national currency issued by the government without the use of intermediary banks, free silver at 16 to 1, a circulating medium increased to not less than $50 (or twice that extant), and a sub-treasury scheme for the extension of low-cost government farm credits.[61]

Official and popular debate over the currency increased between 1890 and 1893, and continued in flood proportions through 1896.[62] In his annual message for 1891, President Harrison asserted that while government purchases of silver had not raised its price to a dollar in terms of gold, the additional currency had benefited trade and prices. He was willing to give the Sherman law a 'full trial" but warned of the dangers of silver monometallism and of the need of international agreement.[63] On March 24, 1892, despite support for a Bland silver bill by Speaker Charles F. Crisp, his fellow Democrats, and the Alliancemen, it was defeated by a tie vote.[64] Harrison's announcement of the holding of an international monetary conference forestalled vigorous action in favor of silver, but now the gold men took the offensive in the form of a bill calling for the repeal of the 10 per cent tax on state bank notes provided in the national banking act amendments. Although the measure would implement the Democratic platform, western Democrats denounced it as permitting "wildcat banking" and as constituting a surrender of the nation's sovereignty over the coinage into the hands of private corporations.[65] His ardor undampened by the nomination of Cleveland in June, Bland introduced another silver bill and the Senate actually passed one by a majority of four on July 1. Bland demanded a showdown. When the bill failed, silver went back to the calendar for the rest of the session and Bland's prestige sank. Now the turn of the gold men, Sherman introduced a bill calling for the unconditional repeal of his own Silver Purchase law, but the Congress adjourned without acting upon it.[66]

In the short session of the 52nd Congress (December 5, 1892 to March 4, 1893) two propositions split the House Democrats. The Andrews-Cate bill would repeal the Sherman law and also permit the national banks to increase their circulation. Another bill would repeal both the law and the tax on state bank note issues. Silverites held that the repeal of the Sherman law, that "cowardly makeshift," should not be accomplished unless a substitute could be secured that would prevent contraction of the currency without at the same time augmenting the powers of either the national or the state banks. Cleveland pressured Crisp, saying that he would approve his re-election as speaker only if the majorities on the Ways and Means, Appropriations, Coinage, and Banking committees were composed of gold and low tariff men. The president also pointed out that in 1889 he had left Harrison a treasury surplus of $226,000,000, of which $196,000,000 was in gold. Now, except for the $100,000,000 reserve, the treasury was practically empty. He and his prospective secretary of the treasury, John G. Carlisle, favored the repeal of the Sherman law, and he warned that he would use the patronage club against those who opposed repeal and that if repeal was not accomplished by March 4, 1893, he would call Congress into extraordinary session to do so.

On February 3, 1893, the Senate defied Cleveland by refusing to pass Sherman's repeal bill. On February 8, the House did likewise by defeating the Andrews-Cate bill, but the closeness of the vote, 153 to 142, showed that repeal and anti-repeal strength was as equally divided in the House as in the Senate. Sponsors of silver, meantime, killed all bills authorizing the sale of bonds for gold, asserting that contraction of the currency would not bring permanent relief to the people. Moreover, they argued, there was no further need for the $100,000,000 redemption fund. This fund had been established when specie payments were resumed, and fear was felt of a drain on the gold reserves. Now $30,000,000 or $40,000,000 would do. Furthermore, the obligations of the United States, whether bonds, greenbacks, or treasury notes, called for redemption in "coin," which meant gold or silver, not gold alone. Of what advantage was it to issue bonds for gold if the gold were obtained in an endless chain by the presentation of greenbacks for redemption? And why issue bonds to buy gold when silver lay ready for use in the treasury? [67] Such arguments were bolstered in the 53rd Congress by the four senators and eleven representatives the Populist party had gained in the elections of 1892.

The financial crisis forced Cleveland to abandon the tariff issue to save gold.[68] Cleveland entered the presidency with only $100,-

942,410 in the gold reserve. Export needs drained $25,000,000 from the treasury in December, 1892 and January, 1893; February started with a reserve of only $108,000,000, and Harrison's secretary of the treasury, Charles Foster, ordered the preparation of plates for a bond issue, an order withheld while he borrowed gold from the New York banks. In his inaugural address Cleveland asserted that he would avert debasement of the currency and disaster to the nation by repealing the Sherman law. To this end he would use the patronage, his party organization, and the influence his position carried in the Congress and with the public.[69] In this, Cleveland opposed such Democrats as Bryan, who believed government was made for the convenience of the people. Cleveland demanded stability while Bryan would experiment. If free silver failed, Bryan would try something else, but above all he would try something.[70]

There was not a single silver mine in the entire South, but the South vied with the West in demanding free silver at 16 to 1, and western and southern Democrats, western Republicans, and the Populists cooperated in mutual defense of their sections and interests.[71] They argued that under demonetization of silver all debtors would pay their debts in a commodity worth far more than at the time the debts were contracted and thus give creditors an unearned increment. By contracting the currency, it would appreciate the value of gold and reduce prices still further, preclude capital investment, prevent re-employment, make competition with the cheap labor of silver countries like India and China impossible, and make debts practically perpetual. Bimetallism would reduce the appreciation of gold, restore the ratio of the metals to near the time-honored ratio of 16 to 1 and also of the fixed par of exchange between countries on different metallic standards, and prove a more stable standard than one metal alone and therefore greatly lessen the evils of fluctuating and falling prices.

To Cleveland's support, in general, came the Democrats and Republicans of the East and of the industrialized portions of the Middle West, and of the business and professional community. These demanded stability of the currency as a basis for confidence of business prosperity in the future. Silver, they said, was bulky and inconvenient as a medium of exchange. Cheap silver would drive gold out of circulation, thereby reducing the amount of money, most of which was in the form of credit anyway;[72] moreover, paper money rather than coins performed about 75 per cent of all business transactions. The fall in prices since 1873 was caused by better methods and more production, not by demonetization. It was a delusion to have any but a single standard, for how could one measure value by two differing yardsticks?[73]

By April, 1893, the gold reserve had dropped below the $100,-000,000 mark. Regarding it as an index by which to measure the maintenance of the gold standard, Cleveland insisted that he would "keep the public faith and preserve the parity between gold and silver and between all financial obligations of the government." When the international monetary conference called in 1891 failed to reach agreement in April 1893, Cleveland and Carlisle began seeking loans in the New York money market. On May 4 the failure of the National Cordage Company ushered in the panic of 1893,[74] beginning five years of falling prices,[75] business failures, unemployment, and severely reduced government income. Western farmers also suffered a partial crop failure. When the price of silver fell by the astounding sum of 20 cents because of the demonetization of silver by India in June, the American farmer believed another link had been fashioned by the gold men in the inexorable chain with which they would bind to earth the debtor classes of the world.[76]

Silverites denied that the government's silver purchases had caused the panic and depression, for the depression was worldwide and affected the gold standard nations as well as the United States. European investors in need of cash had sold their securities in the United States, they explained, thereby draining our gold reserves, and American banks had ruined many sound businesses by "running scared" and refusing ordinary credits. What should be done? Restoration of confidence, asserted the silverites, would follow if the people would put their money back into the banks. Then loans could be made and business would revive. The power to issue currency should be taken from the banks and placed where it rightfully belonged, with the government. And the Sherman law should remain untouched, for it was a sure way of getting money into circulation during the hoarding of gold.

Two weeks prior to the convening of the special session of Congress called by Cleveland on June 30 for August 7, 810 delegates representing forty-two states and territories attended an American Bimetallic League convention in Chicago and planned strategy for warding off the repeal of the Sherman law. Weaver's suggestion that all free silverites embrace the Populists' Omaha platform of 1892 was declined, as was that of the creation of a distinctly new national silver party. The delegates agreed that all legislation unfavorable to silver must be defeated, that the financial policy of the nation must remain free from dependence upon that of any other nation, and that the only remedy for current conditions lay in the unlimited free coinage of silver at 16 to 1.[77]

The battle over the repeal of the Sherman law had political as well as economic significance, for Bland, recognized as the outstanding silver leader, must defeat Cleveland in order to win the presidential nomination in 1896 or give way to some other silverite, perhaps Bryan. Seeking a compromise, Bland offered a series of bills providing for free coinage at ratios from 16 to 1 to 20 to 1. All of Bland's bills were defeated, as was the proposal to return to the Bland-Allison Act. On the repeal of the Sherman law, which was accomplished by a vote of 239 to 108, four-fifths of the Republicans voted aye while the Democrats divided, 138 aye to 78 nay. Since only two-thirds of the Democrats stood by Cleveland, he won because of Republican support.

While the Senate Finance Committee worked on its repeal bill, the House silverites struck back with a demand for the coinage of the seigniorage,[78] castigated Cleveland for his obstinacy in pushing repeal, and charged him with causing "the disintegration of the Democratic party in the South and West." For eighty days, free silver senators conducted the longest filibuster then on record. On October 20, the repeal bill passed nonetheless, 48 to 27, with the Democrats dividing equally, 22 to 22. Almost all of the nays came from the South, and all but one of a dozen Republican votes cast against the bill came from the representatives of silver-producing states.[79] On November 1, before an excited House, the silverites failed to jam the proceedings by offering obstructionist motions and finally admitted defeat, but they left predictions of dire consequences. The unconditional repeal of the Sherman law would stop the purchase of silver and the issue of new treasury notes and limit the currency to gold and to whatever notes the national banks found it profitable to issue. Moreover, to support the gold standard the administration must issue gold bonds, and the national debt should not be increased in times of peace. Repeal, in sum, was the "Crime of 1893" which would bury the Democrats in the next elections.

By a captivating *post hoc* argument, inflationists insisted that silver was not wholly to blame for the depression of 1893 because economic conditions got worse immediately following repeal and did not improve materially for more than four years.[80] As prices dropped, unemployment spread, and farm foreclosures increased, free silver loomed large as the principal issue for the campaign of 1896. And for his last two years the Congress denied most of Cleveland's demands for additional financial reform legislation.

The Resumption Act of 1875 authorized the sale of government bonds only for the redemption of greenbacks, not for maintaining monetary parity. Attorney General Richard Olney ruled that such bonds could not be sold if they called for payment in gold alone, and Congress refused Cleveland authority to sell gold bonds. But Cleveland meant to issue bonds whether the Congress liked it or not. Using the only authority available, that for long-term issues at high interest rates in the refunding acts of 1870–71, Carlisle ordered the issue of "coin" bonds. Then Cleveland put pressure on Speaker Crisp, who narrowly defeated a move to pass a seigniorage bill over his veto. This bill, the silverites believed, would have obtained sufficient profit for the government to make the sale of bonds unnecessary, and its defeat further widened the gulf between the eastern and western wings of his party. On April 4, with the defeat of the seigniorage bill, the government was out of the silver business altogether for the first time since 1878.

Cleveland's two sales of gold bonds in 1894 were made through syndicates including J. P. Morgan and Company. When much of the gold paid for the bonds was found to have been withdrawn from the treasury, the government, in 1895, resorted to foreign gold via a private contract with J. P. Morgan and Company and sixty-one European associates. This incited raucus western and southern cries against the "cursed plutocracy" which had "seized control of the government," for Cleveland could have sold the bonds by popular subscription, and assertions that "Wall Streeters and their gold roam through the administration like panthers through their native jungles," for the syndicate had measured the emergency of the government with little mercy. The last bonds sold by subscription (January, 1896) gained the government little because of the paper money endless chain.[81]

Cleveland had consciously cast his weight toward those with vested interests. Far removed from the people, he took advice from Wall Street friends and refused to permit the government to aid the millions of unemployed. By selling bonds he saved the gold standard but saddled the country with a debt of about $262,000,000 from which the bankers profited. Lacking sufficient imagination to perceive the sincerity of silverites, he shattered Bourbon control of his party.[82]

Neither gold man nor silver man was wholly right, for neither at the time envisaged currency plans based upon the nation's wealth in resources other than gold or silver, although irredeemable paper money was vaguely based upon the government's ability to pay. Free silver would not have provided the just and flexible currency the silverites demanded. Nor would it have provided the "complete justice" they sought. But they were at least willing to experiment to relieve the nation's financial distress and prophetic in their demands that the federal government take the lead in solving a problem national in scope.

In 1896 Bryan, the choice of the Democrats, was endorsed by the Populists, the silver Republicans, the National Silver party, and all the minor parties worth noting. He erred in waging a sectional war of the West and South against the East and in campaigning on free silver almost exclusively, but he followed logic which told him that free silver must serve until an "honest" or "commodity" dollar could be obtained, that reform of the currency was the most important of all issues, and that less important problems could be solved later.[83] McKinley's currency plank called for the maintenance of the gold standard until international bimetallism could be attained. In 1897 he tried unsuccessfully to get the important nations of Europe to convene an international conference, and was forced to wait three more years before the Gold Standard Act of 1900 officially made gold the monetary standard. He was indeed fortunate that the South Africa and Alaska gold finds of 1896 and the cyanide process of extraction furnished enough currency to serve the nation's and the world's growing needs for a decade. In 1906 Bryan asserted that the influx of gold and resulting prosperity proved the quantity theory of money.[84]

What moral followed the story of the currency issue for students of American politics? How could an issue which died so quickly have been so consuming and the cause of such intense partisanship to the last generation of the nineteenth century? What men thought, not what they knew, as is so often the case, made history in these years, and many men thought that currency reform was the solution of their ills. Like all great political issues, free silver rose above either the force or weakness of its inherent facts to become an emotional touchstone to the politics of the day. The secret of its appeal lay not in its complexity, which was apparent to the careful student, but in the paradoxical simplicity by which it seemed to many to be an easy solution to the social, economic, and political ills of the day. If free silver were adopted, they reasoned, the economic barons would lose control of the economy, thus restoring equality of opportunity in the market place; they would lose their privileged social positions, thus opening social vistas for more men; and they would be driven, along with special privilege, from the government, which would thus be returned to the people. Currency control was the keystone in this complex arch of special privilege in all spheres of American life; once removed, the arch would fall.

And so it went for a generation, as orators and writers of both parties poured out a stream of persuasive propaganda on behalf of their cause. Like most magic potions, free silver was to cure all ills. In that tacit understanding lay its vast and often hectic appeal to many alienated groups in American society who either did not understand or would not see that the ills for which the medicine was prescribed were susceptible to no such easy cure.

7

Rumblings Beneath the Surface
America's Outward Thrust, 1865-1890
MILTON PLESUR

HISTORY is a continuous drama, and the events of today are later acts to previous settings. Thus today's great debate over the complexity of our foreign entanglements can be related to post-Civil War America and the new role that international relations began to play on the morrow of Appomattox. Diplomatic historians have generally underplayed these post-bellum years, treating them as but an interlude before the grand and romantic climax of spread-eagle expansionism.[1] Undoubtedly during these decades, preoccupation with internal improvements and the westward push precluded a vigorous overseas program. Men of the Grant era concerned with exploiting the natural resources of the trans-Mississippi empire were not prone to lust for even more distant adventures. Controversies over the national debt, taxation, the currency, the New South, superimposed upon the time-hallowed isolationist complex explain this apparent lack of interest in classic imperialism.[2] The Pax Britannica and the limitation of the American horizon to factory smoke on the one side and the vanishing frontier on the other produced a complacent feeling of ocean-locked security.

Moreover, even the most superficial scanning of contemporary records reveals the "Little America" spirit of the times. In an oft-quoted statement, the erudite politician, Henry Cabot Lodge, summed up this sentiment: "Our relations with foreign nations today fill but a slight place in American politics, and excite . . . a languid interest. We have separated ourselves so completely from the affairs of other people." [3]

Surprisingly, even William H. Seward, who spent much time trying to acquire territory, noted, "the United States are not seeking . . . any conquest." We desired only to improve the abundant space already occupied.[4] Every chief executive in this period echoed similar thoughts. Rutherford B. Hayes felt that our country deserved congratulations in 1878 since no grave questions arose to disturb our European relations, and Grover Cleveland could declare unequivocally in 1885 that he opposed territorial acquisitions.[5] A common admonition was that it would be a "bad day" when the people let any "jack-o'-lantern," however brilliant, lure them from the safe road marked by George Washington.[6]

Foreign events counted little in the platforms of the major parties. On the whole, the politicos seemed oblivious to external problems except to reaffirm the necessity of protecting the rights of Americans abroad, emphasizing the need to cultivate friendly relations, and urging the new demands of American commerce.[7] But such sentiments were mere platitudes and, in the manner of party platforms, offended no potential voters and marked no new milestones on the road to world leadership.

The underlying theme of American foreign relations since William McKinley has been the persistent conflict between those forces favoring the assumption of the obligations of a world power and those seeking to avoid the inevitable.[8] This dichotomy was not a new one. Seward's plans for the acquisition of Cuba, the Danish West Indies, and Hawaii foreshadowed a later imperialistic urge but with the exception of Alaska, the New Yorker's program outran the possibilities of public support.[9]

Hence, the purchase of Alaska aside, all other Republican expansionist schemes were stillborn. In those languid years, foreign concerns were usually reactions to specific crises such as the celebrated *Alabama* and *Virginius* cases, the defense of the Monroe Doctrine, and a desire in some quarters for the annexation of Canada with its relatively homogeneous population. Grant's Santo Domingo fixation contributed to the 1872 G.O.P. schism. A dozen years later the Mugwump malcontents opposed expansion, and for the sake of political expediency the once land-hungry Democrats abandoned their former stand. Hawaiian reciprocity talk in the 1870's excited little nonbusiness attention because the Beecher-Tilton scandal crowded it out of people's minds! Soon the public became preoccupied with disclosures of official corruption and proposals for civil service reform. Americans were too busy making money and expanding the domestic economy to concern themselves seriously with the potentials of Pearl Harbor or Pago Pago.[10]

The rest of the world seemed to count for nothing as the country celebrated the centennial of independence. The diplomatic service was denounced as a costly luxury. It was variously labeled as a "humbug," a "sham," a "relic of mediaeval and monarchial trumpery" and a nursery for snobs.[11]

Though to the world the minister or ambassador is the face and voice of the United States, every president since Thomas Jefferson has had to justify increased expenditures to suspicious congressional committees. Diplomacy, especially before 1941, seldom enjoyed a favored position in the perennial struggle over the "pork barrel." Each Congress had its "watchdogs" who favored the closing of less important missions, wanted to eliminate positions, or wished to abolish the entire service on the grounds that more rapid means of transportation and communication made missions and embassies superfluous.[12] Long before George Harvey amused Americans of the 1920's by sporting knee-breeches at the Court of Saint James's it was charged that our "codfish aristocracy" went abroad preferring the "spotted peaches" of European baskets to our home-grown products unmarred by "freckle or spreck." [13] Mugwump reformers of the E. L. Godkin type often advocated the abolition of the service on the grounds that our isolated position precluded an elaborate system of ministries. If a serious crisis arose, so this argument went, able international lawyers could be recruited on a militia basis.[14]

But under the placid surface there were rumblings of future storms. In the wake of rapid industrialization some recognized the need for improved foreign representation.[15] In marked contrast to the hostility shown to the diplomatic service, the congressional leaders were increasingly sympathetic toward consular appropriations. The consular branch performed a practical function and politicians became ever more sensitive to its place in the growth of American business.[16]

The final quarter of the nineteenth century was a seedbed of the future.[17] These were years of flux, when the nature of American expansionism was changing along with so much else in the burgeoning country. The transition from an agrarian to an industrial economy was bound to affect the concept of our global role. After the mainland was riveted with bonds of steel, continental expansion gave way to the seductive thought of overseas empire. Were not, as Alfred T. Mahan later pointed out, the oceans express highways rather than obstacles? The day could be foreseen when more would be produced than consumed and hence attention slowly turned beyond the water's edge. The by-products of this new interest were the demands for a refurbished merchant marine, the acquisition of distant bases and coaling stations, a *sine qua non* to power in an age of steam.

To the small coterie of intellectuals who revolted against the complacency of the Gilded Age, growth beyond our borders was something absolutely necessary to refreshen the wellsprings of American nationalism. The rationale of these men was destiny, a sense of mission and race, the usual arguments of the Social Darwinists. Spencer's influence reached its peak in the United States in the 1880's.[18] In a classic summary of this "New Manifest Destiny," John Fiske proclaimed:

> I believe that the time will come when . . . it will be possible . . . to speak of the United States as stretching from pole to pole. . . . Indeed only when . . . [this has been] realized can civilization, . . . be said to have . . . begun. Only then can the world be said to have become truly Christian.[19]

Another herald of American imperialism, Josiah Strong, was certain that in the hands of the Anglo-Saxon race lay the destiny of mankind. He predicted that the United States would become the center of this beneficent influence and would expand its blessings into Latin America, "the islands of the seas," Africa, and "beyond." [20] As general secretary of the Evangelical Alliance of the United States, the Reverend Mr. Strong stressed the need for rapid-fire evangelization to save America so that it in turn could save the world.

Looking backward in 1900, the sage Brooks Adams declared that the new expansionist phase had indeed begun in 1870. The seat of wealth and power, he argued, was moving westward and America must meet the challenge. The brothers Brooks and Henry Adams, Theodore Roosevelt, Henry Cabot Lodge, and Alfred T. Mahan were basically conservative and imbued with the eastern

genteel tradition, but favored an aggressive foreign policy. Thus
they were sharply critical of the reluctance of the business moguls
and their political vassals to think in terms of larger national goals.[21]
Instilled with the racism of their time such men felt expansionism of
the "fit" a biological necessity. They were more than ideologists,
for they had a blueprint for the implementation of their program.
America, the chosen land, was to hold a beacon out to mankind as
the time-proven exemplar of freedom's banner. This was a heady
view; we could transform any backward country into a miniature
United States by simply extending to them our democratic institutions. The solutions to man's problems in those uncomplicated
times lay in a form of cultural union, spread through imperialism,
and with the United States assuming its part of the "white-man's
burden." [22]

When Harrison entered the White House in 1889, America's
industrial might had made supply exceed domestic demands and the
need for foreign markets was increasing. For a nation with a favorable balance of trade,[23] dreams of commercial isolation were no
longer possible. As a leading cotton and wheat producer, the United
States was involved in the world economy long before the Civil
War, but the increased volume and variety of exportable finished
goods accounted for the difference between ante-bellum and post-
bellum commerce. In 1889, Speaker Thomas Reed could talk of a
"billion dollar country" and excess capital and exports were seeking
additional outlets. In the roseate years just before the 1893 slump,
all America was "breaking out," and the intellectuals were awaken-
ing the "large spirit."

Agricultural products had long been the chief American staple,
amounting in 1880 to 84.3 per cent of all products exported. Unquestionably the ability of the European market to absorb our agricultural surplus was one of the chief factors in our national growth.
America, as the chief granary of the world, gave a fillip to the comfortable belief in our invulnerability. The "myth of the garden"
increased the farmers' indifference to Europe and formed the core
of his isolationism. And yet the effects of the "myth" projected his
look outward and as overproduction became more chronic, he paid
increasing attention to foreign outlets.[24]

Despite the growing overseas market, farm journals regularly reported on foreign agricultural developments and displayed anxiety over increasing harvests overseas and resultant lower prices for American goods. The demand for agricultural products overseas was not constant and depended upon such intangibles as war scares and foreign droughts. Hence, the farmer was skeptical of such trade that made him produce for a "blind market." In the 1880's, there was a sharp price decline and the grain-trade periodicals urged farmers to sell at lower prices to retain their share of the British market. The English leverage on American prices and eventual increase in exports from Russia, Egypt, and India stirred agitation for new markets in South America and the Far East. Farm prosperity was untenable and it is significant that the rise of organized agrarian discontent and the push for new markets both came during the heyday of Populism.[25]

Glowing and rosy statements on the promise of America's increased stature in world markets became increasingly commonplace. From London (1892), Minister James Russell Lowell emphasized that if commerce was not inherently a great "civilizer," it has always been an agent of civilization. A commercial journal declared that even in a country studded with isolationists, one could hardly find a person not anxious to increase business entanglements.[26]

Part of the marvelous growth of America's export trade was due to Secretary of State William M. Evarts' revitalization of the consular service. He believed that the federal government, rather than the self-appointed captains of industry, should nourish our overseas trade. Hence Evarts sought out consuls with business experience, "investigated" the diplomatic corps, and inaugurated a system of reports to assist his department in developing foreign markets. The consular officials helped improve our trade policies. Their suggestions included establishing foreign exhibition houses, displaying prices and samples of goods, improving the quality of exports, and increasing the language and cultural outlook of American businessmen abroad. From Berlin (1881), Minister Andrew D. White prematurely suggested the creation of a department of commerce in order to lend prestige to American commerce beyond the waters.[27]

The perennial tariff issue affected the debate over foreign economic commitments. The high rates of the post-Civil War era spelled increased prosperity to some, while importers, middlemen, and transportation moguls felt the tariff should be lowered in order to increase trade.

Appeals for tariff reduction usually fell on deaf ears, for it was axiomatic that foreigners had to buy from us. Some more enlightened protectionists, however, did favor tariff reciprocity as a compromise measure. The sectional nature of the cleavage was apparent, since the Midwest pictured commercial-minded New York and Boston as centers of free-trade agitation. That the tariff curtailed trade was denied by the scientifically oriented *American Economist* on the ground that if we bought fewer domestically produced articles our trade would increase in other areas.[28]

From one point of view, the irrepressible conflict of the nineteenth century was not over the nature of the Union, but rather the commercial conflict between the United States and Europe for trade supremacy. An unreasoned fear of foreign competition stymied attempts at a more enlightened policy. The new European aggressiveness for commercial gain that followed 1870 became a common news story. England's control of world finances and commerce was questioned in the light of America's economic growth and the tilting of our balance of trade. The weakness of foreign competitors and our own strength were obvious to some. Americans even talked about economic retaliation against Europe since our imports were chiefly in the form of luxuries and manufactured products not produced here in sufficient quality and abundance. Europe, on the other hand, was thought dependent on the United States for the very necessities of life.[29]

From the present-day vantage point, nineteenth-century Russo-American economic relations take on heightened interest. Trade with the land of the czars was slight, and our consul in Odessa emphasized the need for trade depots where we could display our wares. While American businessmen found a relatively small market in Russia, their interest was unflagging. The Latin American market, peculiarly prized and jealously guarded because of proximity and the Monroe Doctrine, formed a subject of constant discussion. Our "legitimate influence" southward, some argued, could only be maintained through closer commercial connections.[30]

American participation at international fairs and exhibitions proved that our inventive resources and mechanical know-how had developed to the point where we demanded a larger place in the commercial sun. Participation in the global shows, beginning with the London Exhibition of 1851 and the Paris Fair of 1867, demonstrated that the United States was a commercial power with which the world would soon need to reckon.[31]

In general, our businessmen were not very aggressive in foreign trade. The central government seemed more farsighted and as in the later quest for colonies, business lagged behind other forces. However, consular files were filled with inquiries from businessmen interested in exhibitions and foreign displays; not all businessmen were satisfied with the vaunted insatiability of the domestic market.[32]

The "pork diplomacy" of the 1880's, the dispute over the western European discrimination against American hog products, illustrated the growing cooperation between business and government. Business wanted to expand its markets while the government smarted at the thought that other powers could so insult the "American Eagle." An unprecedented pork supply coupled with declining American livestock produce created a brisk trade. Then Europe charged that trichina had spread from American hog meats and several countries instituted a series of regulations followed by a ban. These measures led to the usual demands "to take the foreigner by the beard." It was obvious that the sanitary-hygienic explanation was a pretext, for Germany and France were seeking protection of home products. The Senate Committee on Foreign Relations recommended a reprisal bill in order to avenge the American hog growers, and this feeling was ultimately embodied in the Meat Inspection Law of 1890. The story of pork diplomacy was but one example of economic nationalism and the growing economic overtones of our foreign relations. As Mr. Dooley so aptly put it: "If all thim gr-reat powers . . . was . . . to attack us, . . . I'd blockade Armour an' Comp'ny an' th' wheat ilivators iv Minnysoty. . . . I tell ye, th' hand that rocks th' scales in th' grocery store is th' hand that rules th' wurruld." [33]

The need for foreign markets compelled some in the United States to think in expansionist terms, and yet business as such never conspired for foreign annexations. The government tried to stimulate our export trade, and Wall Street only belatedly jumped on the colonial bandwagon after events called attention to the Far Eastern market. There was, however, a steady rise in American foreign investments, and a discernible trend from a debtor to a creditor nation. But the United States had not yet entered the economic stage where outlets for surplus capital and goods were recognized necessities.[34]

Labor unions were too preoccupied with organizational disputes and ephemeral domestic problems to be seriously concerned with foreign affairs. Except for its stand against open-door immigration, harsh treatment of Irish workers by the British, and armed service which depleted its ranks, labor was generally silent on matters of foreign policy. Such interest as it displayed reflected specific reactions to a particular country's attitude toward the labor movement. Labor did, in the fashion of reform movements of the day, espouse the cause of international arbitration.[35]

The businessman and, to a lesser extent, the laborer were beginning to consider the implications for their future welfare of events that took place beyond the shoreline. Practically every outside interest was economic in tone. Such was the over-all importance of commerce in American foreign policy long before Calvin Coolidge curtly noted, "The business of America is business."

The potential right arm of diplomacy and commerce in those leisurely days was the American naval and merchant fleet. A refurbished merchant marine was sorely needed for overseas carriage while our new warships were to become the backbone of a more spirited and aggressive foreign policy. The realization that our once proud and glorious navy had succumbed to "rot, rust, and obsolescence" and was at the mercy of tenth-rate powers began to arouse comment. The supposed immunity of the United States from attack nursed a sense of security and fostered a conservative military and naval policy. Congressional misers chosen by tax-conscious rural constituents thought of military expenditures as a waste of money.[36] The Jeffersonian belief lingered that the chief tasks of the navy were to protect our merchant vessels and to provide immediate coastal defense in event of an invasion that no one anticipated.

Both political parties eventually realized the need for a naval overhaul. In 1884, the Democrats and the Republicans alike called for rethinking of the question. However, the Democrats were mired down in their small-navy tradition, and it was not until both houses were controlled by the G.O.P. that a new navy was assured. President Arthur argued that the navy would not have declined if we had given it but a portion of the bounty bestowed on industry. Secretary of the Navy William H. Hunt added that since the mercantile interests of our country had now extended over the globe, our business-minded citizens should look to the navy for increased protection of their widespread interests.[37]

Though Congress was checked by public inertia, hard times, and see-saw party control, some men recognized the problem. Geographical isolation and a placid foreign policy had long detached the United States from *Realpolitik,* but this attitude was anachronistic in the day of the screw propeller, with Liverpool but six days from New York. The creation of a Naval Advisory Board in 1881, the adoption of the Navy Bill of 1883 providing for the construction of steel ships, and the establishment of the Naval War College all heralded the future acceptance of Mahan's teachings. As business recovered from the depression of 1873, and the treasury surplus mounted once more, naval improvement became politically feasible.[38]

Sea power was then as much a political and diplomatic affair as a military shield or a commercial agent. Naval officers frequently served as roving diplomats forming in effect the "right arm of diplomacy." An adequate navy was the first step toward the preservation of friendly relations with other powers and the best guarantee against aggression. There was no more popular argument for increased maritime strength than the vexing problem of Isthmian defense and the need for bases to supply battleships with larger cruising radii. Alfred T. Mahan's writings serve as eloquent testimony to America's shrinking provincialism. Mahan's mission was to rekindle his country's former interest in sea power, contending that power and national prestige resulted from the proper use of ocean highways, ships, and bases. In less than a decade, the navy was to be transformed from an "atrophied arm of national power" to an assertive force in American foreign policy. A former Civil War general (1886) foresaw the day when the Atlantic would be crowded with American ships and we would ask what right other nations had to hold naval bases adjacent to the water avenues washing our shores. By 1891, Secretary of the Navy Benjamin F. Tracy was predicting that the sea would be the future seat of empire and that the United States would rule it as certainly as the sun rose each day.[39]

Prior to the 1860's, American shipping was second only to that of Great Britain in tonnage and carrying trade; but here too, deterioration and neglect had set in. Five years after Lee's surrender, only one-third of our import-export trade was carried in American bottoms. The reasons for this decline included the refusal of Congress to grant mail subventions to encourage shipbuilding, the absence of government subsidies, the efficient work of the Confederate raiders, and our lethargy in changing to steam at a time when wind power was clearly obsolete. A few American shipping companies did brave the waters. In the early 1870's, the Pennsylvania Railroad launched the American Steamship Company, the Red D Line ran three iron steamers to Venezuela, and the Ward Line provided service to Cuba and Mexico. Together, the United States and Brazil subsidized one minor mail line operating between the United States and Rio de Janeiro.

Various business groups, aided by such eager politicians as James G. Blaine, pressed constantly for subsidies. In 1880, a national commercial convention petitioned for a national policy to foster commerce while shipbuilders flooded Congress with similar requests. But politics inevitably hamstrung such assistance, for the Democrats opposed assistance to private shipping while the G.O.P. favored subsidization.[40]

Gradually, however, the United States could boast of a fleet in Europe, the North Atlantic, the South Atlantic, and the Pacific. Aside from tensions with Germany over Samoa and the troubles inherent in the Chile-Peruvian War, there was no major international crisis in the eighties. Nevertheless, naval reform was making rapid progress.

Meanwhile, the tempo of foreign missionary activities accelerated. Long before Kipling came up with his "white man's burden," the implications of his challenge became clear. The credo and primary task of these traveling evangelists was religious propagation, but their activities encompassed a variety of other fields, diplomatic, commercial, and humanitarian. Missionaries served as pioneers, furnishing valuable information to both government and businessmen, interpreting and popularizing far-off areas and cultures. Their influence extended over the entire face of the globe, helping to modify American parochialism, promoting a more world-oriented outlook,[41] and even contributing to the rationale for the imperialist upsurge at the turn of the century.

Especially noteworthy was the increased missionary work in Hawaii and Korea. In the Sandwich Islands, as Hawaii was called, the first whites were missionaries and, more often than not, their sons entered the business world. The founder of the Dole canning empire is a case in point. In Korea, diplomatic relations with the United States were facilitated by Dr. Horace N. Allen, the first American missionary to the Hermit Kingdom. Other men of the cloth who worked in foreign climes helped dispel ignorance and apathy about Asia. Because of the novelty and the challenge it presented, the Congo also served as one of the most attractive areas for proselytization. Missionaries helped advertise the resources of the Dark Continent and the merchants followed quickly on their heels.[42]

In the propagation of commerce, however, the missionaries especially shone. Salesmen's sample cases followed their portable altars. Christianity introduced new conceptions of wealth in underdeveloped areas, for the American Protestant ethic taught that if an honest man is God's noblest work, the merchant was an honor to commerce. Missions attempted to redeem the market place from the spirit of greed and lust, maintaining that through the pursuit of trade the Protestant conception of "service" would prove higher than that of mere "pay." [43]

The *fin de siècle* witnessed a growing affinity between commerce and imperialism as the missions stressed the enlightenment and moral transformation that would come in the wake of westernization. Some wearers of the robe and frock gave heed to the clarion call of imperialism. The religious press was replete with ideas of destiny, racial superiority, and religious zeal. Missionaries in far-off Micronesia or in any underdeveloped area would have hailed prompt annexation to the United States. Furthermore, the missionary work was related to expansion because it was conceived in terms of the subjugation of enemy territory, territory either pagan or in need of reconquest by the true believers. Consciously or unconsciously, these zealots were advance agents of the Western way of penetration.[44]

The American government traditionally guaranteed its citizens the protection of the flag. Stringent enforcement of this rule was but one more example of the growing importance of the United States in world affairs. Representations, petitions, and instructions dealing with America's attitude toward its overseas travelers and residents flooded the understaffed State Department. Giving voice, and more often lip service, to the protection of citizens overseas was an ideal way to suggest the country's strength. Political parties utilized this issue to generate enthusiasm. Both parties gave the British lion's tail a vigorous twist in 1868 by criticizing the ancient dictum of indelible allegiance.[45]

American missionaries in foreign parts were constant victims of discrimination. Secretary of State Thomas F. Bayard and Minister Samuel S. Cox in Constantinople were in regular communication over missionary treatment at the hands of the Sublime Porte. The diplomatic dispatches of the period were filled with representations made in behalf of American nationals discriminated against by Russia and Turkey. The United States spoke, too, against German treatment of our missionaries in the Caroline Islands.

Nevertheless, the government refused to single missionaries out for preferential treatment. It recognized their need for protection, but the core of American policy was that all citizens were entitled to the same privileges and the same protection. That the United States had to protect its citizens abroad, regardless of race or religion, became a cardinal American principle and drew Washington further into the international whirlpool.[46]

Despite the fact that many vocal segments regarded participation in international conferences as inconsistent with American tradition, there was a growing awareness of indirect benefits of co-operation in nonpolitical areas.[47] In the 1860's, a slight but rather futile move toward internationalism was apparent. Paris and London, already having devised a merchant marine signal system, called a conference, but Washington chose not to attend. There followed an attempt to standardize weights, measurements, and coinage; but the Paris Conference of 1867 revealed only that no nation (including the United States) was ready to modify its own monetary system.

By 1864 the major European countries had adopted the International Red Cross, but it was not until eighteen years later that the United States adhered to the Geneva Convention. Hidebound isolationist sentiment delayed even such limited cooperation. By 1882, however, the first hesitating moves toward broader global participation were in the making, and the Red Cross Convention was no longer considered a violation of American aloofness.[48]

Differences in postal rates and variant units of weights provided the impetus for the International Postal Union established at Berne in 1874. The agreement provided for a uniform rate in a single postal territory of all the attending nations for the conduct of a global mail service. The United States postmaster general enthusiastically reported that the movement for postal uniformity contributed to the dissemination of truth and civilization. Reflecting the growing business orientation, the United States also participated in conferences which dealt with the protection of widespread industrial holdings. However, European patent grants faced trouble in the Senate and ratification of the 1883 convention was consequently withheld. The money issue, which was intimately bound up with the growing reform impulse, also had certain international ramifications. Unless the United States was prepared to embark on free silver at a higher ratio than the existing values, the only alternative was an international agreement on the silver issue. Fearing unilateral action on the part of Europe, Washington arranged for the Paris Conference of 1881. While this country could not convince other Atlantic powers that she intended to suspend silver coinage unless an international agreement was reached, the overriding fact is that the Senate approved participation.

Other matters settled by international congresses in which the United States participated included the fixing of the prime meridian, the delineation of the time zones, standardization of navigation charts, and an agreement on the exchange of public documents. Conferences were also held regularly to encourage trade and to celebrate important anniversaries, promoting a more international atmosphere. For a country supposedly preoccupied with political strife and weighted down by isolationist anchors, the United States participated in and at times initiated a large number of such conferences. Such action was a startling innovation spurred on by the development of a new national self-consciousness which reflected growing interest in the wider world.[49]

That our literary people used foreign themes as sources of inspiration and themes is still further testimony of an expanded horizon. American artists, "troubled souls" and "passionate pilgrims," were drawn to Europe and a spate of travel books produced by such writers as Mark Twain, William Dean Howells, and Henry James rolled off the presses.[50] Whether it was eternal Rome or exotic Paris which inspired the artist, the reciprocal influences of contrasting civilizations were potent forces in the development of a more cosmopolitan spirit.[51]

Another literary manifestation of our world interests was the development of the international novel, associated chiefly with the restless Henry James. James, a lifelong pilgrim to other shrines and the most famous literary expatriate of his day, was convinced that the materialistic, acquisitive, and thin American intellectual climate was uncongenial to the creative artist. His works generally took their theme from the conflict between innocent, loyal Americans and wiser, more sophisticated Europeans.[52]

James Russell Lowell, diplomat and writer, performed yeoman service in improving strained Anglo-American relations. He once asserted, "The dust that is sacred to [the Englishman] is sacred to [the American]." [53] Such remarks helped meliorate cultural relations in an age marked by Britain's "splendid isolation" and America's traditional apathy. Many other writers also turned outward for inspiration. William Dean Howells interpreted Italy to his countrymen. Bret Harte, famed as a western regionalist, left for Europe in 1878 never to return. Lafcadio Hearn was drawn toward tropical, primitive, and oriental themes. Henry Adams, in his quest for the meaning of life, wrote about many distant lands.[54] The *literati* who lived overseas or those who merely wrote on foreign themes were in reality advance agents of Americanism rather than a lost generation of exiles. Many of them possessed a "world vision," a haunting nostalgia for the older culture which had given birth to ours.[55]

In the brownstone age the utopian novels achieved popularity. Because they dealt with imagined life in a far-off dreamland, these books were also part of the movement which looked outward. Ignatius Donnelly's *Atlantis* (1881), dealing with the idea of a lost continent, reflected man's search for a Shangri-La. Donnelly's expansionism sought to carry his indigenous Populism to frozen continents and to the heat of the tropics. He was outspoken in predicting that the United States would eventually "swallow up" Canada. Edward Bellamy's world, as described in *Looking Backward*, was probably inspired by his travels to Germany and Hawaii and his dabbling in Hindu, Judaic, and European thought. Bellamy's nationalist movement took as axiomatic reciprocal peaceful relations between America and the rest of the world.[56]

With marked improvements in steamships the oceans became highways rather than roadblocks, and by the time Reconstruction was completed, some 30,000 American travelers were reported in Europe. Business expansion in the 1880's meant more money, leisure, and travel for the restless *nouveaux riches*. A young aristocrat like Franklin Delano Roosevelt was abroad eight times before he entered adolescence, and such well traveled intellectuals as Nicholas Murray Butler, Charles W. Eliot, and Henry L. Stimson were in time to become arch enemies of isolation and champions of world cooperation. The traveling sophisticate was apt to combine an appreciation for foreign culture with an increased understanding of his own. Travelers were repeatedly warned to become familiar with the history, customs, and people of foreign lands. So early was advice given not to be "ugly" Americans! [57]

One of the largest groups of itinerant Yankees were the students and artists. In a speech made before the American Student's Association in Paris (*circa* 1888–90), Minister Whitelaw Reid noted the great concentration of art students and lauded the effort. Some feared that our youth abroad might become "un-Americanized" and return after having enriched the hotelkeepers of "effete despotisms" with tastes, habits, and ideas foreign to our own way of life.[58]

Perhaps it was Germany which exerted the greatest influence on American higher education in this period. Ever since 1766 when the aging Benjamin Franklin visited in the University of Göttingen, Teutonic universities had attracted thousands of American students.

Inadequate graduate instruction in the United States and the popularity of German *Wissenschaft* attracted young scholars eager to spend their *Wanderjahre* abroad.[59] Perhaps the most influential social scientist to study in Germany was Herbert Baxter Adams, later of Johns Hopkins University. Importing the seminar method, Adams did much to professionalize historical scholarship. The Graduate School of the Political Sciences, founded at Columbia University by John W. Burgess, owed much to his German tutelage. The idea of welfare economics and the state as an agency for the good life was first popularly advocated by Richard T. Ely, who learned at Heidelberg the Prussian concept of the role of the trained expert in civil service and welfare activities. The American who returned bearing a German doctorate had acquired the "intellectual point of view" which stressed thoroughness in thinking and research.

Exploration also brought the United States into vital contact with strange parts of the earth. Men of the present are concerned with reaching the moon and orbiting in outer space; during this period, the great powers still had much to learn about their own world. By 1869, Major John Wesley Powell had explored the last unchartered American terrain in Colorado, and now men's minds could speculate beyond the shoreline with surer confidence. Before 1850, the United States had already sent an expedition to Antarctica, and after the Civil War, Henry M. Stanley's exploits in the Congo gripped the popular imagination. But it was the arctic that presented the major challenge to the restless late nineteenth-century pioneer.

While it was not until Peary's expeditions that the ultimate goal was achieved, there were many preliminary attempts to reach the North Pole through an open polar sea. In 1871, Captain Charles F. Hall, commanding the ill-fated *Polaris*, was instructed to investigate the land and waters beyond eighty degrees north latitude. Eight years later, George Washington De Long, U.S.N., moved along the Siberian arctic coast in an expedition financed by James G. Bennett of the *New York Herald*. Three relief cruisers were sent to rescue his drifting ship, the *Jeannette*, and while De Long perished, his reports remained intact. In 1881, Congress appropriated money for an expedition to settle a colony in the Lady Franklin Bay area as a base for the scientific explorations undertaken as part of the International Polar Year activities. The expeditions of Lieutenants Adolfus W. Greely to Lady Franklin Bay and Patrick H. Ray to Point Barrow, Alaska, were among the finest domestic scientific achievements of the age. Not only was much learned of the natural and geologic life, but our first genuine knowledge of Eskimos was established. Pecuniary gains resulting from increased commerce colored our early arctic dreams. The *New York Daily Tribune* predicted that far-northern exploration would yield new trade routes and reopen competition with England for Asiatic commerce. But it was mercy, glory, and science that called forth the arctic explorers who carried Old Glory into the northernmost reaches of the earth.[60]

Intellectual horizons were also broadened by various scientific explorations of the "Plant Explorers." Their travels in South America not only resulted in the introduction of new seeds and plants, but also generated wider general and scholarly interest in the southern hemisphere.[61] Whether one speaks of big-game hunters or writers or explorers, the professional and nonprofessional wanderers had the unquenchable pioneer spirit, and their urge to discover and to expand geographical knowledge ranks them high on the list of those who broadened Uncle Sam's horizon.

The children of the 1890's lived to see their country intimately concerned with the peace of every quarter of the globe, but what did Americans think of the rest of the world in that far-off peaceful age? How did their elders react to our growing role in the determination of world affairs?

Most Americans thought European militarism, warfare, and colonialism but another illustration of Old World degeneration and hence little or none of our concern. Was not Europe the home of destitute noblemen in search of American heiresses? We were proud of our divorce from troublesome foreign machinations. Satiated and peaceful, with militarism limited to the hyperbolic tales of graying G.A.R. veterans, our tranquility stood in sharp contrast with the European "circle of camps and barracks." [62] We lost sight of the fact that our oceanic moats and the absence of aggressive neighbors made possible a minimum of military expenditures, and even these shrunk for a spell after Chief Joseph of the Nez Percé Indians surrendered.

Unlike the press, official circles in Washington usually regarded reports of foreign expansionist efforts more as news stories than as stringent facts. The rumors that flooded the State Department were patiently checked, but usually discredited. Our attitude was one of detached amusement rather than fear. European conduct was just one more proof that here in the New World the *summum bonum* of all existence had been reached. Having absorbed the choicest sections of the continent in our own "expansion," the United States felt free to criticize "imperialistic" nations. Like Great Britain, we shared all too often the feelings of the retired bank robber turned honest until 1898, when we went on the prowl for new territory.

Despite the fact that the United States looked with a jaundiced eye at some European institutions, there was a paradoxical twist to this attitude. Joined to the older idea of disgust and scorn came a new deference to the Old World on the part of some restless souls anxious to escape from the mundane realities of the new industrialism. Our ideas about Europe were at the same time parochial, antipathetic, patronizing, and yet envious. Sensitive Americans still felt a magnetic pull toward the matrix of our culture. European homes, fashions, polite society, sports, reform movements, labor, religion, and culinary habits were all of some interest to Americans. English and French best sellers often outdistanced native efforts, and the highest aim of our literary journals was to emulate the English or continental periodicals. Such imitative magazines featured discussions of less romantic foreign developments as well as descriptions of the economic and political life of other countries.[63]

On the other hand, Europe had long regarded the United States as an uncouth upstart. Matthew Arnold summed up a segment of British sentiment when he made his celebrated trip here and found considerable fault with so much of what he saw. Some British travelers to America noted our frontier mannerisms and criticized its rowdyism. James Russell Lowell predicted that it would take the English a great deal of time to rid themselves of their patronizing attitude since in their eyes we were but "lusty juveniles." Young James Bryce, however, was more sentimental and optimistic. He was convinced of the efficacy of travel improvements in fostering Anglo-American amity.[64]

A persisting charge leveled against the United States involved the copyright issue. With the absence of an international agreement, literature prospered, though this American piracy often reduced home royalties. Great controversy ensued among authors, publishers, and printers. Finally by 1891, a lame-duck G.O.P. Congress, faced with a Democratic majority in the House, passed the Platt-Symonds Bill, and the United States was no longer the "literary Ishmael of the Civilized World." [65]

The flood tide of immigration from Europe lent new shape to our foreign conceptions. Business, reputed to be pro-immigration, was in fact rather hostile to unskilled foreigners who came during slack times, thus aggravating existing problems.[66] Some of the most volatile immigrant publicity stemmed from Irish activities. The postwar Fenian raids raised the problems of enforcing American neutrality laws against a popular cause and defining the rights of Irish-Americans in view of the stubborn British notion of indelible allegiance. Hence, our press constantly "twisted the Lion's tail." The cry against immigration was further heightened as the foreign-born came to be closely linked with increased radicalism and labor unrest. The emerging socialist movement gave a fillip to a new form of know-nothingism culminating in the formation of the American Protective Association.[67]

If America's attitude toward Europe was ambivalent, our concepts of Latin America were more positive and always encased in the elastic frame of the Monroe Doctrine. Such expansionist sentiment as there was—the desire for bases and an American-owned canal, the promotion of Pan-Americanism, and even the movement for reciprocity—were sanctified in Mr. Monroe's name. The enhanced popularity of the doctrine after Maximilian's fiasco caused Americans to be increasingly wary of European wiles. Our concern with the War of the Pacific (1879–82) arose in part over resentment of Old World control of the Chilean and Peruvian markets and reflected a nascent maturity.[68]

A pet Washington dream involved the acquisition of Central American bases. There was considerable support for such projects even before the keels of the Great White Fleet had been laid. Resolutions authorizing the government to secure calling stations were common even before the voices for an American-built canal became a crescendo.[69]

Central American union, long envisioned by the State Department, was intended to facilitate commerce, to further the cause of republicanism, and to forestall possible European intervention. The press generally blessed such schemes as consistent with our traditional hegemony in the area. Pan-Americanism, the single constructive policy of James G. Blaine's long public career, was in time to evolve into the Good Neighbor Policy, but if there was enthusiasm for closer contacts in these years, it resulted from the commercial potential of such a union.[70]

Although the United States evinced general interest in all areas south of the Rio Grande, our relations toward Mexico, the West Indies, and the Isthmus took on a special significance. With the pro-Yankee stabilization brought by Porfirio Díaz, our official attitude toward Mexico combined respect for her territorial sovereignty with respect for her seeming achievements. A perennial problem that threatened relations was the raids of the bandits and cattle thieves across the Rio Grande. "Hot pursuit" of Mexican marauders in the interest of protecting life and property became standard practice, and occasional war cries arose on both sides of the river. The Mexican market aroused unflagging interest in the United States, and talk of a *Zollverein* was a staple of every congressional session. American commercial interests in Mexico by the time of Díaz's exile were spread heavily among railroads, mining, land, and oil interests.[71]

From the earliest days of the Republic, the Caribbean Islands attracted the attention of both theoretical expansionists and practical businessmen. Officially, the United States assumed the role of big brother in order to uphold the territorial integrity of these states. While we were cool to the idea of more territorial grabs, some Americans always thought that in due time the islands would fall like ripe fruit into Uncle Sam's lap. Ever since the Ostend Manifesto of Pierce's day, there was special interest in the "Pearl of the Antilles," and talk of acquiring Cuba always aroused interest. The island's commercial advantages and the fact that any power controlling it might convert the Gulf of Mexico into a *mare clausum* were not overlooked. However, if the South's desire for Cuba died with Lee's surrender, public opinion was not adverse to establishing commercial supremacy in Havana, and in 1884 a reciprocity treaty was signed with Madrid.[72]

No matter of foreign policy so gripped the popular imagination as the long-mooted piercing of the Isthmus. While some quarters denied the wisdom of acquiring a unilaterally owned canal and enlarging the Monroe Doctrine so as to control foreign enterprise in this area,[73] the majority hailed the cry, "America first in the digging." A canal linking our oceans would have obvious commercial benefits, and the Clayton-Bulwer Treaty notwithstanding, Washington was no longer prepared to share canal rights with Britain.[74] President Rutherford B. Hayes affirmed most forcefully American ownership and control, but characteristically the cautious Grover Cleveland was opposed to our exercising paramount authority outside our own territory. James G. Blaine, of course, could be counted on for an unequivocal endorsement of the "American first" view. Even the pacifist and Anglophile Andrew Carnegie agreed that the 1850 treaty needed modification, and he predicted, "America is going to control . . . everything on this continent." Congress, too, championed an American canal as long as it involved no great financial gamble.[75] Thus, while the regnant point of view was that America should act, and "canal fever" was rising, its champions had to await another day and more propitious circumstances to consummate their plans.

Economic motivations rather than grandiose political ambitions characterized our relations with Samoa, Hawaii, and Canada. The vast Pacific with her untold island treasures had challenged the imagination of Americans since the ginseng traders of Confederation days. Despite the fact that the United States received the right to establish a naval station at Pago Pago in 1878, we firmly denied interest in political control or direct annexation.[76] Certain business forces, especially Pacific merchants and western farmers, were aware of Samoan potentialities, and many advocated plans for making Pago Pago the commercial focal point of that section of Polynesia.[77] It is not surprising that in this remote paradise the United States would break from its traditional policy of noninterference in the external affairs of other states, a stance so characteristic of our trans-Atlantic relations. Sometimes denials, like Shakespeare's lady who protested too much, actually indicate interest. State Department official Alvey A. Adee tended in the direction of nascent imperialism, concluding that only through an assertive policy could we hope for a permanent foothold.[78] The basic cause of our concern was the preponderance of foreign influence and the desire to assist Samoan authorities in maintaining a stable government. Rumors of sinister English or German plots filled dispatches from Samoa, and Secretary Bayard made it clear that America's Pacific interests were real and urged increased concern with the ambitions of other powers.[79]

"To take or not to take Hawaii" was a never-ending question from the days of John Tyler. Political concerns, commercial possibilities, and the fear of undue foreign interference long dominated American thinking about Hawaii. Once more James G. Blaine symbolized the "large spirit." Obviously intending to reactivate the Monroe Doctrine, he marked out a sphere of American influence in the Pacific, including of course the Hawaiian archipelago. Democratic Secretary Bayard took a more aggressive stand on Hawaii than on the canal. He stated categorically that while we did not wish to dominate the Pacific, we opposed the "roaming" of any other nations in its waters. The newspaper press generally supported this stand, linking American prestige and nationalism with an all-inclusive Hawaiian policy.[80]

The roundly debated Hawaiian Reciprocity Treaty of 1875 was renewed in 1884, but it was not approved until the Senate added the proviso that Pearl Harbor be secured as a naval station.[81] Reciprocity became the economic substitute for political annexation. Interest in Hawaii's domestic policies, investments, and trade reports revealed that the Kingdom of the Kanakas was becoming more and more linked to our own defense and economic systems.

In regard to Canada, interest wavered among men concerned with commercial possibilities, North Pole expansionists, and subtler spirits who regarded commercial union as a step toward eventual political union. Charles Sumner's ambitions persisted even in the "mill pond" diplomatic years, and Benjamin F. Butler, always fishing in troubled waters, urged America northward.[82] Arguments advanced in favor of political ties included the greater prosperity that economically depressed Canada could enjoy and the continental solidarity which would follow from cementing two English-speaking peoples.[83]

Though the advocates of political union made considerable noise, the most feasible plan for closer relations lay in the commercial field. Canada, many predicted, would have to become part of a North American *Zollverein*, much like the one projected by Blaine for Latin America. Canadian Liberals desired closer ties with the United States in an attempt to pull out of the disastrous depression of the 1880's. Businessmen and politicians generally aired their views in favor of reciprocity, the leader of the movement and chief lobbyist being S. J. Ritchie of Akron, Ohio, a capitalist and president of the Canadian Ontario Railroad.[84] Booster organizations discussed the question and passed resolutions while Congress debated and committees reported. However, reciprocity was far from being universally popular. Zealous advocates of such a program could not dispel the notion that reciprocity was but a veiled attempt to seduce our northern neighbors into full *Anschluss*.[85] In sum, the United States remained indifferent to both annexation and commercial union, except for ephemeral and localized concern.

The fisheries dispute plagued diplomats from John Jay to Philander C. Knox. Business thought on foreign policy matters was often divided, but this issue reflected a high point in its concern. Following the fisheries arrangements made in Washington in 1871, Canada retaliated, and pleas were heard that our honor as well as our pocketbook were involved. Protests reached fever pitch in 1887 when the House authorized President Cleveland to retaliate against Canadians by barring their ships from our ports. The next February the Bayard-Chamberlain Pact furnished the cue for Senate Republicans. The vigorous jingos and election-minded conservatives helped spike Democratic chances in 1888 by defeating compromise.[86]

Americans paid the least attention to the Orient and Africa. The Far East did not make American headlines until Dewey steamed into Manila Bay but, as with Latin America and Occania, interest was slowly if unnoticeably mounting. America's conception of the East was often based on a romantic image, as the later Fu Manchu or Mikado figures, rather than on facts or sympathetic understanding.

The United States had long favored the open-door policy and the maintenance of the territorial integrity of Asiatic nations, and as with other areas, we acted either to keep Europe out or to regulate her endeavor.[87] Especially aggravating were French threats against Indo-China and Russian intrigues in China and Korea, but our refusal to take a positive stand in Asiatic affairs reflected ambivalence.[88] Many Americans were especially interested in Japan, for it was a commonplace that the Land of the Rising Sun looked up to the nation which had introduced her to the West. The spectacle of a people surging with vigor and ambition of a rediscovered youth excited much American curiosity.[89]

China aroused much romantic interest in a nation so often captivated by travelogues and fiction. Despite the numerous incidents that arose over the Chinese reluctance to observe treaties and over their treatment of missionaries, the conclusion of the Burlingame Treaty in 1868 was generally interpreted as assurance that American-Chinese relationships were at last established on a friendly basis. The work performed by Commodore Robert W. Shufeldt as special advisor to the government of the Manchus is striking testimony of the new role China was beginning to play in our foreign policy. Shufeldt's task was to strengthen Chinese naval forces because of the threat of war with Russia. James G. Blaine noted that Shufeldt's presence in China might prove advantageous to our Far Eastern position. Traditionally, Paris or London had led in the task of modernization, but China was becoming apprehensive of their voracious appetites for territory and turned more and more to Washington.[90] The links between a hoary China and a youthful United States were pointed up in predictions that within a century the two nations would be *the* two powers on earth.

One subject, however, vexed Sino-American relations. By the 1870's the coolie had outworn his usefulness in America's internal development. While Asiatic immigration was a domestic question, it had broad foreign implications. Opinions in the United States were sharply divided between those that felt that the influx of more Chinamen would endanger our institutions and the business-religious Sinophiles. Presidents Hayes and Arthur generally sided with this latter group, and Hayes's veto of the immigration restriction bill was lauded as preventing the "obloquy that Congressmen tried to fasten on our national reputation." [91] As a matter of policy, some felt that the United States could not afford to treat any nation in this manner. Ambivalence was apparent even this early between those who had larger horizons and the older isolationist tradition with its racist overtones.

Serious American concern with Korea did not begin until that fateful Sunday in June, 1950. That peninsula, still a global pressure point and in recent years all too often the subject of headlines, had been in the American "sphere" ever since the United States opened the Hermit Kingdom to world trade. In response to a congressional resolution, the Navy Department commissioned Commodore Shufeldt on a long and detailed mission which included the task of opening the Land of the Morning Calm to world commerce. Shufeldt, enthusiastic and persistent, predicted that the Pacific would soon become America's commercial domain and a treaty with Korea would form another link in the chain uniting East and West.[92]

In May, 1882, the sailor-diplomat reported success, but the Shufeldt mission attracted little attention at home except for the world-minded *New York Herald* which was so proud of the treaty that it suggested that it be pasted in everybody's hat for reference! [93] Official and unofficial American influence persisted even after the treaty was ratified. Secretary Bayard instructed Chargé d'Affaires George C. Foulk to use discretion in the current diplomatic tug-of-war in the Far East, and he insisted only on an independent Korea. It was an American judge, Owen V. Denny, who served as the king's chief foreign counselor, while Horace N. Allen was to establish himself as a prime purveyor of Korean culture to the United States.[94]

America's Far Eastern policy was basically commercial and philanthropic. To that end, we insisted that the door to trade, real or potential, be left open, and we closely watched any European advance that threatened to close the gateway to Eastern riches. We jealously guarded the "most-favored-nation" clause in our treaties [95] and insisted on the security of life and property of our citizens. Our attitude was at once moderate and humanitarian but also practical in that it satisfied our material desires. By maintaining the political status quo, we were setting a foundation for the more concrete policies of a later day.

Despite America's concern with Africa ever since the Liberian experiment began in 1817, it was only in the Grant era that the spotlight really began to illuminate the Dark Continent. Africa, the realm of romance, fascinated the scholar, explorer, philanthropist, businessman, and layman alike. It was not unusual, then, that on his return Stanley received a huge ovation replete with the inevitable banquet at Delmonico's.[96]

Tangible evidence of this concern was the 1878 mission of Shufeldt to West Africa, which formed the first leg of his eventful voyage to the Orient. His chief recommendation was for the establishment of consular service in West Africa, the "great commercial prize of the world." Bennett's *Herald*, sponsor of the Stanley mission, naturally hailed Shufeldt's work. President Arthur recognized the importance of Africa to America's economic destiny. In his annual message of 1883, he suggested cooperation with other powers in opening the door to the Congo. Congress, too, was not immune from "African fever." Petitions calling for land surveys, railroad establishments, or setting up trading posts were quite common.[97] Talk eventually became action, for six years after Shufeldt's probing expedition, Willard P. Tisdel introduced American products into the Congo. Tisdel was instructed to secure only commercial privileges and his reports were generally encouraging.[98]

Exclusive foreign control of the Congo and other underdeveloped areas was anathema in American diplomatic and commercial circles. French efforts to gain commercial supremacy in the rich interior of Africa were noted by the State Department, and Alvey A. Adee suggested an investigation of African potentialities. Rumors of a French protectorate over Liberia met spirited warnings from the State Department. While our concern was genuine and we used our good offices in her defense, the United States consistently refused to make firm commitments to Monrovia.[99]

Ostensibly, in order to encourage the work of King Leopold's International African Association in promoting trade, in introducing the benefits of white civilization, and in ending the slave trade, a concerted movement was undertaken to secure American recognition. Two Americans, General Henry S. Sanford, a former minister to Belgium, and the legendary Stanley lobbied in influential circles, and finally President Arthur extended recognition to the Association in April, 1884. Interest in Africa was great, but the "fever" was not so high that the United States could break with tradition and ratify the proceedings of the 1884 Berlin Conference on Congo affairs. Our delegate, John A. Kasson, was instructed to confine his attention only to commercial topics and not to enter into the eternal wrangling over Africa's political future. The politicians on Capitol Hill debated, and despite the fact that our delegate's hands were tied, we did participate in an international conference limited to political and economic action. But Grover Cleveland, foreshadowing his later action toward Hawaii, stuck to a Jeffersonian isolationist position. Hence, the work of the Republican Kasson came to naught.[100]

By 1890, the possibilities that Africa presented were common knowledge, and her coastal cities had been opened to Western commerce and civilization. No longer could she be regarded as a place simply in need of Sunday school pennies. It was not even uncommon to predict that the whites would in time swallow up the African Negro in the same way the North American Indian had all but disappeared.[101] While political concerns were minimized, the events of those days prepared the stage for the tragic role that Africa plays in today's American foreign policy.

The pitfalls of exploring public opinion toward foreign affairs are obvious. Cumulative thought is awkward to describe and hard to gauge. Frequently, it is impossible to determine whether a given expression is a reflection of public thought or merely an attempt to mold or create it. As nineteenth-century simplicity gave way to twentieth-century complexity, there was bound to be some overlapping between the shades of the past and the portents of the future. There was latent expansionist sentiment at all points. Butting this rising spirit, there stood the rock-bottom foundations of the later anti-imperialist movement.[102]

However, interest in foreign policy during the post-Reconstruction period was quiescent rather than dead. America's concern with an overseas economic destiny gradually quickened and the newer business entanglements preordained a broader outlook. There was a growing awareness on the part of interested groups of these newer horizons. Alfred T. Mahan summed up the newer feeling toward foreign problems: "I am frankly an imperialist, in the sense that I believe that no nation . . . should henceforth maintain the policy of isolation." [103] Yet Mahan was the result rather than the cause of the impulse that he did so much to enhance. It would be all but impossible to conceive of an American Mahan in the days of Lincoln or even Grant.

This period was not a low point in American diplomacy, unless "low point" is taken to mean the beginning of bigger things. The "large policy" had its origins in the very years of our supposed land satiation and rapid industrialization. Eventually it was rationalized on the basis of racial and moral superiority, a sense of national mission, strategic considerations, national prestige, and aversion to a worldwide imperialism from which we were economically excluded. While not originally seeking territory for ourselves, we could not allow other powers to jeopardize what we considered our legitimate interests. The restless pioneer spirit whereby unspanned streams had to be bridged and the bridge crossed typified the "Expand or Bust" philosophy which came as the depression clouds of 1893 lifted and revealed the sunshine of McKinley prosperity. Amid this *Zeitgeist*, the United States took its place in the front ranks of the nations of the world. As the new century dawned, America embarked on the path that was to bring war, world leadership, and a never-ending series of unprecedented dilemmas.

8

Gilt, Gingerbread, and Realism:
The Public and Its Taste

ROBERT R. ROBERTS

*T*HE popular culture of the Gilded Age does not need a reappraisal so much as a serious appraisal. Earlier and later eras have had their historians of manners and mores,[1] and several special phases of the popular culture of the Gilded Age have been treated—in the fields of books, magazines, literature, and the theater, for example—but the record is spotty and unfocused.

The scene is generally set by repeating with dramatic and telling enunciation of the vulgarity and crassness of the era, pointing with scorn at the usual objects of contempt—the gingerbread French chateaus on Fifth Avenue, iron deer on front lawns, and bric-a-brac in the cluttered middle-class living room, or "parlor." This opinion divested, the historian leaves the impression that no other age would be guilty of such crass and patent bad taste, and then shies by saying "yet," indicating the vitality and strength of a nation bursting with economic growth, population increase, and even attention to things of the mind. This usually leads to a discussion of certain seminal and exceptional minds—the artists, scientists, writers—who save the age from total disgrace. Somewhere in the discussions of Mark Twain, the Darwinists, Josiah Willard Gibbs, William James, and C. S. Peirce, the whole notion of popular taste or culture disappears and is never touched upon.

Examples abound of this "on the one hand but on the other hand" approach in the historical literature. A basic and excellent text starts its treatment of the era with the unambiguous statement, "The years between 1865 and 1890 were an era of parvenu standards, eclectic architecture and exotic art, literary sterility, and derivative, rather than indigenous culture." It continues thus: "Yet the post-war period was, withal, a robust, fearless, and not ungenerous age, lawless and picturesque, full of the old-time gusto and joy of living, giving large scope even in corporate form to individual energy and material creation, and challenging, by its very shoddiness, the genius of men." [2] Not so bad after all. Another widely used basic text points to the gaudiness and hypocrisy of Jim Fisk and Henry Ward Beecher and then returns to comment on the era's basic strength and growth.[3] Some texts simply gloss over or ignore the period, telescoping a generation into a series of bad epigrams and inadequate generalities, remarking that the people tended to "focus on the gaudy symbols of wealth," which is true but hardly adequate.[4] There are, of course, some exceptions in the text literature, but in the main they conform to the stereotype.[5]

The general pattern for evaluations of the culture of the Gilded Age goes back to V. L. Parrington, who, in his colorful section on the thought of this era, so tellingly characterizes the corruption, the brassiness, the hypocrisy of the dominant figures from Jim Fisk to Dwight L. Moody—perhaps not always justly, but always entertainingly. And, of course, there is substantial justice in this approach; there was corruption, it was a gaudy age, and the contrasts between public professions of morality and actual behavior were frequently glaring. The unfortunate results of this approach are twofold: first, the fundamental nature of the popular culture of the age is lost in these generalizations; and second, the results of a closer examination tend to be prejudged by these popular views. Let us eschew some of these preconceptions, if possible, and direct attention to some of the basic factors which ought to be a part of a serious study of the popular culture of the Gilded Age.

There is always the preliminary question of definition. It is quite obvious that the enduring works of art and the far-ranging works of the mind are likely to attract more attention from historians than the more ephemeral products of popular appeal. It may even be that the artist has insights and understanding which the purveyor of popular entertainment cannot afford, even if he were capable of them. But such rules are not invariably true and the works of Mark Twain might be cited as evidence that art and popularity are not necessarily incompatible. Nevertheless, in attempting to define what is meant by popular culture the historian must first respect the adjective in that phrase. As Carl Bode said in introducing his study of popular culture: "Popularity has been my touchstone. . . . This is a book on the people's choice." [6]

There are more pretentious definitions:

> The counterconcept to popular culture is art. . . . Schopenhauer remarked that music is "the world once more." This philosophical aphorism throws light on the unbridgeable difference between art and popular culture: it is the difference between an increase in insight through a medium possessing sustaining means and mere repetition of given facts with the use of borrowed tools.[7]

The doctrinaire qualities of this definition impede rather than assist the understanding of popular culture, particularly in the pronouncement of the "unbridgeable difference" between art and popular culture. Such dramatic claims are often easier to make than to sustain in an actual historical analysis of the art and popular culture of a given period. But part of this definition does produce results in assessing the popular culture of the post-Civil War years—that part which refers to popular culture as the "repetition of given facts." It applies with great accuracy to the Gilded Age. The time was one of rapid change, of the introduction of much that was new and disturbing in American life; traditional values were severely tested, some of them not surviving and others surviving only in modified form. To be sure, this process occurs to some extent in any historical epoch, but in the Gilded Age it was carried to great extremes. In the face of these trials, the popular culture was overwhelmingly a "repetition of given facts." Never, perhaps, did the old values reign so completely in the realm of popular culture. The artists were fumbling for new modes of expression, but the popular writers were repeating the familiar situations. Popular culture is something less, therefore, than art in the capacity to sustain insight into the human situation, in its intellectual power, and in its aesthetic sensitivity; to see popular culture as something less, however, does not mean to see an unbridgeable gap nor to see art and popular culture as "counterconcepts."

Obviously popular culture can cover a vast number of activities, from the daily newspaper to the mass revival meeting, from the Chautauqua lecture platform to the touring Shakespearian troupe.

A useful beginning here is once again that of Carl Bode. He indicates that his definition of the scope of the term lies between that of the cultural anthropologist, with his interest in all aspects of a culture, and that of the literary historian with his restricted field of interest.[8] To Bode, the definition would include the popular forms of painting and sculpture, literary productions, music, and the theater. This flexible approach can be broadened or restricted to cover the typical popular activities of any given period. Together these areas make up the means of expression of the ideas and beliefs accepted by the majority and the institutions to which the people turned most frequently to hear the various expressions of their ideals and aspirations. Whether it was to hear Dwight Moody in the pulpit, Russell Conwell on the lecture platform, or Joseph Jefferson behind the proscenium arch, the American people of this era assembled in large numbers, paid admission fees or took up great collections, and listened patiently as these culture-heroes declaimed on what seemed to the audiences to be the eternal verities.

Another phase of popular culture rarely dealt with, especially in this period, is the extent to which the traditional classical culture of western Europe belonged to the people and flourished on a popular level. In the novels of this era there remained a fundamental stratum of the great tradition of the eighteenth-century English novel, though heavily covered by Victorian ideas of morality and propriety. Dickens had not yet become a "classic," but was simply a popular writer, very likely the "world's most popular author."[9] Dickens belonged to the world of art and also to the popular culture of the America of the middle and late nineteenth century.

The arts also permeated American life. Russell Lynes begins *The Tastemakers* with some quotations from one George Makepeace Towle, a traveler returned to America from England, who wrote that he heard "boys in the street singing and whistling Mozart and Rossini, and hand organs grinding out the arias from *Faust* and *Lucrezia Borgia*," as well as the usual ballads, minstrel songs, and patriotic hymns. Towle was also impressed by the liveliness of the American theater, including "more performances of Shakespeare in America . . . than . . . in England" and "tragedy, fine old comedy and the 'free and easy' burlesque."[10] This is certainly a notable commentary on the state of the arts in America in the

Gilded Age. Further evidence of the permeation of the arts is in the pages of the cheap story-papers, where authors of accepted stature appeared side by side with the most popular writers, or in the popularity of great actors and actresses such as Edwin Booth or Sarah Bernhardt. Or one might cite the immediate hit made by Gilbert and Sullivan musicals, assuming that they can be classified as art as well as popular stage fare. In the theaters Shakespeare was followed by *East Lynne*, and Samuel Smiles or Mrs. E. D. E. N. Southworth might outsell Thomas Hardy or the Brontë sisters, but the classics were on the same lists and the same programs.

Such examples testify to the extent to which the traditional culture of the Western world, albeit sometimes in debased forms, continued to hold sway in America. There was a healthy mingling of popular and classical culture in the years of the Gilded Age. It is quite unfair to dismiss the culture of these years without noting this important fact. It may well be that one opera house in a middle-sized American town in the 1880's offered more of the classic tradition in music and drama in one year than the combined television networks of the United States do in the same period of time in our own age.

This was hardly an idyllic society of popular acclaim of great art and happy and wholesome popular arts without exception; the general trend was actually in the opposite direction. These years saw the rise of magazines and newspapers of mass appeal and of transformation in the theater and other forms of entertainment that produced an increasingly wide gap between popular culture and higher standards of art. And, of course, there were exceptions all through the years of the Gilded Age. There was the difference between the public image of Mark Twain and the skepticism and bitterness of his private world; there were the lonely paths of such artists as Albert Ryder and George Inness and the anti-philistinism of James M. Whistler. There were also the remnants of the world of the Boston Brahmins in the persons of the Adams brothers or Francis Parkman, who believed that the American people were patronizing shoddy lectures and buying tasteless magazines. And there were such pre-Civil War monuments as Longfellow and Emerson who lived on into the postwar decades and did not find them good. Still, in none of these instances nor in the era itself was there any extensive spirit of "épater le bourgeois." The coterie artist and the self-conscious rebel against middle-class values were not in evidence in any major way. This familiar schism, so characteristic of the twentieth century, had yet to appear significantly in America in the Gilded Age.

On the mingling of traditional and popular culture in the Gilded Age, it is pertinent to point out that the description of this culture as "derivative" is quite true. England, naturally, contributed most heavily to American popular culture. The common name for the then prevailing moral view of the universe has come to be "Victorian," obviously not a native American product. The most popular style of middle-class domestic architecture was called the "Queen Anne." The arbiter of this architecture and of home decoration and landscaping was one Charles Lock Eastlake, Englishman and disciple of Ruskin and William Morris.

The area in which European standards cast the longest shadow was that of literature, especially the novel. It has been estimated that more copies of Dickens were sold in the 1880's than in the 1860's, and his influence clearly was maintained in the Gilded Age.[11] Not only Dickens, but such distinguished names as Thackeray, Anthony Trollope, George Eliot, Jane Austen, and the Brontës regularly appeared on American publishing lists. Indeed, good reading seems to have been more readily available than at any time prior to the modern paperback book movement, and the press and magazines of that time show that, in proportion to the literate population, good reading was more widely indulged in then than now.

It was, however, not only in the area of quality literature that English standards carried over to America. The most celebrated novel of the sensational-romantic school, *East Lynne*, was the product of a native of London, Mrs. Henry Wood. A second Englishwoman, Mary Elizabeth Braddon, contributed the "preposterously successful melodrama," *Lady Audley's Secret*, and many other such romances to eager American readers. A third of the English lady romancers was the famed author of French origins with the unusual pen name of Ouida, who contributed tales like *Under Two Flags* and *A Dog of Flanders* to her audience. The American reading public was not alone in its thirst for melodrama and romance. As literacy increased steadily and, particularly, as more women received education, the audience for the mass sale and distribution of reading matter increased, and the adventures and romances appealed to readers whether they lived in Chicago or Manchester, New York or London.

The years of the Gilded Age do not constitute a convenient, closed unit in the area of popular culture. In almost every activity in this era a considerable change was taking place, usually at a different rate. The press, for example, remained from the 1850's (having emerged from the stage in which newspapers were purely party organs) to the 1880's in the phase of personal journalism in which a few great editors such as Bowles, Dana, and Greeley dominated. In the early 1880's the American theater entered a new stage which came to be called the "Golden Age of the Road." Equally significant changes were taking place in the field of minstrelsy and in the Chautauqua movement. American popular culture in this period defies exact classification or precise chronological limitations. Generally, the American popular culture of the 1870's resembled that of the 1850's more closely than it did that of the 1890's, and the 1880's probably witnessed the greatest changes. The transitions were often still ahead or were in beginning stages.

An excellent example is the area of popular arts. There was a continuity and unity from the 1850's through the 1880's, which period has been called the "hey-day of cheap and popular art for everyone." [12] But this began before the Civil War. The much praised "simple arts," whether hooked rugs or clipper ships, had gone into decline in the 1850's. Lewis Mumford in his *Brown Decades* delivers this judgment: "When the Civil War broke, architecture in America had been sinking steadily for a generation. Order, fitness, comeliness, proportion, were words that could no longer be applied to it: construction was submerged in that morass of jerry-building, tedious archaism, and spurious romanticism that made up the architectural achievements of the nineteenth century." [13] In the decades after the Civil War there was tastelessness in art and architecture; showiness and gaudiness appeared alongside of the factory and the tenement house in unhappy juxtaposition, and there was a flowering of exotic styles and excess ornamentation. But it is patently unfair to charge the men of this era with sole responsibility for casting off a valuable tradition and replacing it with shoddy vulgarity. The Gilded Age was to a great degree, particularly in the popular arts, a product of the techniques and tastes of pre-Civil War America.

Two notable examples of this general point would be the continued popularity of Currier and Ives prints and Rogers sculpture groups. Currier began his print business in 1835, the partnership with Ives was formed in 1857, and they published and sold their prints with tremendous success until 1907.[14] Today these prints have become collector's items; what was then produced to meet the broadest possible tastes is today valued as art. Another popular phenomenon of the world of art was John Rogers the sculptor. His first popular work was "The Checker Players" in 1859, and he went on to become "not only a household name but a household ornament."[15] In both cases talent and honest craftsmanship gained a deserved popularity from the American public and serve as an index to public tastes as well as to the continuity of the period from before the Civil War well into the late nineteenth century.

In the area of the popular novel this basic continuity is also obvious. The names that emerged in the 1850's continued to rank among the best sellers throughout the years of the Civil War and the postwar decades. Mrs. Mary J. Holmes, described a trifle cruelly, if accurately, by Frank Mott as "that prolific favorite of the unthinking," is a case in point.[16] Her publishing career began in the 1850's and continued on into the 1880's at roughly the rate of a novel a year. Her protagonists were paragons of perfection, physically and morally, and her villains were veritable monsters of evil—the outcome was never long in doubt. In general, her books belong in the sentimental-moralistic school of writing, one much favored by the writing ladies of the mid-nineteenth century. One of the foremost students of popular literature has commented: "Publishers in the 'fifties learned to welcome any woman who turned up at their offices with a novel in bulky manuscript under her arm."[17] The publishers of the Gilded Age did not forget this lesson. The sentimental-moralistic novel continued to be a staple of the weekly story-papers and the publishers' lists.

It would be improper to leave this vein without some mention of Mrs. E. D. E. N. Southworth. By all who count publishing figures, Mrs. Southworth is accounted the queen of what Nathaniel Hawthorne once called that "d——d mob of scribbling women."

The leading authority on best sellers has pronounced her the "most popular authoress in the annals of American publishing"—no mean achievement in a field in which the ladies have excelled.[18]

Mrs. Southworth generally set her stories in Virginia or Maryland, though occasionally a craggy mountain pass might defy the known facts of geography; a fine old plantation served admirably as the background for a romantic tale. In this setting her handsome heroes of slim and graceful carriage (she frequently sounds the same note as Metrecal commercials) and her pure and lovely heroines could win through to true love in spite of fearsome villainies, ancient curses, and assorted trials and tribulations. An example of a setting and plot idea can be gained from one of her books, *The Malediction; or, The Widows of Widowville*, in which a mysterious stranger, of slim and graceful carriage and patrician features, learns that a noble plantation house, rising above the Chesapeake Bay, is the home of a beautiful heiress who is prevented from marrying by an old family curse of a most peculiar, but unknown type.[19] Who could resist a situation fraught with such peril and promise? Obviously not the reading public of the Gilded Age who continued to buy Mrs. Southworth's books for over sixty years; her works were still selling in considerable numbers at the time of her death in 1899.

A variation on the sentimental-moralistic romance was the type of novel that had something more of the sensational element, usually in the form of more violence or a hint of sexuality or exposures of vice in high places. The English best sellers, *East Lynne* and *Lady Audley's Secret*, were of this type. There were, of course, numerous practitioners of this school of writing, including Sylvanus Cobb, Jr. and Charles Reade. Cobb began publishing in the cheap story-paper, the *New York Ledger*, in 1856 and was still going strong in 1885. James Hart has noted that Cobb was looked on with disdain by the more "cultivated and genteel" readers, but he also noted that Cobb had a contract for thirty years at $50 per week with the *New York Ledger*.[20] Reade was also a perennially popular author whose sensational tales appear and reappear on publishers' lists from the 1860's to the 1880's. In *Griffith Gaunt* (1866) and *A Terrible Temptation* (1871) he proved that a taste for exposés of vice and sin in high society had as solid an appeal in the moralistic middle class of the Gilded Age as in any other era.

No popular literature is so well remembered as the famous "dime novels." The history of this genre—its beginnings in the fertile mind of Erastus Beadle, its noblest examples, such as Edward Ellis' *Seth Jones; or The Captives of the Frontier*, and its degeneration into cheap hackwork for children, as the famed Nick Carter series—has been told before. The usual story in these books, of heroic deeds on the wild frontier, maintained the prevalent celebration of the individual and the persistent moralism of the popular literature of the Gilded Age.

The religious novel was still another genre which had its seed-time before the Civil War and blossomed luxuriantly in the immediate postwar years. The persistent interest in such novels in these years is not difficult to understand. These were years of challenge and trial for American churches, particularly for the traditional Protestant denominations. Orthodox theologies which had been subject to liberalizing influences in the pre-Civil War decades were now abruptly challenged by currents of scientific thought, notably, of course, the Darwinian hypothesis of the evolution of species. Probably no other topic occupied so much time in pulpit discourse or space in the religious press, and this interest was bound to carry over to the general public. Furthermore, the ethical ideal and social programs of the churches were being severely tested by the social and economic problems of an urban-industrial growth of nearly frightening proportions. When the faith of the fathers and the traditional values are being sorely tried, people often eagerly grasp for reassurance in most guises, and perhaps most eagerly in a happy fictional world where an omnipotent author can manipulate the plot to produce the triumph of those same ideals and beliefs. This was the case in the three major best sellers of this type, Augusta Jane Evans' *St. Elmo* (1859), Elizabeth Stuart Phelps's *The Gates Ajar* (1868), and the Reverend E. P. Roe's *Barriers Burned Away* (1872). In *St. Elmo* a beautiful and brilliant girl (or presumably so, though the modern reader may find this brilliance a bit difficult to grasp) convinces St. Elmo to turn from atheism to the ministry; *The Gates Ajar* ignores theological problems and vanquishes doubt by descriptions of the beauties of an extremely worldly sort of heaven; and in *Barriers Burned Away* the great Chicago fire and spiritual truths are combined in a "sure-fire" formula. These books were leaders on the publishers' lists throughout the late nineteenth century testifying to the appeal of simple faith in a complex age.

In the 1880's there appeared one of the major popular novels in American history. In the pages of *Ben Hur*, General Lew Wallace successfully combined the powerful appeal of religion, the glamor of an historical setting in the Roman Empire, and the sheer excitement of plain old melodrama. It should not be difficult for those of us who have recently witnessed a vast and costly version of this story in motion picture form to understand its tremendous vogue. Professor Hart has said, "If every American did not read the novel, almost everyone was aware of it." [21] This novel was the precursor of a rage for historical fiction in the 1890's and, of course, continuing into our own time. But it is doubtful if any of this type, from the crude sensationalism of Sylvanus Cobb, Jr., to the slick productions of Thomas Costain, has had the impact and persistent appeal of *Ben Hur*.

Perhaps the theme most often used for critical treatment by the historians of the Gilded Age is that which may be described as the self-help and success theme, with a strong admixture of inspiration. Here is the most undisguised worship of success and, outside the pages of Herbert Spencer or William Graham Sumner, the most unalloyed celebration of individualism. The theme was begun early in childhood with the widespread use of the McGuffey readers; there was an edition in 1857, to which a High School Reader was added in 1863, and further editions in 1879 and on into the twentieth century. These readers conveyed the well-known lessons of honesty, industry, obedience, thrift, piety, punctuality, and many other such virtues.[22] Fame and fortune were likely to result from the strict adherence to these rules of living. This was reinforced by the popular Horatio Alger books in which the young hero would find that a life of virtue and a chance to save the daughter of a rich man from drowning could lead to an opportunity and ultimate success. The role of chance in these success stories and the hackwork literary quality seem to escape the memory of those who recall the books with great fondness.

This early training with McGuffey and Alger might well have

been responsible for producing a taste for the books of the Englishman, Samuel Smiles. Four of his works have been accounted as best sellers by Frank Mott, and the titles alone should be sufficient to describe their content: *Self-Help, Character, Thrift,* and *Duty.* By the late 1880's two famous essays had appeared which further reinforced the gospel of uplift and success. The first of these, and the most widely read and heard in ensuing years, was Russell Conwell's *Acres of Diamonds,* in which this Philadelphia minister insisted that a man could find wealth in his own backyard if he but looked, and that it was every man's duty to acquire wealth. The second was Andrew Carnegie's formulation of the value of competitive individualism in selecting those best fitted to have wealth and the obligations of ownership of wealth, all of which can be summed up in the title of his essay, *The Gospel of Wealth.* All of these works obviously suited the tastes of the dominant middle class of the Gilded Age and certainly reflected the ideas of a nation that was engaged in the tasks of building a transportation system and an industrial machine, and of exploiting the natural wealth of a great continent. But such tastes were not peculiar to that age or to America. Englishmen were buying Samuel Smiles in as great numbers, and the uplift theme in America has always been a favorite. From Benjamin Franklin's *Poor Richard's Almanac* to Dr. Norman Vincent Peale's *Power of Positive Thinking,* Americans have been eager patrons of this brand of literature.

The American public did not, however, patronize only historical or religious fiction or self-help literature; it was also eager to read and to listen to the boisterous company of humorists that flourished in these years. The techniques of these humorists were not new in American life—the grotesque exaggerations of the Davy Crockett type of story, the rural parody of the style and manners of "city folk," and the artful mishandling of the English language were all inherited from an earlier America. After the Civil War, there was an increasing consciousness of the peculiar traits of regions and localities. The fact that the economic forces of the time were driving the nation toward a greater degree of nationalism and a diminution of the differences between the sections and regions produced an audience for those writers and lecturers who specialized in the portrayal of the unique and disappearing types in American life. The Yankee, the middle western "hayseed," the rough and ready westerner, and various southern types all found a public for their brands of humor.

The leaders of this school of humorists included such men as David Ross Locke (Petroleum V. Nasby), Charles Farrar Browne (Artemus Ward), and Henry Wheeler Shaw (Josh Billings). From their poses as "hayseeds" or other types, these humorists poked fun at the customs and conventions of the Gilded Age. Josh Billings wrote in his *Farmer's Allminax*, "Most people repent ov their sins bi thanking God they aint so wicked as their nabors." [23] Artemus Ward got off his share of quotable remarks, such as: "I tell you, feller citizens, it would have been ten dollars in Jeff Davis' pockets if he had never been born," or "Old George Washington's fort was not to hev eny public man of the present day ressemble him to eny alarmin extent." [24]

The sale of books of collected works of these men testifies to their popular appeal; Billings's *Farmer's Allminax*, for example, sold 90,000 copies in its first edition of 1869, and in ten years subsequent versions sold as high as 127,000 and never less than 50,000 copies. [25] These men and others—Bill Nye, Opie Read, Stanley Huntly, to mention a few—served up a pungent brand of humor based on strong characterizations, parody, and broad social satire. In an age of colorful individuals, these folk figures did not need to take a back seat to business barons or political bosses. They added a large dose of earthy, lusty humor to an age not especially known for its delicacy or refinement.

From the ranks of these regional humorists came two men who deserve special attention, Bret Harte and Mark Twain. Harte's sentimental tales of rough and ready characters with hearts of gold do not belong to the annals of great literature, but in him the frontier produced a writer who could give life to its experiences. This vein must have run out for Harte, however, for after his great success with *The Luck of Roaring Camp and Other Stories* he seems to have lost his artistic touch and his popularity. Samuel Clemens belongs to the realm of great literature; suffice it to say that in him the local colorists, the parodists, and the rough humorists of the West produced a genius, and his genius transmuted this raw material, just entertainment in other hands, into the closest thing to an epic of the Gilded Age.

In the field of magazine publishing there is a certain unity in the years of the Gilded Age, though the major innovations in this field came in the 1890's. On the other hand, in newspaper publishing there took place in the 1880's a major change, the fall of great editors and personal journalism to powerful owners and syndicates. The difference in response appears to be more a matter of difference in rate of change than anything else. Actually only a few years separated the "new journalism" from such magazine innovators as *Forum, Arena, Cosmopolitan,* and others. In both cases new business methods, decreased costs, lower prices, the demands of advertising, and the need for mass distribution diminished the personal note and encouraged the rise of the merchant of news.

The content of the newspapers of the Gilded Age resembled that of the pre-Civil War years. The changes that would be called "yellow journalism" had not occurred; the sensationalism, the comics, and other attributes of modern newspapers were not yet noticeable in the newspapers of the 1870's and just beginning in the 1880's. An upstate New York farmer continued, after Greeley's death, to subscribe to the *Tribune* in the belief that Horace was still responsible for its contents, and, if he missed the news of the death of the great editor, this mistake was understandable.[26] Technical changes took place; the telegraph and the cable, the press associations, expensive new machinery, labor unions, and advertising revenue were transforming the newspaper from a personal organ to a big business. By the time Pulitzer and Hearst had emerged as major owners in the 1890's, the style and content of the newspaper would be transformed to accord with this technical revolution.

In magazine publishing, these were years of "boom."[27] The number of magazines increased from 700 in 1865 to some 3,300 in 1885, and circulation figures show corresponding increases.[28] There was also a major trend toward more dependence on advertising, and in the early 1880's advertising "demonstrated its value and established its place in the general magazine."[29]

It is doubtful that the average reader (whoever he may have been) of the Gilded Age was conscious of, or seriously affected by, these changes. The effects of these profound revolutions in publishing were more clearly evident in the twentieth century than in these early years. The content of the magazines, as in the case of newspapers, resembled the traditional models more than the types that would emerge by the turn of the century.

Among magazines the cheap story-papers which had held sway prior to the Civil War continued to attract large numbers of readers. Such publications as the *New York Weekly*, the *New York Ledger*, or *Frank Leslie's Chimney Corner* combined fiction, poetry, essays, joke columns, and advice columns in such a way as to appeal to a wide variety of readers. The *Ledger* and *Weekly* claimed over 300,000 circulation, and the other shorter-lived story papers had circulation figures in the thousands for a few years.

The content of these popular, weekly periodicals reflects the tastes and beliefs of the period, as it seems safe to assume that the publishers of these competitive enterprises tried to give the American middle class what it wanted. The moral tone was smugly proper. In words reeking with self-righteousness, the publishers assured their readers that their particular publication was a family paper and the innocent daughters of the household could be permitted to read it in complete confidence.[30]

The bulk of the material in these papers was fiction, largely serialized versions of the romantic or historical novels of such authors as Mrs. Southworth or Sylvanus Cobb, Jr., if the publisher was fortunate enough to have one of these popular writers under contract; if not, of course, there were always imitators who could produce remarkably similar tales. Interspersed among the chapters of fiction there would be some poetry, always that of the pre-Civil War style and manner of Longfellow or Bryant, and never the unconventional barbarities of a Walt Whitman. There might well be something from Dickens or some other noted English author, and for patriotism and inspiration, respectively, historical sketches of the founding fathers of the nation and essays by Horace Greeley or Henry Ward Beecher. There were also, in one series of the *Ledger*, regular columns on "Advice to Young Women" by such authorities as Mesdames Horace Mann, Horace Greeley, Lydia Maria Child, and others.

The subheading of the *New York Ledger* proudly announced

that it was a paper "Devoted to Choice Literature Romance The News and Commerce." Neither "The News" nor "Commerce" were much in evidence; stories, essays, advice columns, poems, and proper (though not, it must be admitted, funny) jokes made up the bulk of these story-papers. Hence, the content of these papers reflects the same tastes as the best seller lists in terms of desire for sentimental fiction and the triumph of the accepted values (which might be expected in any popular writing). To these one can add a taste for some uplifting essays and appropriate poetic sentiments, all of which produced thousands of readers in the years of the Gilded Age.

Though not so widely read as the story-papers with their popular appeal, the actual leaders of the magazine world in these years were the genteel, learned, and massive aristocrats such as *Harper's Weekly* or *Monthly*, *Atlantic*, *Galaxy*, or *Scribner's*. Some of these, notably the Harper publications, can be called popular; all of them reflect the tastes and ideas of the middle class and could be found on parlor tables whether they were read or not. They were badges of serious intellectual interests and sound opinions. They were part of popular culture, since their contents reflected what the dominant class believed and what they thought they should know and talk about.

It is more difficult to know what to do with a periodical such as the *Nation* and its small circulation of some 8,000 as compared, for example, with 100,000 for the Harper magazines or 200,000 in 1885 for *Scribner's* (known by then as *Century Magazine*).[31] Certainly the *Nation* seems to have been the journal of the intellectual classes; yet it usually demanded improvements and reforms of certain types. The mild liberalism of the Cobden or Manchester school of economics, the moral rectitude, and the authoritative tone that Edwin Lawrence Godkin instilled in the *Nation* were not suited to a popular magazine but were eminently suitable for a successful class which believed that things were going well on the whole and that certain improvements could be made by men of good will and upright character, but that no fundamental changes were required.

The wider following of other journals came from a less circumscribed subject matter than that of the rigidly intellectual *Nation*. These other journals were of "miscellany and opinion,"[32] and one cannot help but admire the dutifulness of the readers who ploughed through their many pages of heavy prose. The editing and the prose were considerable improvements over the weighty and ponderous style of the pre-Civil War periodicals, but even so it was no small task to read through a typical issue of *Harper's* or *Scribner's*. Possibly the upper middle-class reader of the Gilded Age had more time for reading and a sterner sense of the duty to be informed. Consider, for example, reading an article on "The Development of the Steamship, and the Liverpool Exhibition of 1886," complete with diagrams of ships' hulls, superstructures, and engines, thirty pages long, and then following with a scientific and equally factual article on the "Forests of North America." But who knows? Perhaps many readers glanced at these formidable articles and hurried on to read "Marse Archie's Flight," a dialect Civil War story, or the last chapter of a long novel of New York family life.[33]

The journals reflected the era's great interest in scientific matters. Economics was another prominent subject. And one could expect to find in almost any issue an article on that topic that so fascinated the public of the Gilded Age, the evolutionary hypothesis and its significance for religion. *Harper's Weekly* described itself as "A Journal of Civilization," a just claim, judging by the standards of the time. This whole group of periodicals were, in fact, the "journals of civilization of the Gilded Age." Their contents ranged from popular fiction to foreign news, humor columns, travel articles, literary essays, political editorials, articles on economic and scientific subjects, and excellent illustrations and occasional poems —taken as a whole, an excellent mirror of the mind of this period. Indeed, after exploring some of these journals, one is likely to come away with increased respect for the breadth of interests and seriousness of purpose of those Americans who supported these magazines.

One might suppose that the American people of the post-Civil War years spent all of their leisure time reading novels, story-papers, newspapers, and magazines. Considering the lower percentage of educated persons in those years, those who did have high school or college educations must have read a great deal for the publishing industries of the era to have flourished so and to have produced such variety. In many cases, the readers were seeking a familiar goal—escape to a world of danger and high adventure, exotic settings, and, occasionally, sex and violence. The urban world of factories and offices must have made such escape ever more necessary since the vogue for this kind of fiction, beginning in the 1850's, constantly increased through the years of the Gilded Age. But the readers also sought reaffirmation of the traditional values, the beliefs and ideals of an earlier America of town and countryside, and these they found especially in the novels and story-papers. The educated minority found the same reassurance in the firm moral tone and the determined factuality and seriousness of the journals of opinion.

In the United States in these same years, industry was going through a time of revolutionary change and growth, and the nation was undergoing a social transformation as industry and urbanism grew with awe-inspiring rapidity; depressions, immigration, labor disputes, all competed for space in the press. Yet the fiction, essays, poems, and editorial advice of the popular publications were all redolent of a rural and village land. The revolution in values lagged behind the revolution in the social structure, and this was most clearly evident in the popular literature of the age.

But Americans then, as now, did not spend their evenings and Sundays solely in reading. They heard lectures, attended the theater, went to curiosity museums and circuses, and participated in self-improvement classes at Chautauqua institutes. In all of these they sought something similar to what they sought in their reading—the escape from reality of Barnum's collection of curiosities or of the artificial world of the theater, the confident proclamation of the "old truths" in a Moody revival meeting, or the self-help and inspiration at a Chautauqua. They may have attended that new phenomenon, organized, big-league baseball. In any case, there were many varied activities available to the public, and most of them flourished in these years.

Religious revival meetings were a national favorite to many, and no revival team compared in popularity to Dwight L. Moody and Ira D. Sankey. Moody in 1875 was "the rising young tycoon of the revival trade as Andrew Carnegie was of the steel trade or John D. Rockefeller of oil." [34] He was the revivalist who coupled businesslike methods with the "old fashioned gospel," and his success was enormous. In this he was substantially aided by Ira D. Sankey, who took charge of the music and contributed stirring solo renditions of popular gospel hyms. But Moody was the driving force in this revival movement of the 1870's and 1880's. He used committees to prepare the way, asked for cooperation of the various denominations, made the act of conversion as simple and businesslike as possible, and he preached in the language of the people; no learned theological discourse or flowery rhetoric ever marred the simple plea to "take Christ now." There were ties between Moody and the popular writing of the time. The popular magazines and novels were building a taste for "sentiment and make-believe," and the revivalist who would succeed "would have to speak the new commoner's tongue." [35] Clearly Moody, the lay preacher, appealed to the same broad audience that read the cheap story-papers and the books of Mrs. E. D. E. N. Southworth, and, of course, to nonreaders and anyone else who would listen. He was a remarkably persuasive example of the peculiar combination of the revolution in techniques and the cultural lag in values which characterized so much of the popular culture of the Gilded Age. His methods were modern but his message consisted of forceful repetitions of the "old truths." This combination made him the most popular and significant revival preacher of the Gilded Age.

There were many famous preachers in this age, some conservative in theology, a few, liberal; some who argued that Christianity should be applied to the social problems of the day, others who preached on sin and salvation alone. But one man stood out as somewhat of a symbol of the middle-class pulpit and created one of the great sensations of the time—Henry Ward Beecher. He was not a typical preacher. The typical minister was more conservative, not nearly so successful, and certainly not as controversial. Yet Beecher spoke with tremendous authority from his Plymouth Congregational Church in Brooklyn, New York, and from his editorial position on the *Independent*. His message had wide popular appeal. He rejected the theology of his Calvinist forebears, influenced in so doing by his father, Lyman Beecher; he preached not orthodoxy, but rather a doctrine of love and an ethic of individualism modified by the demands of brotherhood. His sermons were dazzling dramatic displays, more remarkable for their emotional appeal than for serious content.

As with Moody, the traditional values, without the complex theology and harsh punishments of the old faith, were restated and combined with considerable dramatic ability and commercial skill to gain tremendous popularity. When Beecher was accused of seducing the wife of a close friend and co-worker, the ensuing scandal, aired at two church councils and a public trial, was a national sensation. The frailties of clergymen and the public interest in such scandal are hardly unique to the Gilded Age, though in an era when sexual morality was considered an essential bulwark of the public welfare the affair was bound to create unique concern and sensation. It provided countless columns of reading matter for months upon months as the councils and the trial dragged on. As much as any other event, this affair raised serious questions about the prevailing mores in the realm of "private versus public conduct, the function of the evangelical church, and the place of women in the social order." [36] Although there is not space here to discuss these aspects, it is too easy to dismiss the whole scandal as a comic episode revealing the hypocrisy of Victorian morality; its meaning and consequences were much deeper.

Another fascinating episode in the history of popular culture in the Gilded Age is the early history of the Chautauqua movement. Most accounts of this movement dwell upon the later phase, known as the circuit or tent Chautauqua. This latter development was the commercialization and standardization of Chautauqua for purposes of taking Chautauqua on the road, and it led to some degradation of the content of Chautauqua as pure entertainment attractions gradually supplanted most of the educational programs (students of educational television may find some historical precedents here). This phase of the story has been told by Victoria and Robert Case in their book, *We Called It Culture*, and of it, they say: "It is the tent or 'circuit' Chautauqua that is remembered by millions today, mostly by those whose origins were in the small towns of the nation." [37] But this was a development of the turn of the century and not part of the Gilded Age.

The original Chautauqua was a summer session on the shores of Lake Chautauqua, New York, begun as a Sunday School Teachers Assembly by Lewis Miller, an Ohio manufacturer, and the Reverend (later Bishop) John H. Vincent of the Methodist church.

Both the program content and the number of such institutes expanded rapidly. Permanent Chautauquas were founded in Ohio, Michigan, Iowa, and eventually in the Willamette Valley at Gladstone, Oregon. The original Chautauqua added, in succession, a Literary and Scientific Circle, a School of Theology, and a College of Liberal Arts with authority to grant a bachelor's degree. The most eminent educators, ministers, and lecturers (eventually including six presidents of the United States) contributed or sold their services. The most prominent educator and a leading figure in the Chautauqua was William Rainey Harper, later president of the University of Chicago, but the champion lecturer must surely have been the Reverend Russell Conwell, who is said to have delivered his famous lecture, "Acres of Diamonds," over 5,000 times.

The self-improvement drive and the success-through-knowledge theme demonstrated again that the American people of the Gilded Age eagerly sought the learning that was available in their time. If this phenomenon is linked with the free library movement, which had tremendous growth in the years 1878 and 1898, the already noted prosperity of the book publishing industry (climaxed by the spectacular royalty check paid by Samuel Clemens for his publishing house to former President Grant for the sum of $200,-000), and the magazine boom, it is obvious that the thirst for knowledge and the desire for culture were prominent characteristics of the public attitude of the Gilded Age. To be sure, this search customarily led simply to the reaffirmation of the values rooted in the experiences of that age. The benefits of private property, the beauties of the law of competition, and the stewardship of men of wealth were main themes of Chautauqua lectures on social and economic subjects. But it would be strange indeed if the popular institutions of a society purveyed ideas contrary to the accepted values of that society. We may expect that the lonely prophet or perceptive intellectual or sensitive artist will confront a society with its failures and injustices, but surely the culture-heroes will not, and the purpose of studying the latter is to identify the popular ideas, not the unconventional ones.

Again the impression may linger that the public of this time devoted itself entirely to reading and listening to sermons and lectures; such was plainly not the case. The Gilded Age was the time of the rise of spectator sports, of the birth of the modern circus; it was a great era in the history of minstrelsy and a "golden age" of the theater. As the people gathered in cities and worked in factories, it became necessary to substitute organized recreation and spectator events for the games and entertainments of a rural society. For these spectacles, on the playing field or on the stage, the audiences were large and enthusiastic. This period witnessed the first mammoth three-ring circus under "three acres" of circus tent and the opening of the nation's foremost opera house, the historic Metropolitan, in New York City in 1883.

In the realm of theater, there were three developments which any student of the popular culture must consider: the dominance of the "road"; the vogue for light musicals and scenic splendors, including the spectacle of the scantily attired female form; and, finally, the popularity and decline of minstrelsy.

The roll call of touring road stars who were available to Americans in towns and cities from coast to coast is enough to arouse envy in the breast of any lover of the stage. The list might include such names as Richard Mansfield, or James O'Neill—assigned to permanent stardom in the role of Edmund Dantes in Dumas's *The Count of Monte Christo*—or Edwin Booth, the supreme Shakespearian, or Mary Anderson, or the brilliant Italian stars, Tammasco Salvini and Adelaide Ristori, or Mme. Modjeska, or that perennial favorite of the time, Joseph Jefferson in *Rip Van Winkle,* or Henry Irving and Ellen Terry, or the Divine Sarah herself, or, near the end of the time, the innovator who helped create the modern style of acting, Eleanora Duse. A rich and varied fare of theater was brought to millions of Americans by the touring companies in these years. *East Lynne*, the popular favorite and money-maker, might have to be played on Saturday nights; but Shakespeare and Dumas, even Racine, and later G. B. Shaw and Ibsen were available.

By 1893 this "golden age of the road" was drawing to a close, and the development of theatrical syndicates foretold the rise of a new kind of theater, one that would culminate in the "star" system and the limited theater of the mid-twentieth century. The story of the American theater has been written from almost every point of view; memoirs, biographies, and critical histories are all available.[38]

but the post-Civil War decades were glorious years in the annals of the American stage. The revolution in organization which occurred at the close of the period, and which affected the twentieth-century theater, left the experience of theater in almost every town and village largely a memory from the nineteenth century.

The second development was the taste for lighter theatrical fare, in this case particularly in the major cities. The origins of this vogue have been traced to the success of a melodrama called *The Black Crook*, which included a Parisian ballet sequence. This theatrical sensation was the most expensive and daring show that Americans had seen as of 1866. Nor could the thunderous denunciations of clergymen and angry moralists contain this trend. *The Black Crook* ran for sixteen months and broke all box office records. It was often revived thereafter and, quite naturally, was followed by a number of similar shows.[39]

The comic opera also profited by this vogue. The sprightly, melodic works of Gilbert and Sullivan were major hits after the first American production in 1878. So popular were these works that the authors opened the *Pirates of Penzance* in New York City. This was partly to prevent the work from being pirated (no pun intended) by American producers. The glamor queen of the Gilded Age, the opulent, beautiful, graceful, queenly—to use a few of the customary adjectives—Lillian Russell was long associated with Gilbert and Sullivan roles.[40] In addition, this taste for *opéra bouffe* enabled several of the works of Offenbach to succeed in America in spite of the usual charge of "French indecencies"—or perhaps, because of it.

The costumes, as illustrated in the newspapers and posters of the time, do not appear so daring to the modern eye, accustomed as we are to the calendar poses of Hollywood starlets and the engineering miracles of the apparently supportless Bikini bathing suit and the strapless gown. Lillian Russell was, after all, acclaimed as a singer; what can be said of Jayne Mansfield? The burlesque was hardly compatible with the professions of Victorian morality, but this gap seems no more ridiculous than some of the dilemmas posed by the existence of off-color productions in the mid-twentieth century. The well-turned ankle titillated the audience, usually all male, of

the Gilded Age; the near-exposure of the breasts titillates the audience, usually mixed, of the 1960's. The Gilded Age does not come
off too poorly if the comparisons are fairly made.

The third of these trends in show business is the role of the
minstrel show. The minstrel show dates back to the between-acts
specialty numbers of black-face performers in the pre-Civil War
era, especially one Thomas Rice, famed for his "Jump Jim Crow"
number. In this period the stock Negro character of the stage
evolved, bearing little or no resemblance to any actual Negroes.
From this came the authentic minstrel company with end men,
jokes, and songs. This form of entertainment had its heyday in the
period from 1850 to 1870. Thereafter, the competition to form ever
bigger and more elaborate shows caused a loss in the quality of the
performances. This loss, plus increasing expenses and competition
with vaudeville, burlesque, and musical comedy caused minstrelsy
to go into a long decline which ended the form in the 1920's.[41]

The success of the minstrel show does cast some light on the
public attitude toward racial minorities in the Gilded Age. Such
stereotypes were a commonplace of that era. In particular, the
Negro was portrayed on stage, in dialect stories, and in illustrations
as a comic fellow, "ludicrously inept," often putting on "airs . . .
above his true station in life," but withal a happy, good-natured
type, perhaps gifted at singing or dancing, but never as a "person
of consequence or dignity." [42] This was an age when racial distinc-
tions were taken as obvious and inescapable. Those who were concerned about the conditions of minority groups acted from pater-
nalistic motives, not from a sense of the legitimate dignity and worth
of all men.

Some of the stock racial stereotypes are well known. The earlier
picture of the Jew as a shadowy and alien figure somehow en-
meshed in the world of international finance became sharper
through its relationship to the anti-Semitism of the Populist movement. The image of the Indian changed—first he was portrayed as
a dangerous enemy, then as nature's nobleman going down to defeat bravely, and then as a romantic figure as that in Helen Hunt
Jackson's *Ramona*. This was also the time of the emergence of the
stage Irishman; such teams as Harrigan and Hart or Kelly and Ryan

began the long career of this favorite comic figure of the vaudeville stage. The Irish were also frequently portrayed as dull-witted workingmen like Sam Sleeny (which apparently is meant to have an Irish sound) in John Hay's novel, *The Bread Winners*. The Irish, along with other and newer immigrant groups, suffered from the prevailing anti-Catholicism of the time.[43] On the Pacific Coast the Chinese were the chief victims of racist thinking. Although Bret Harte may not have intended it, this was the result of his oft-reprinted poem popularly known as "The Heathen Chinee."

The popular culture of the Gilded Age cannot be encompassed in an essay. There is too much to consider. Nothing has yet been said about the giant figure of P. T. Barnum, for example, whose promotions were of more than passing importance in the field of entertainment. Though it was not so much Barnum himself as it was his partners—W. C. Coup, in particular—who created the modern circus, the "greatest show on earth," Barnum remains the symbol of this achievement. Obviously the growth of the circus was tied to the growth of railroads and centers of population adequate to support such an enterprise. In the field of entertainment the gigantic circus was related to the spirit of the age, an age of great enterprises of all kinds, from spanning a continent with iron rails to building a multimillion-dollar business empire. P. T. Barnum belongs among the empire-builders of this era.[44]

Still another fascinating episode in the popular culture of the Gilded Age was the drawing power of the famed agnostic, Robert Ingersoll. It was not just Moody or Beecher or Barnum who could attract crowds with ideas and attractions that were plainly acceptable to most people, but a brilliant orator could bring large crowds into the lecture halls to hear their own religion criticized and challenged.[45]

The ballads of the time, as might be expected, reinforced the accepted values found elsewhere in the popular culture. The moralistic note is at least detectable in "Always Take Mother's Advice"; the sentimental-religious theme might be represented by "Flowers from an Angel Mother's Grave"; the hallmark of respectability was a rendition of "In the Gloaming"; and surely everyone has shared at some time in the nostalgia of that romantic ballad, "Down by the Old Mill Stream." [46] The lyrics of these ballads and others would be excellent guides to various facets of the popular mind in the Gilded Age.

Several general propositions can be ventured about the popular culture of this period, all of which deserve consideration in any lengthy study. There was a revolution in the technical phases; because of improved transportation, large cities, and improved business methods, as well as a changing society, all of the institutions that purveyed popular culture were being transformed. The newspapers and magazines had to revise their methods and their appeal; the Chautauqua was commercialized and standardized; revivalism took on business methods; minstrelsy could not survive the competition of this new age in entertainment. The changes that grew out of this revolution in methods, however, were felt in later years with more force than in the Gilded Age itself. But the need for greater sales was surely evident in the popularity of the sentimental-romantic stories in magazines in serial form and then in book form, both of which were major features of the post-Civil War decades.

The degree of continuity between the Gilded Age and the pre-Civil War years deserves notice. The years before the Civil War have been called the "Sentimental Years," but this characterization with its implication of sentimentalization of human relationships could with equal accuracy be applied to the Gilded Age. The death of loved ones, the idealization of the family, and the celebration of romantic love were all powerful themes through the Civil War and into the postwar years.

Closely related to this continuity is the degree to which the popular works of the Gilded Age clung to the values and beliefs of an earlier time. Indeed, the insistent celebration of these virtues of an earlier America leads to the conclusion that there was an awareness of the forces that were transforming the nation and a fierce resistance to them.

But in spite of these continuities and the characteristics shared with American popular tastes of any period, there was something of a characteristic quality to the Gilded Age. The period came to an end as the 1880's drew to a close. The transformation of the publishing industry, the rise of theatrical syndicates, the passing of the "golden age of the road," the decline of minstrelsy, the disappearance of the cheap story-papers, all marked the change. Something would be lost, perhaps best described as the folk element, that which had endured into an industrial age from an earlier America. Another casualty of the more highly organized society was the uninhibited individualism, which for all its unfortunate results, lent a colorful and fascinating quality to this era. And, finally, there was a loss of that sense of assurance and abundant optimism which, though a substantial part of the American character in all periods, was assuredly at a high point in the Gilded Age.

These losses were bound to occur as the technology of an industrial society advanced, and mass markets for art and entertainment were made possible, even necessary. It is probably well that artists and entertainers or, at least, their promoters and business managers should have organized for this new age, but it is also permissible to feel a twinge of nostalgia for an age when the individual seemed a bit more significant. The Gilded Age was still a time when a bold editor could display his personality in his paper, a colorful preacher could become a national figure almost in the manner of a motion picture star, and every housewife could hope to become a famous writer with her latest romantic tale. And all of this they could do with a firm belief in the triumph of their cause and surpassing faith in the imperviousness of their moral armor.

9

The Search for Reality:
Writers and Their Literature
ROBERT FALK

TO REASSESS the literature of the Gilded Age in a brief chapter is a problem of synthesis. Selection from many facts in the interests of unity and freshness is required. One must set the scene, name the main factors, and write the play. And it cannot afford to be another Victorian melodrama. On the other hand, it must not fall into the opposite cliché, a sophisticated assault upon proprieties and genteel attitudes à la H. L. Mencken and Sinclair Lewis. We are too far past the 1920's for that, and too far past the 1930's to make the Gilded Age a scapegoat for those seeking in business enterprise and the "gospel of wealth" historical causes for the economic dislocations of the depression decade. Since 1945, however, there has been a continuing revisionist body of scholarship consisting of biographies, collections of letters, editions, and critical studies centering primarily on the major writers of the period—James, Mark Twain, and Howells—and a lesser current of reinterpretation of the minor ones.[1] The effect of this has been to correct previous orthodoxies in critical points of interpretation such as, for instance, the vitiating influence of genteel emendations of Mark Twain's writing by his wife, Howells, and others. The nature of this work has been analytical, detailed, and specialized. Meanwhile, the larger historical framework, the relation of literature to the period, has been relatively untouched or treated in accordance with the earlier orthodoxies of historical writing. Broader questions must now be asked. Has any clear outline emerged from the scholarship of the past two decades? What is the picture of the Gilded Age in its literary phases now that it has been retouched—now that familiar landmarks have been removed, major and minor figures given new emphasis, and relative values revised and adjusted?

The fundamental question is this: can we proceed beyond the negative implications of such epithets as "The Gilded Age," "The Genteel Tradition," and "The Age of Innocence"?

"Don't forget to speak scornfully of the Victorian age. There will be a time for meekness when you seek to better it." [2] Thus James M. Barrie defended his age against the younger generation in 1922. Now, more than a half-century after the first use by George Santayana of the phrase "genteel tradition," and thirty years after Mencken, Van Wyck Brooks, Parrington, and others launched a concerted broadside of anti-Victorianism, we are better equipped to evaluate the literary thought and expression of that time. We are no longer impelled to see it as the reverse image of our own generation or to disparage the culture of the Gilded Age as justification for our own deficiencies. Brooks himself has gradually recanted. " 'The Genteel Tradition,' " he wrote in 1941, is a phrase which "has had too long a run. It has been stretched in so many directions that it is as useless as old elastic." [3] Such phrases have little validity in accounting for the climate of opinion which produced writers of major stature. And they need redefinition when applied to some of the special literary accomplishments of writers like John W. De-Forest, Bret Harte, George W. Cable, Sidney Lanier, and Edward Bellamy. The Gilded Age was the environmental background for the careers of a number of distinguished men of letters of whom it is in poor taste to speak condescendingly. Henry Adams, for one, was as much a part of his time as he was in revolt against it. Such original minds as William James, John Fiske, Charles Peirce, and Chauncey Wright belonged to the best American intellectual tradition of that era, and their writing was closely interwoven with the texture of their generation.

In more strictly literary circles the period contained such skilful practitioners of regional fiction as Eggleston, Catherine Anne Woolson, Sarah Orne Jewett, and Joel Chandler Harris, all widely acclaimed during the 1870's and 1880's. There were influential editors in this period of the magazines. Howells of the *Atlantic Monthly*, R. W. Gilder of the *Century*, G. W. Curtis of *Harper's*, and J. G. Holland of *Scribner's*—all tastemakers charged by some later critics with perpetuating the canons of propriety. At a time when the literary essay was still an art in itself, there were men like

Higginson, Aldrich, and H. H. Boyesen to carry on the tradition of Emerson, Holmes, and Lowell. Literary criticism, slowly emerging from the conventional book-review columns, became during these years a profession in its own right.[4] James, Howells and other liberal-minded critics like Thomas S. Perry, Brander Matthews, W. C. Brownell, and E. C. Stedman did much to advance the cause of realism in fiction and helped work out a rationale for the novel which allowed for some of the facts of life without excluding the imagination and espoused a scientific discipline of method without quite sacrificing a healthy moral tone or, in the best sense, an idealized view of human nature.

Poetry, with the notable exceptions of Whitman and Emily Dickinson (the latter not even published until after 1890), remained derivative and conventional. The influence of English romantic verse and the towering figure of Tennyson overshadowed the younger poets, while readers and critics were content with the greater names of the mid-century, Whittier, Lowell, Bryant, and Holmes, all of whom were still active well beyond 1870. Bret Harte's verses found a momentary audience and so did Joaquin Miller's, but the Gilded Age produced no new forms of poetry or lasting poetic influences. Popular and sentimental fiction flourished, however, as a sign of a generally low level of taste among the juvenile and somewhat arrested adult readers of E. P. Roe, Frances Hodgson Burnett, Horatio Alger, Lew Wallace, Marion Crawford, and others. But cataloguing of names can only serve to suggest the variety of writing and the manifold levels of literature found in this twenty-year period, much of which has been too easily crowded under a few pejorative epithets. Like all such "periods," this one was composed of at least three generations. There were the older voices of romanticism, the younger antiromantic novelists and critics, and the still younger generation which was to espouse naturalism in the 1890's. To understand the "tone" of the time one should be aware of all of these, but the prime concern must be with the middle generation, that of James, Howells, and Mark Twain, which came of age in the 1870's and produced much of its finest work before 1890.

Certain themes in fiction may be found at all levels of writing during the Gilded Age, showing a mingling of romantic and realistic elements. The Civil War, strangely neglected, was touched only lightly in a few stories of Henry James and in Melville's Battle Pieces in verse. It was realistically handled in DeForest's *Miss Ravenel's Conversion from Secession to Loyalty*, an advanced work which failed to make the impression it deserved in a national mood which was not yet ready for actual battle scenes in literature. Feminism was one of the central preoccupations of the time. The theme was mingled with national pride and native innocence, as well as old-fashioned "romance," but in their search for anti-romantic attitudes James, Howells, DeForest, Henry Adams and others treated the young American woman with psychological insight, irony, and penetration. Money, in this 'golden age of business,' was a frequent literary motif. Juvenile readers eagerly swallowed the long series of success stories by Horatio Alger, Jr., which painted the rainbow possibilities of wealth amidst degradation and poverty. Absurd and mawkish as they were, these tales were among the first to depict city life with a certain accuracy, and one suspects that farm boys were less impressed by Alger's moralizings than by the fascinating details of street life in New York which they found in his homely pages. Mark Twain used the success theme to expose the hypocrisy of dreams of unlimited wealth and the corrupting effects of greed. James and Howells both devoted long novels to the analysis of the man of property and the self-made businessman. Politics was only cautiously employed in the 1870's as a literary theme, but a few novels, notably *The Gilded Age, Honest John Vane*, and *John Andross*, opened up the vein of social criticism which reached full expression in the 1880's in the work of Tourgee, Hay, Adams, Howells, Bellamy, and others.

If one were to summarize the influential forces underlying the literary mind of the Gilded Age, he would list them somewhat as follows: (1) the new evolutionary science of Herbert Spencer, merging with Comtean Positivism, to reinforce the genial romanticism of the 1870's; (2) the increased interest in *milieu* as a determining factor in the development of character; (3) the new nationalism and the rediscovery of America in fictional terms; (4) the cross-currents implicit in the rapidly rising urban culture of the east and the still-uninhibited expansion to the west; (5) American innocence and European experience; (6) regionalism and local color; (7) naturalistic and scientific literary attitudes deriving from French fiction in conflict with inherited idealism and certain Victorian proprieties; (8) the mingling of reality and romance; and (9) western humor versus the genteel tradition (especially in Mark Twain and Bret Harte). Such a listing is, of course, incomplete and oversimplified, but it can provide a basis for an attempt to understand the paradoxical character of Victorian realism in the Gilded Age. It is not enough to call the period "transitional" or to speak of its eclectic or disparate tendencies. All literary periods thus overlap and intermingle, and intellectual conflict is more the rule than the exception. The task will be to illustrate with certain selected authors, themes, and literary methods the ways in which these currents of thought came together to form a literary "center." What, in short, *was* "realism" in those years? What did the best writers intend to accomplish? What theories did they follow and how were they received?

Realism, as a literary phenomenon of the Gilded Age, began tentatively in the late 1860's as a protest against mid-century romantic literary attitudes and conventions. During the 1870's it was in an experimental and transitional stage. By 1880, one can recognize an authentic movement of realism in the novel, and it was during the 1880's that the best writing of the period was done. After 1886 a different climate of opinion began to alter the character of fiction, and a new and younger generation began to express itself. The gradual beginnings about 1865 may be found in some of James's early reviews in the *Nation*, in Howells' Italian sketches, DeForest's two best novels, Twain's *Innocents Abroad*, and Bret Harte's stories. It was presaged, too, in the transitional nature of the national mind. Henry James assayed the tone of the age as a "romantic vision of the real." A strong current of nationalism and optimism helped form the literary tone of the 1870's. The mood was one of anticipation and hope for the coming dispensation, combined with a considerable naïveté as to what that dispensation would be. A spirit of progress and melioristic growth, based in part upon the lure of material advancement, helped America forget the tragedy of the recent war over slavery. Walt Whitman expressed this somewhat vague idealism: "All goes onward and outward, nothing collapses." Whitman was one of the few who sensed the evils of a materialistic plunge toward outward expansion with its consequent neglect of larger ideals, but the general mind in 1870 was impatient of restraints, unwilling to brood over ultimate truths and somber realities. Still in its teens the American psyche was only beginning to sense the coming responsibilities of middle age. Three things mainly helped to preserve the illusion: mid-century idealism (what Parrington called "the twilight of transcendentalism") carried over into the postwar years; positivistic science; and the buoyant atmosphere of an expanding frontier.

When Howells made his pilgrimage to Boston and was received with favor by Lowell and Holmes and other of the Cambridge gods, Holmes described it as a kind of apostolic succession, or laying on of hands. As successor to Fields in the editor's chair of the *Atlantic Monthly*, the leading literary periodical of the 1870's, Howells was personally responsible for the persistence of certain earlier attitudes into the new age. In his theories of realism, only gradually formulated through the 1870's, he was a great compromiser between the new and the old. His fiction, too, was tentative and flexible, skilful and subtle, but lacking in conviction and the qualities of ripeness. He sided with Boston in the struggle for cultural supremacy against New York. He was, in his younger years, unable to grasp the significance of the chasm which separated the late writing of Lowell and Whittier from the early work of Mark Twain and Bret Harte. In the enthusiastic atmosphere of the 1870's, he looked before and after and admired what he saw.

The *Atlantic* moved cautiously in these years away from its classical moorings toward the fascinating and untried waters of the Darwinian controversy, adding the word "science" to its subtitle in 1868. *Appleton's Journal*, edited by E. L. Youmans, the *North American Review*, the *Popular Science Monthly*, the *Scientific American*, and many other periodicals devoted their pages, wholly and in part, to the new ideas emanating from Darwin, Spencer, Huxley, Tyndall, and Mill. But the ideals of human perfectibility and the Enlightenment were firmly rooted in the national mind, and the naturalistic implications of the new science were for the moment ignored in the general optimism. Chauncey Wright, O. B. Frothingham, John W. Draper, and John Fiske all sought to bridge the gap between a materialistic and a churchly view of human origins, employing the newer terminology to support the pre-existence in the mind of self-consciousness and moral reason. The result of such positivist speculation for fiction lay in a gradual shift in the treatment of character. No longer regarded as a static concept, the mind was studied under environmental conditions. The brave hero and virtuous heroine, the black-and-white school of fictional portrayal in Cooper, and the symbolism of Hawthorne gave way to an interest in the "complex" character. Howells' delicate penetrations into the feminine psychology and Henry James's explorations into the mental reactions of highly sensitive individuals had a basis in such theories as that of William James on the spontaneous variation of species. These variations from the norm come about in a mysterious way, but once appearing they are evaluated in the direction of morally useful and valuable ends. Thus pragmatism, arguing from Darwinian premises, was able to support a conventional, even an idealistic, ethical system.

Although the new science thus lent its weight to the postwar idealism, there were disturbing implications of naturalism within it. These had to be reckoned with by liberal-minded men and women of letters who recalled for instance that Huxley had cynically described poetry as "sensual caterwauling." Nowhere was there a readiness to grapple with the more violent aspects of man's inhumanity to man, but here and there were chinks in the façade of what Howells once called "the large, cheerful average of health and success in America." Deft strokes of nongenteel dialect, hill-country speech and characters began to appear in the work of such otherwise "correct" local colorists as Sarah Jewett and Catherine Anne Woolson. Still greater fidelity of language informed the pages of Joel Chandler Harris and G. W. Cable in their sketches of the Negro and Creole types. Realism entered in these gentle ways into the select literary circles and periodicals of the East, and was mingled with tears and laughter, regional eccentricities, humor, and sentiment.

In the West, however, Mark Twain and Bret Harte set off minor explosions of laughter and crudity which heralded a fresh style for American prose. In 1867 there appeared both *The Jumping Frog* and Harte's *Condensed Novels*, the latter opening a vein of parody and deflationary attitudes toward romantic fiction. The following year *Innocents Abroad* administered a staggering blow at gentility by its parody treatment of cultural monuments and pretentious attitudes, incidentally flattering the American middle-brow by viewing the Old World through frontier spectacles and showing him "how *he* would be likely to see Europe and the East if he looked at them with his own eyes instead of the eyes of those who travelled in those countries before him." [5] In 1870 *The Luck of Roaring Camp and Other Stories* was published. This volume made its author one of the most widely known reputations of the period. Its tremendous popularity can be explained in part, at least, by the fact that Harte's method mingled old and new elements and brought about a literary vogue which somehow typified the extremes of realism and sentimentalism which marked the Gilded Age as a whole. His plots were melodramatic and his philosophy meretricious. His characters were burlesque versions of the real thing, his style elegant and precious. But in the skilful juxtaposition of East and West, in the fine writing about degraded scenes and characters, in humor mixed with condescension, realism compounded with romance, "The Luck of Roaring Camp" was somehow a microcosm of the America of the 1870's. In his Dickensian contrasts of frontier scamps and card sharks, self-sacrificing friends and idealistic vagabonds Harte struck a literary vein reflecting accurately the admixture of gentility and awkwardness which historians have found in the social nexus of the age.

Despite indications of economic dislocation and protest among the Grangers in the Middle West, the formation of the Greenback party, the economic depression of 1873, and the Erie Railroad scandals, the American literary scene was not yet ready for collective protest or critical realism. Only occasional works of fiction like DeForest's *Honest John Vane* or Twain and Warner's *The Gilded Age* touched upon political matters in pungent terms. For the time being realism would concern itself with externals, matters of dialect, dress, local character-types, regional contrasts, wedding journeys, schoolmarms on European holidays or in country inns—in short, the smiling aspects. Social criticism, muckraking, factual reporting of the low tone of politics in the 1870's—these were not regarded as material for the novelist. The characters of a work of fiction, as one writer expressed it, "must move on an ideal plane, parallel with yet

above the real. . . . It is in this respect that his work differs from
that of the photographer and the newspaper reporter." [6]

The decade of the 1870's produced only a handful of important
works of fiction and almost no significant poetry; yet one can trace
in some of the short fiction and longer novels of Henry James and
Howells a gradually evolving method and aesthetic philosophy
which were coming to be identified with the spirit of the time. This
style revealed more than a superficial coloring of reality. It showed
marked changes from English fiction of the mid-century, though
influenced by George Eliot, Dickens, Trollope; and it was considerably in advance of current aesthetic theory on the novel. Except in the case of James, American fiction of realism suffered from
provincialism, adolescence, a want of cultural shadow, and a somewhat strident nationalism. Only James, of the writers of the decade,
was acquainted with the French school of realists, Balzac, Turgenev,
Zola, and Flaubert. Still, the decade which saw the publication of
DeForest's *Kate Beaumont*, Eggleston's *The Hoosier Schoolmaster*,
Mark Twain's *Roughing It* and *The Gilded Age*, and Howells' *A
Foregone Conclusion* and *The Lady of the Aroostook*, James's *Roderick Hudson* and *The American*, plus some of his finest early short
stories and two books of criticism, is not a period to be discounted
in the development of American literature and in the slowly evolving conception of realism.

A renewed spirit of nationalism stirred in these postwar years.
The temper of the period was expressed, for instance, by Thomas
Perry, one of the most balanced and articulate literary minds of the
younger generation: "We ourselves know," he wrote, "that even
out of Civil War there may arise a grander comprehension of
patriotism, fuller national growth, a broader view of the nation's
duties and responsibilities." [7] Howells, appointed editor-in-chief of
the *Atlantic* in 1871, was eagerly in search of new material. It was
he who opened the theme which was to concern much of this new
fiction with his *A Chance Acquaintance*, the first in the series of
delicate penetrations into the psychology of the young American
woman. James followed his lead with "Madame de Mauves" and
later the greatly popular novelette, *Daisy Miller*. Feminism in the
1870's was mixed with politics, doctrines of free love, spiritualism,
table-rapping séances, sentimentalism, and national honor. In the

best fiction of the period, however, the subject was treated with psychological realism, stimulated by such scientific studies as those of the German behaviorist, Wundt, who investigated psychic states as a means of understanding the mind. Novelists began to discover the "complex" character and to analyze the American female as a product of regional or national social characteristics.

Henry James was himself a product of the Gilded Age and the genteel tradition. Certain Victorian reticences and proprieties were imposed upon him, but he was in his own right a Victorian gentleman and an American of his time. His early travel to Europe, his exposure to the richer civilization and the centers of art and culture there saved him from a narrow provincialism and provided him with a deeper center for his literary theory and practice than that of most of his literary contemporaries. He worked out, for instance, in many reviews and critical essays a wholly original and nearly impressionistic position in conflicting debates over realism-idealism, art and didacticism, Anglo-Saxon "decency" and French license, romance and reality, science and art, all the literary currents of the age. He admired the devotion to technique and the serious view of art he found in Daudet, Goncourt, Balzac, and the French writers, but deplored their moral lightness. On the other hand, he praised Anglo-Saxon wholesomeness and idealism. But his artistic sense and his cosmopolitanism could not accept the over-insistent didacticism of George Eliot whom he considered to lack a deep sense of the sterner realities because "her colours are a little too bright and her shadows too mild a gray." [8] His theories of realism in the 1870's were subtly expressed, never orthodox or provincial, and were guided by the best European models. Especially in the pages of Ivan Turgenev, James discovered the balance he was searching for. The great Russian writer satisfied James's "puritan habit" without violating his need for honesty and realism. Like his age, James was not ready for naturalism. Temperamentally, he would never accept it even during his late years when it became the dominant tone in fiction. "We value most the 'realists,'" he said (using the term in quotes), "who have an ideal of delicacy and elegists who have an ideal of joy." [9]

Recent criticism of James has explained the "revival" of his reputation as a phenomenon of world literature, an anticipation of modern techniques of fiction, and an exploration of "the role of the American in the world; not in the passing terms of international struggle, but in the eternal terms of civilization and the world." [10] But in making him a world figure, his admirers have tended to overlook and minimize the early American roots of his genius; his intense respect for intellectual freedom, for example, his distrust of social tyrannies over the minds and sensibilities of his heroes and heroines. That James was superior to the taste of his time and international in his viewpoint does not quite alter the fact that he was, in his way, a product of the Gilded Age and that his work may be one of the redeeming factors of the period itself. He converted certain genteel reticences and Victorian proprieties into enduring literature, and somehow discovered a method which would outlive the style of the later naturalists whose work was shaped in reaction to the Age of Innocence.

The earlier period of James's work has not received the critical attention it deserves. It has often been condescendingly compared to the "complex" method of the later novels and seldom interpreted in terms of the currents of doctrine in the America of the 1870's. Yet it seems clear that much of his early writing was formed by the aesthetic idealism of that decade. His stories often ran toward allegory and symbol in which he turned into skilful narrative the intellectual conflict of his time between "ideality" and "reality," or to put it more simply, between art and worldliness. "The Madonna of the Future" (1873) exposed the weaknesses of both extremes. In this admirably posed parable of the two attitudes toward art, James wrote one of his best early stories. On the one hand, there is Theobald, a pathetic and ineffectual dreamer whose aspirations are high but unrealized; on the other is the vulgar and cynical realism of the artist of the cats and the monkeys. As between the two viewpoints, James left the paradox unresolved, not so much from intellectual vacillation as from an unwillingness to accept oversimple absolutes and a continuing search for some mediating philosophy of art which could encompass both extremes. In short, James was seeking in these early works a literary response to the conflicting aesthetic tendencies of the 1870's.

In his vast curiosity and experimentation with technique in fiction, his verbal solution to intellectual problems, and the strong carry-over into a more materialistic age of transcendental and meta-physical thought, James was slowly becoming recognized by a few perceptive people of the time as the leading writer of fiction during the Gilded Age. In *Roderick Hudson* and *The American* he suc-cessfully transformed some of the provincialisms, pruderies, and insularities of the period into enduring literature. Satire was one of his weapons, but the most effective of all and the source of much of his power was what Frank Moore Colby called the "verbal hedge" of his style, the nervous power of his attempt to reveal all sides of a question, to suggest realities without bluntness, to conceal and re-veal truths at the same time. He could, for example, deal with the mysterious intrigues of Madame de Bellegarde in *The American* in such a way as to suggest adultery without incurring editorial censorship. He could stay within the moral spectrum of the Gilded Age and still write a novel which satisfies a twentieth-century audi-ence totally emancipated from the confining taboos and niceties of the 1870's.

The relation between James and his friend and admirer, William Dean Howells, constitutes a valuable chapter of the literary history of the 1870's and after. Each reviewed the other's work with generosity, curiosity, and mutual respect. They differed about Eu-rope. James was the "passionate pilgrim" exploring with youthful enthusiasm the art treasures and the rich traditions of the Old World. Howells, though he had spent four years as consul in Venice during the Civil War, wrote to his father in 1876: "At my time of life one loses a great deal of indefinable, essential some-thing, by living out of one's country, and I'm afraid to risk it." [11] His middlewestern roots were strong. He looked both east and west but took his stand with American nativism and innocence, the reality of the commonplace, a love of country inns, and a sympa-thetic interest in the people who inhabit them. Like James, Howells was not, in the 1870's, ready for economic novels, critical realism, or even for "a large canvas with many people in it." The real dramatic encounter for him was always between two persons; in other words, "romance." But his sensitivity to the growing scientism of his time gave his fiction a probing quality and his love stories a social depth beyond conventional romance. In his own fiction of that decade he showed a mastery of dialogue, a love of the charming and the picturesque, a shrewd observation of regional types of character, and most of all a subtle penetration into the whims and moods of Puritan maidens from Florida or Massachusetts or Erie-creek, Ohio.

Howells' writing mirrored the tastes and needs of middle-class readers of the *Atlantic Monthly*, mostly women, whose scruples he loved to titillate but not offend. Twentieth-century critics have been patronizing about the early Howells. To Sinclair Lewis, Mencken, and others, he was "old maidish," "spinsterish," effeminate. Recent scholarship has emphasized the later work, his realism, his strong social conscience, the influence of Tolstoi, and his humanitarian sympathy for the underprivileged. But the special quality of his early realism took its direction from a temperament essentially poetic, dreaming, aesthetic, and idealistic. There is a genteel preciosity in his much-cited sentence from *Their Wedding Journey:* "Ah! poor real life, which I love, can I make others share the delight I find in thy foolish and insipid face?" [12] It is easy to find, after the revolution of public taste and morals of the 1920's, an excessively romantic quality in such a pronouncement, coming as it did in the midst of the era of Jim Fisk and the Erie Railroad affair, the aftermath of Civil War, economic dislocation, and political malpractices. We learn from it something of Howells himself and of the aestheticism of the 1870's, and we can clearly see the division between social facts and literary tastes of that decade when we read Howells' early travel sketches and such early novels as *A Foregone Conclusion* and *The Lady of the Aroostook*. His realism was negative and antiromantic. He preferred man in his habitual moods of "dullness" and vacancy, and he consciously avoided sharp dramatic conflicts or violent situations.

Nonetheless, Howells, as editor and critic, sensed the prevalence of a new spirit in fiction which, he once said, for want of a better name we call "realism." In his reviews of the period he steadily praised such qualities as truth, actuality, lifelikeness, verisimilitude, and honesty in the work of Bret Harte, Twain, DeForest. He wavered between "romance" and the "novel" as terms to describe the fiction of the period, and he admired the realists who stressed commonplace events—Trollope, Jane Austen, George Eliot. He liked Turgenev, but disapproved of Dickens' "theatricality" and

Zola's "bad French morality." One can discern in Howells' vacillation on critical matters a fundamental separation of mind between what his own literary taste and sensitivity told him, and the element of Puritan morality and genteel propriety which prevailed and dictated in large measure the editorial policy of the *Atlantic*. It would require a notable change in the atmosphere, after 1880, to turn him in the direction of a stronger and sounder basis for his fiction and an altered terminology for his critical beliefs.

Regional patterns were fast crystallizing during the 1870's. New York was beginning to emerge as a cultural entity and rival of Boston. Howells wrote to a friend: "I like Boston best and Cambridge best of all. New York is large and jolly, but it's too much of a good thing." [13] New York was to become synonymous with the more utilitarian and realistic elements in American culture, while New England remained as the stronghold of a neo-romantic tradition. The South, too, clung to its prewar inheritance of an aristocratic cultural tone, opposed in principle to a literature which took its character from the fast growing, industrial society and free enterprise system in the North. The work of Sidney Lanier exemplified best the split in the southern mind between traditional modes of thought and a conscious effort to align the agrarian system with contemporary economic practice. Uncle Remus gradually became a force for compromise and reconciliation in the tales of Joel Chandler Harris, while Timrod, in what has come to be regarded as the finest technical achievement of postwar southern poetry, continued to glorify the Confederacy.

But it was the West which provided the strongest impetus for a new literature of realism. The qualities of pretentiousness, sentimentalism, artifice, decorum, those tendencies recognizable even in the work of James and Howells and which we can only describe as "genteel," were steadily confronted in the West by masculinity, a distrust of imitativeness, by parody, burlesque, satire, and all the weapons of a frontier psychology seeking a hearing in eastern literary and cultural circles, but at the same time bent on expressing its own individuality. Goody-goodyism, flim-flam charlatanism, and all evidences of prudishness, gentility, or sentimental artifice which afflicted the popular literature and affected in certain ways the best writers of the Gilded Age were soundly attacked by the western humorists. Bret Harte, Mark Twain, Bill Nye, Artemus Ward, John Phoenix, and others were not quite "realists" in the doctrinaire sense, but their work as a whole provided an amorphous body of criticism which lent impetus to the declining romantic tradition. "If the saddest words of tongue or pen," quipped Harte in a burlesque of "Maud Muller," "are these / It might have been, / Sadder still, we daily see Are these / It is but hadn't ought to be!" Mark Twain parodied Franklin, Cooper, burlesqued the noble savage, and rebuked in *Innocents Abroad* the culture seekers. Slang, dialect, misspellings, colloquialism, exaggeration, the tall tale, buffoonery, all contributed to the cause of preparing the ground for a more serious aesthetic of fiction. In certain ways, however, even these iconoclasts belonged to the genteel tradition. They almost never overstepped the bounds of propriety which the period held sacred, the subject of love, women, the relations of the sexes. Twain seldom went beyond Tom Sawyer's adolescent flirtations with Becky Thatcher, Harte went further by implication in "The Luck of Roaring Camp," but concealed himself effectively behind a polite style. Henry James likewise hinted at unmentionables in *Daisy Miller* and *The American*, and a few of the short stories with European settings. But these were allowed to slip by, partly because of the "innocence" of the readers themselves, an innocence described by Edith Wharton as an "inexorable convention" of pretended respectability, a "factitious purity" manufactured by a conspiracy of long-dead ancestresses, aunts, and grandmothers. And they were unnoticed, too, because James himself concealed them behind the "fig leaf" ambiguity of his own impeccably Victorian pose.

It is generally correct to say that western literary methods and those of the middle border gave an impetus to the sociological trends of the Gilded Age in contradistinction to the eastern preference for individual character studies and psychology. Eggleston's *The Hoosier Schoolmaster* applied Taine's environmental determinism to rural conditions in Indiana, showing a regional interest in native social conditions. Twain and Warner successfully combined social satire and politics in *The Gilded Age* (1874). Bret Harte and Joaquin Miller exploited picturesque aspects of the far West, as did Mark Twain in *Roughing It*. A natural harmony existed between native humor and politics, a combination inherited from as far back as Seba Smith and Lowell's *Biglow Papers*. But the frontier reinforced its own brand of individualism parallel to its interest in the land and in political and agrarian protests. A kind of rough-hewn, bragging, show-me attitude, partly defensive and partly provincial in origin, underlay even the best parody-burlesque writing of Mark Twain, Harte, John Phoenix, and others. In the West the two discordant forces of individual and collectivist thought were present, as they were among the more serious writers of the eastern seaboard, but its writers lacked the intellectual roots and philosophical influences to bring about a satisfying synthesis. As a result, western literature gained something in freshness, immediacy, and honesty, but contributed less to a growing awareness of the meaning of realism for fiction.

Beginning around 1880, many of the vacillations, hesitations, and uncertainties of the 1870's began to come together and provide for the historian a certain coherence and an authentic indication of a literary movement. By this time the older voices had begun to fade from the scene. Howells, James, and Mark Twain were in their prime and ready to write some of their finest books. Sectional rivalries and bitterness were gradually softening; a broadly national mood of harmony and progress prevailed. For the moment at least the economic turbulence of the 1870's was over, the Reconstruction era was at an end, and the time was ripe for accomplishment in fiction. The elements of artifice, aestheticism, and "romance" which marked much of their earlier work now wore off, and Howells and James produced some of their best novels in the opening years of the 1880's. *A Modern Instance* and the *Portrait of a Lady* appeared first, followed by Mark Twain's *Life on the Mississippi* and *Huckleberry Finn*. *The Rise of Silas Lapham* was published in 1885, *The Bostonians* and *The Princess Casamassima*, both in 1886. Meanwhile James was writing some skilful short stories and some of his best essays in criticism, collected in 1888 as *Partial Portraits*. The year 1886 was a pivotal one for Howells, who turned from realism to social and humanitarian themes in fiction and in his column for *Harper's Magazine*, The Editor's Study.

To put it simply, realism (however one defines it) became less talked about and more successfully practised in the early 1880's. These half dozen years may justly be called "The Triumph of

Realism," but not of a realism which denied the earlier idealism. Rather it absorbed and included it in a new kind of synthesis and harmonized it with the more pragmatic tone of the new decade. The bright Victorian skies, as Parrington wrote, now deepened in tone, but had not yet been darkened by the approach of continental naturalism, scientific determinism, or native agrarian and Populist protest. Intellectual America had somehow become more settled, more mellow. An adjustment of the nervous apprehensions over evolution came into sight, and for literature and criticism the self-conscious nationalism of the earlier decade gave way to a certain acceptance and maturity which in another context has been called "The Pragmatic Acquiescence."

The fiction of Henry James now began to shift away from the European scene to American conditions. *Washington Square* was his first attempt to apply realistic methods to a native locale, showing an awareness of the effects of environment upon character in the destiny of Catherine Sloper. In his critical study of *Hawthorne* (1879) James had complained of the want of "realism of spectacle" in *The Scarlet Letter*, "that vague hum, that indefinable echo, of the whole multitudinous life of man, which is the real sign of a work of fiction." [14] In the early 1880's he concerned himself with broader themes, multiple characters, descriptions of places and social conditions in response to the new literary climate. Neither *Washington Square* nor *The Bostonians*, his two most "American" novels, were favorably received, and James's own discouragement at the public indifference to them turned him away from the national scene as material for fiction and motivated his omission of them from the later collected edition of his work. The "great American novel," about which there was much discussion and excitement in those years, was not to be his forte, and after the indignation caused by his brilliant satire of bluestockings and feminine suffragists in *The Bostonians* he turned to the English scene for his next novel, *The Princess Casamassima*. But he was not temperamentally suited to the social novel, for all of his admiration of Balzac and Zola, and he failed to find in the American scene a tradition or a coherence which could hold his imagination.

It was, instead, another international novel, this time on a grander scale, which marked the best of James's writing in the

early 1880's. *The Portrait of a Lady*, as one reviewer put it, fulfilled all the conditions of a portrait in oils. It was a series of portraits with the central figure of Isabel Archer giving unity to the
whole. Although the book was clearly oriented away from the
sociological trend of the time, it showed a harmonizing of romantic
and realistic elements beyond what James had done before. W. C.
Brownell, one of the most perceptive critics of the Gilded Age,
called it a work of "romantic sociology" giving "an imaginative
treatment of reality." [15] Several years later, in the most famous of
his critical essays, "The Art of Fiction," James defined the novel as
falling between history and portrait painting. Character was his
primary interest, character revealed not through environmental
determinism but through depth and perspective as by an artist.
Deterministic elements were strongly written into the fate of
Isabel Archer, but the direction of James's aesthetic philosophy was
clearly toward a synthesis of conflicting views. In the interplay of
character and circumstance lay the dramatic qualities of this exter-
nally unexciting story.

Howells, meanwhile, was at the peak of his powers as a novelist.
Between 1880 and 1886 he wrote his three best works of fiction,
A Modern Instance (1882), *The Rise of Silas Lapham* (1885), and
Indian Summer (1886). In its specially American manifestation,
realism found its finest expression in these books. Character delineation was Howells' prime interest still, but a relentless accumulation
of circumstantial detail marked out a predetermined fate for the
well-meaning but weak Bartley Hubbard in the first of these novels.
Howells balanced off the naturalistic and the idealistic elements of
the story by the somewhat awkward device of an ethical spokesman and commentator who represented the moral viewpoint of
the author upon his own story. He was more successful in *The Rise
of Silas Lapham* in integrating the forces of reality and ethical
idealism by combining them both in the single main character. Silas
is the first self-made businessman to be fully depicted in an American novel, and he has remained the classic example and reference
point for all succeeding attempts. Howells' literary portrait of a
Jay Gould or a William K. Vanderbilt was skilfully blended of
satire and sympathy after the manner of Jane Austen, and with
touches which recalled Balzac. At this time Henry James wrote

Howells from Europe, calling him "the great American naturalist" and shrewdly advised him against a tendency to vitiate his realism with certain "romantic phantoms and factitious glosses." [16] At almost the same time Howells was writing in *The Century* in an effort to reply to critical indifference toward James's work. He called James the shaper and leader of the new fiction which, he said, derived from Hawthorne and the milder realism of George Eliot and Daudet rather than that of Zola.[17]

James himself was beginning to tire of the critical terminology of American reviewers and was less concerned with such dichotomies as "realism" or "romance." Instead he was moving toward an impressionistic position which allowed the greatest freedom to the novelist to work within his own literary domain. In his now widely known essay "The Art of Fiction" (1884), James rested his case upon a paradox, but it was a subtle and refined paradox which amounted to a synthesis of the opposing tendencies of his time and of his own nature. The novel, he wrote, aims primarily to "represent life" in its broadest and freest sense. On the other hand, art is a "selection whose main care is to be typical, to be exclusive." [18] A moral conscience and a social responsibility belonged to the highest art; yet the artist must not be deprived of his freedom of subject. In his succeeding essays, later collected as *Partial Portraits,* James produced the most distinguished body of critical writing of the decade. It was distinguished both for the verbal skill and flexibility of the language and for its formulation, in the 1880's, of an aesthetic of taste and intelligence which somehow harmonized native Anglo-Saxon "decency" and French license, without quite espousing either one.

Mark Twain's relation to the Gilded Age has baffled criticism ever since 1920 when Van Wyck Brooks developed his genius-thwarted-by-commercialism-and-Puritanism thesis in *The Ordeal of Mark Twain* (1920). Brooks's denigration of the American scene which blunted Mark Twain's idealism and turned his satire into crude humor and vulgarity was echoed by later critics and blended with the Marxist criticism of the 1930's. Mark Twain was, it is true, typical of the age whose name he coined. He was typical of its puzzling contradictions and cross-currents. He shared, for instance, something of Colonel Sellers' dream of sudden wealth. Money was

the theme of many of his stories, but unlike Horatio Alger his end-
ings were more often bitter and disillusioning. He was defensive
about art, Europe, age, tradition, culture, and bookishness; yet he
was one of the most cosmopolitan travelers of his time. He possessed
broad humanitarian sympathies and reformist tendencies; yet he
condemned the human race as selfish, cynical, brutal, and deterministic. He was full of ribaldry and profanity, and he was one of
the most sensitive and "exquisite" of men. He detested "novels,
poetry, and theology," he once said, but in "What Paul Bourget
Thinks of Us" he defended the authenticity of local color and regional fiction which could be written only by a man who has had
years of "unconscious absorption" and prepared himself to report
the soul of a nation, its very life and speech and thought.[19]

He was not at home in philosophy or in theoretical criticism.
His standards were those of reality, fact, verisimilitude, and he did
not write from any conscious theory of what the novel should be.
Recent scholarship has shown that Mark Twain was a conscious
literary artist, not a spontaneous genius. If he was, he was not a be-
liever in literary schools or doctrinaire definitions. His was a special blend of realism, born of experience and frontier skepticism,
schooled by such hard disciplines as the printing office of a newspaper or the pilot house of a Mississippi steamboat. Travel made
him the more conscious of his own limitations and threw him back
upon the main affirmation of his life, a democratic faith in the dignity and worth of the individual. In his own way, however, he
worked out a synthesis of the conflicts of his personality and of his
time. In the two books of the early 1880's, *Life on the Mississippi*
and *Huckleberry Finn,* Twain achieved a kind of equilibrium of
the varying elements of his nature and talents. If it was not the
middle zone between romance and naturalism which Howells
sought, nor the special "ideal reality" of James, the balance in Mark
Twain's best books was between the youthful, frontier humorist
and the aging misanthropist of the 1890's. In these books he found
the most successful expression of his strain of idealism and his love
of accurate dialects and local places and people. He could not hold
this balance long, for his next book, *A Connecticut Yankee,* for
all its brilliance and bitter satire, exhibited less of the control and
sustained writing that had marked his earlier two masterpieces.

For the three major first-generation realists, James, Howells, and Mark Twain, the "interregnum" of the 1880's provided a congenial atmosphere for some of their best fiction. All three were able to bring to fruition the experimental work of the previous decade. By 1884 Howells felt that "realism was almost the only literary movement of the time that had vitality in it." [20] He associated the term with the novel, as opposed to his first love, "romance." But the fundamental element in the new fiction was a harmonization of the two broad tendencies of the period—psychological studies of character, on the one hand, and sociological fiction in which environment became a determining factor, on the other. After 1886, the "social" novel came into its own. Howells, deeply affected by the Chicago anarchist trials and by his reading of Tolstoi, turned polemical in his criticism and his fiction. James turned away from American currents of opinion toward the London stage as a new outlet for his talents. Mark Twain grew embittered by personal tragedies and found it increasingly difficult to recapture the mood which had produced *Huckleberry Finn*. One measure of the "Triumph of Realism" is to compare the work of these three writers after 1886 with their books of the early 1880's. Howells never again achieved quite the subtlety of characterization or the balance between satire and idealism which *Silas Lapham* demonstrated. James, after almost a decade of disappointment with the theater, managed to achieve a new method for his fiction in a final burst of productivity around 1900 which has been called "The Major Phase" of his career. Mark Twain struggled to rewrite his boys' books, but he was unable to sustain his muse and revealed only flashes of his best writing in brilliant passages in *A Connecticut Yankee* and in the strangely beautiful *The Mysterious Stranger* written around 1898 and published after his death.

Recent criticism of Mark Twain swings from exaggerated praise and symbol-hunting in *Huckleberry Finn* to denigration of the provincial iconoclast who has been mythologized as a popular hero. The extremes of comment testify to the contradictory nature of his mind and that of his age. In one sense he belongs to world literature; in another his work is related to the vogue of juvenile literature which included Horatio Alger, Aldrich's "The Story of a Bad Boy," and *Treasure Island*. A strain of adolescence and an element of eternal youth in him partly accounted for his great popularity in the Age of Innocence. *Tom Sawyer*, the "Innocent" abroad and at home, Colonel Sellers, and Sir Boss all share this trait of their author. At the same time he possessed the mark of genius, an acute sense of the possibilities of evil and tragedy in the world, and the gift of transforming commonplace experiences into enduring prose. Somehow he managed to remain a part of the Gilded Age in all its typicality and to emerge from that time as a writer whose reputation is based upon more than the gift of laughter. A child of his time, youth and innocence could shape Mark Twain's mind only because on the border of his consciousness lay a powerful presentiment of reality and truth.

A large unlettered class of readers was being courted in the 1870's by the flood of popular dime novels which poured from the presses of Beadle and Adams, DeWitt's Ten-Cent Romances, Street and Smith, Munro's Seaside Library, and other cheap-book publishers. "Pocket" and "handy-size" volumes replaced the older quartos. Many of these entrepreneurs of the publishing business brought good literature, some of it pirated, to a wide uncritical audience. Thomas Hardy, Blackmore, Zola, Maupassant, Dickens, George Eliot, Stevenson, and Charles Reade were either serialized in the magazines or pirated in inexpensive editions during the 1870's and 1880's. The "juveniles" flourished. Horatio Alger's writing, for instance, appeared in *Student and Schoolmate*, *Ballou's Dollar Monthly*, the *Golden Argosy*, and other serial publications. Beginning his rise to fame with the appearance of *Ragged Dick* in 1868, Alger's incredible speed of writing produced no less than twenty-five separate boy-novels between 1868 and 1875. In all he wrote 109 books, averaging 50,000 words each, marketed at from $1.50 to ten cents. Estimates of the total sales of Alger books reach astronomical figures, but the greater portion were sold after his death in the first decades of the present century. In his lifetime, his total sales may have amounted to about one million dollars. Aggregate sales may have reached the hundred million.[21]

What was Alger's relation to the dream of success which historians have traced to the rapidly expanding frontier psychology and railroad-baron period of the Gilded Age? Like some estimates of his sales figures, accounts of his contribution to the gospel of money in America are easily exaggerated. The emphasis in his titles upon "luck" and "pluck" in the success of the Alger heroes places him clearly in the two traditions of protestant piety and romantic melodrama. Hard work, patience, and resignation are high among the Alger virtues. For the Alger hero success and wealth were rewards, but they came not through struggle and competition, but as gifts of providence. Alger's own evangelical background combined with the mawkish melodrama of popular romance to produce the money and happiness of his books. It was not, as serious critics have charged, an adolescent form of the gospel of wealth or a juvenile ethic of acquisitiveness.

The Gilded Age was a fertile period for the procreation of the kind of popular fiction Henry James described as depending on "a 'happy ending,' on a distribution at the last of prizes, pensions, husbands, wives, babies, millions, appended paragraphs, and cheerful remarks." [22] There were "good" and "bad" boy or girl stories. Frances H. Burnett's *Little Lord Fauntleroy* was one of the best sellers of the time, as was Peck's *Bad Boy*, *Helen's Babies*, *The Five Little Peppers and How They Grew*, and *Heidi*. Equally popular were the more masculine juveniles like *Tom Sawyer* and the Uncle Remus stories. Foreign imports helped establish the taste of the Age of Innocence: Stevenson's adventure fiction, Anna Sewell's *Black Beauty*, Jules Verne, Rider Haggard, R. D. Blackmore, Marrie Corelli, and Ouida must be listed along with their American counterparts, E. P. Roe, J. G. Holland, Lew Wallace, and F. Marion Crawford, and Helen Hunt Jackson. Henry Adams' efforts to combine romance and social commentary proved unsuccessful, but the right blend of utopian romance and economics was struck by Edward Bellamy in *Looking Backward, 2000–1887*, one of the runaway sellers of the 1880's and 1890's. After 1887 the Populist movement and sympathy for inequities between the haves and have-nots directed the fiction of Howells into humanitarian channels, and the popular taste for historical romance or juvenile tears and laughter was temporarily diverted until the resurgence of such themes in the 1890's.

Literary humor is a perishable commodity at best, and aside from Mark Twain and perhaps Bret Harte very little has survived from the Gilded Age. It lacked bite. Van Wyck Brooks maintained that the age dampened Twain's ebullience and emasculated his novels, a thesis now pretty thoroughly discredited. Nevertheless, even he was able only rarely to rise above buffoonery and burlesque to the level of genuine satire. He theorized frequently about humor as a necessary training for the lecture platform. As early as 1870 he recognized the difference between travesty and satire in a passage which indicated his own weakness for burlesque humor.[23] At its lowest level his humor turned upon vulgarity, jokes, puns, mild ribaldry, and physical discomfiture. At his best he raised the tall-tale exaggeration of the western storytellers to the level of literature. Twain's satire may not, as Van Wyck Brooks showed, have achieved the level of a Voltaire, a Swift, or a Cervantes, and in an age when literature depended more than ever upon popular sales, he courted certain of the tastes and inhibitions of his time. Nevertheless, his humor was itself a protest against propriety,[24] and in its way it performed an important step in the direction of antiromantic and antisentimental literary expression in America.

The controversies over realism continued in critical circles through the 1890's and beyond, but the best fiction and criticism of Howells, James, and Mark Twain had been written before the end of the 1880's. Younger voices were beginning to be heard—Hamlin Garland, for instance, and Stephen Crane. They belong essentially to a changing literary climate, although their theory and methods were shaped in great measure by the work of the best writers of the Gilded Age. Like other such literary cycles, realism modified the conventions of its predecessor and, in turn, established its own. After 1890 it was destined to have its ideals changed by a younger generation. In summary the 1870's and 1880's formulated and gave expression to a realistic philosophy of art, centered primarily upon the novel. In the work of its two major practitioners, Howells and James, the novel of psychological realism merged with sociological trends to produce the most balanced fiction of the period. Of equal significance was the career of Mark Twain. The age which has been termed "genteel," "innocent," corrupt, and culturally provincial produced two of America's major novelists and one of near major stature. In addition it was a period in which a number of lasting novels by lesser figures were written, such books as those of DeForest, Bret Harte, Eggleston, and Edward Bellamy.

Henry James and Mark Twain were the most original of these writers, and they have left the strongest impression upon their successors, James for his experimentation and discussion of the novel as an art form and Mark Twain in his creation of a native American literary idiom. Howells possessed less creative talent than either, but his large sympathies extended to the recognition of the genius of both of his remarkable contemporaries. Howells' temperament, his humanitarian impulses, his strong admixture of Swedenborgian thought and democratic idealism, and his influential position as dean of American letters were sometimes at odds with his championing a kind of critical realism which he could not quite achieve in his own fiction. But among three such different talents there existed a compatibility and a harmony which in itself almost characterized the essence of American realism in the late Victorian period. The reputations of all three are firmly established in American letters.

It is no longer necessary to apologize for the literature of the Gilded Age, nor do we any longer have the need to denigrate the age in order to explain the faults of our own. Powerful intellectual conflicts such as the new science versus the older idealism, regional antipathies, labor and agrarian protests, national self-consciousness and Victorian reticences, all were converted somehow into a literary philosophy which, for want of a better name, was called realism. In half a dozen novels and a few books of criticism this synthesis found brilliant expression. The revolution of taste and morals which followed the end of World War I found Victorianism a convenient target for its own critical and literary aims and a justification of its own struggles to come of age. But the age of Howells and James has now survived that phase of criticism and achieved its own status in the history of American letters. Recent scholarship has found it more rewarding to discover the affirmative values and aesthetic principles which produced an important body of literature during a highly critical stage of the national development.

10

New Men and New Ideas

Science and the American Mind

PAUL F. BOLLER, JR.

*I*N an informal poll taken by a group of British scientists in London some years ago, Sir Isaac Newton was rated the greatest scientist to appear since the Renaissance. Charles Darwin's name was second on the list, and Michael Faraday and Albert Einstein tied for third place. The fourth highest was an American: Josiah Willard Gibbs, professor of mathematical physics at Yale from 1871 until his death in 1903. Henry Adams regarded Gibbs as "the greatest American, judged by his rank in science," but Adams, as usual, was exceptional.[1] Few Americans during the Gilded Age, outside of the scientific community, would have been able to identify his name. Indeed, even in academic circles, there was a tendency to confuse him with Wolcott Gibbs, the Harvard chemist. When a new university was founded in the United States in 1887, Sir J. J. Thomson, the British physicist, recalled,

> The newly elected President came over to Europe to find Professors. He came to Cambridge and asked me if I could tell him of anyone who would make a good Professor of Molecular Physics. I said, 'You need not come to England for that; the best man you could get is an American, Willard Gibbs.' 'Oh,' he said, 'you mean Wolcott Gibbs,' mentioning a prominent American chemist. 'No, I don't,' I said, 'I mean Willard Gibbs,' and I told him something about Gibbs' work. He sat thinking for a minute or two and then said, 'I'd like you to give me another name. Willard Gibbs can't be a man of much personal magnetism or I should have heard of him.'[2]

Until the Royal Society of London awarded Gibbs its highest honor, the Copley medal, in 1901, Gibbs's reputation was far higher in Europe than in the United States. Clerk Maxwell very early recognized his genius and acted as a kind of publicity agent for him among British scientists. Wilhelm Ostwald introduced his work into Germany and Henry Louis LeChatelier did the same in France, while Dutch chemists were the first to make practical use of his suggestive formulas in the new science of physical chemistry. When Irving Fisher went to Berlin for study in 1893, he had only to mention the name of Gibbs to German mathematicians to elicit the exclamation: "Geebs, Geebs, jawohl, ausgezeichnet!" Unlike Fisher, however, most graduate students had to go abroad to hear of Gibbs for the first time.

Fisher, who later applied Gibbs's concepts to the field of economics, was one of a very small group of students who studied with Gibbs at Yale. The majority of students, Fisher recalled, "did not know of his existence, much less of his greatness." [3] To the handful of graduate students able to profit by his instruction Gibbs gave courses of lectures on vector analysis, multiple algebra, thermodynamics, theory of light, theory of electricity, and statistical mechanics. And in a small room in the Sloane Physics Laboratory he worked late at night on the series of remarkable scientific papers in which he applied the laws of thermodynamics to chemistry. Somewhat shy and modest, though by no means lacking in confidence in the value and validity of the work he was doing, Gibbs cared little or nothing for public recognition. His was apparently an aristocratic view of intellectual endeavor: he directed his findings to the small elite of fellow workers in science who could converse in the abstract language of mathematics. His work was described as "severely mathematical, and incapable of being translated into common language"; and few American chemists during his lifetime were sufficiently trained in higher mathematics to comprehend him.[4] Editors of the *Transactions* of the Connecticut Academy of Arts and Sciences, in which his major monographs appeared, confessed that they could not understand what he was saying. When Clerk Maxwell died in 1879, one of the members of the Academy said ruefully: "Only one man ever lived who could understand Gibbs's papers. That was Maxwell, and now he is dead." [5]

Maxwell's attention was first drawn to Gibbs in 1878 when the latter published two papers discussing geometrical methods of representing by diagrams the thermodynamical properties of homogeneous substances. The distinguished British physicist paid the young professor the immense compliment of constructing a plaster model for water, illustrating Gibbs's diagrams, and sending a cast of it to Yale. Gibbs was doubtless pleased, though he invariably shrugged it off evasively when queried about it by his students. More impressive than his first two papers, however, was his monumental memoir, "On the Equilibrium of Heterogeneous Substances," which appeared in two parts in 1876 and 1878. In this memoir, which raised him to first rank as a scientist, Gibbs, striking off on entirely new paths, brought physics and chemistry together and laid the foundations for the science of physical chemistry. It was in this monograph that Gibbs introduced his famous "Phase Rule" (which so enchanted Henry Adams), a formula, as he put it, capable of "giving shape to research." By means of the Phase Rule (water, for example, can exist in three phases: vapor, liquid, and ice), it was possible to discover: (1) under what conditions of temperature and pressure different substances (and the same substances in different phases) can exist together in equilibrium; and (2) what effect changes of these conditions will have on the composition of various mixtures. By establishing principles by which the heterogeneous substances occurring in nature could be understood and handled most efficiently, Gibbs's formulas were to be of great importance for industry as well as for science.

For years, however, Gibbs's epoch-making monograph was almost completely neglected. Apparently content to leave it to others in their own good time to make practical use of his formulations, Gibbs turned his attention to developing a system of vector analysis for the use of mathematical physicists. Toward the close of his life, he also did pioneer work in the field of statistical mechanics. Ostwald, who translated "Equilibrium" into German in 1892, found "treasures in the greatest variety and of the greatest importance to the theoretical as well as to the experimental investigator" in its pages. LeChatelier, who put it into French in 1899, declared:

> Gibbs was able by a truly extraordinary effort of the scientific imagination and logical power to posit all the principles of the new science and to foresee all its ulterior applications.

. . . To Gibbs belongs the honor of having fused the two sciences into one, chemical mechanics, of having constituted a completely defined body of principles, to which additions may be made in the future, but from which the progress of the science can take nothing away.[6]

In time, Gibbs's work came to have wide application in the fields of metallurgy, mineralogy, petrology, and theoretical chemistry. In the twentieth century his formulas were utilized in the manufacture of hundreds of plastics, drugs, dyes, and organic solvents.

Gibbs was not a prolific writer. ("A person who writes so much," he once remarked, "must spread his message rather thin.") [7] But almost everything he published had, ultimately, some relevance to the world of industry which was coming of age during his lifetime. Living and working unobtrusively in New Haven most of his life, he seemed unconcerned by the leading issues of the day. He went to church, voted Republican in every election but that of 1884 in which he voted for Cleveland, but, for the rest, revealed almost nothing about his attitude toward political and social questions during the Gilded Age. Still, to think that he was indifferent to the practical applications of his theoretical work would, as Charles Peirce pointed out, come close to "making Gibbs a gifted idiot, rooting up his mathematical trufflles like a Perigord pig, and as oblivious of being deprived of them." [8] Mathematics, for Gibbs, was no mere intellectual game; it was indispensable for interpreting and thus mastering nature. He told members of the American Association for the Advancement of Science in 1886,

> The human mind has never invented a labor-saving machine equal to algebra. It is but natural and proper that an age like our own, characterized by the multiplication of labor-saving machinery, should be distinguished by an unexampled development of this most refined and most beautiful of machines.[9]

"Mathematics *is* a language," he insisted at a Yale faculty meeting; and by speaking this language Gibbs contributed enormously to modern industrialism.[10]

If Clerk Maxwell was the first to recognize Gibbs's genius, he was also among the first to see promise in the gifted young Henry A.

Rowland who was teaching physics at Rensselaer Polytechnic Institute in Troy, New York. As early as 1868, while the "Erie War" was raging, Rowland, not quite twenty, had decided against seeking wealth as a primary goal. "I intend to devote myself hereafter to *science*," he resolved. "If she gives me wealth, I will receive it as coming from a friend, but if not, I will not murmur." [11] In 1873, he submitted to the *American Journal of Science* a paper on the magnetic properties of iron, steel, and nickel; it was rejected by the editors. When Maxwell saw the paper, he arranged for its immediate publication in England, and Daniel Coit Gilman, impressed by Maxwell's judgment, selected Rowland as first professor of physics at Johns Hopkins University. Before going to Baltimore, Rowland spent some months working in the laboratory of the great German physicist, Helmholtz, in Berlin, conducting experiments (of some importance in the development of the modern theory of electrons) to investigate the magnetic effect of moving electrostatic charges. At Hopkins, he studied the effect of the rotation of the earth on terrestrial magnetism, and made improved measurements for certain electrical units which were internationally adopted. In a long series of experiments, he obtained a numerical value for the mechanical equivalent of heat (the "Golden Number" sought by many investigators in the nineteenth century) which was universally accepted. But perhaps his greatest achievement lay in the field of spectrum analysis. The exquisitely delicate concave grating which he devised for an analysis of the solar spectrum produced such magnificent results that men of science in France and England were "actually dumfounded." [12] With this apparatus (adopted in physics laboratories everywhere), Rowland produced his famous "Photographic Map of the Normal Solar Spectrum" and launched his systematic study of the spectra of the elements. In his later years he studied alternating currents and their application to motors and measuring instruments, and he invented a printing telegraph which won a prize at the Paris Exposition of 1900. Rowland, one of his colleagues said, "had a triumphant joy in intellectual achievement such as we would look for in other men only from the gratification of an elemental passion." [13] His political as well as his scientific ideals were high, and he looked with disapproval on men like James G. Blaine who set the tone for American politics in the Gilded Age.

Though accepting the basic principles of Christianity, he looked primarily to the "scientific mind" for advances in civilization. "This is the mind," he declared, "which is destined to govern the world in the future and to solve the problems pertaining to politics and humanity as well as to inanimate nature." [14]

For Rowland's somewhat younger contemporary, Albert A. Michelson, science was fundamentally an art. "If a poet could at the same time be a physicist," he told the Lowell Institute, "he might convey to others the pleasure, the satisfaction, almost the reverence, which the subject of light inspires. The aesthetic side of the subject is, I confess, by no means the least attractive to me." [15] Determination of a more accurate figure for the speed of light than had yet been obtained, "one of the most fascinating problems that fall to the lot of the investigator," [16] was a lifelong interest of the German-born physicist. While teaching physics at the United States Naval Academy, young Michelson made his first measurements with equipment he had built himself and which cost about ten dollars. He also published his first paper, "On a Method of Measuring the Velocity of Light," in the *Journal of Science* in May, 1878, and presented to the American Association for the Advancement of Science in St. Louis a new figure for this velocity, 186,508 miles per second, which he estimated to be correct to within one part in 10,000. With Michelson, the first American to receive a Nobel prize (1907), real precision in measuring light speed was achieved; and until his death in 1931 he continued to refine his measuring techniques and obtained increasingly accurate figures.

The invention of the Michelson interferometer, an instrument for measuring small lengths, for determining the wave lengths of light, and for analyzing a narrow spectrum region, was even more important in the development of modern physics. Michelson invented the interferometer in 1881 in order to ascertain the effect of the earth's motion, as it traveled through the "ether" (a motionless substance, filling all space, postulated by physicists to account for the travel of light through space), upon the velocity of light. His results were negative. ("The hypothesis of a stationary ether is . . . incorrect," he concluded.) [17] So momentous, however, were the implications of his findings for classical physics that he determined to improve his investigative techniques. In 1887, with the help of Edward A. Morley of Western Reserve College, and utilizing an interferometer with a higher order of accuracy, he renewed his efforts. The Michelson-Morley experiment has been called "the most important experiment-that-didn't-work in the whole history of science." It demonstrated that: (1) the concept of a "luminiferous ether" must be abandoned; and (2) with the abandonment of a motionless ether, in terms of which the motion of the earth and other heavenly bodies might be measured, the concept of "absolute motion" itself must be discarded. "The foundations of physics tottered," says Isaac Asimov. " 'Classical' physics—the physics of Newton—had had the rug pulled out from under it." [18] Einstein's famous relativity theory, the conclusion that measurements of space and time are "relative" to some arbitrarily chosen frame of reference, was based, in part, on the work of Michelson, as the great mathematician freely declared.[19]

If American scientists played a creditable part in the "new" physics that was developing in the last part of the nineteenth century, they also made contributions of value to the "new astronomy." The old astronomy had been largely concerned with position and motion; the new astronomy, utilizing physics, investigated the physical structure of celestial bodies. In the United States, the transition from positional astronomy to astrophysics was made when Edward C. Pickering, physics professor at M.I.T., became director of the Harvard Observatory in 1877. At this time comparatively little was known about the nature of stars, and Pickering concentrated on accumulating masses of data in the new field. Calling himself a "collector of astronomical facts," he constructed a meridian photometer for measuring the magnitude (brightness) of stars as they cross the meridian and devised a system of visual stellar magnitudes that was adopted internationally.[20] He was also a pioneer in stellar photography and created a library of celestial photographs, the famous "Harvard Photographic Library," containing thousands of glass plates on which the history of stars was recorded. By means of astrophotography, moreover, he collected the spectra of thousands of stars (yielding valuable information about the composition, temperature, and physical condition of the stars), and worked out a standard of classifying stellar spectra. Meanwhile, at Dartmouth and later at Princeton, Charles A. Young (known to his students as

"Twinkle") was conducting his pioneering studies in solar physics; and Edward E. Barnard, astronomer at the Lick Observatory at the University of California and then at the University of Chicago's Yerkes Observatory, was applying celestial photography to the Milky Way with excellent results. James Lick, a San Francisco philanthropist who had amassed a fortune in real estate speculation, had left a bequest in 1875 for "the greatest and most powerful telescope" ever made; and the observatory bearing his name, with its 36-inch telescope, was completed in 1888. The Yerkes Observatory, with a 40-inch telescope, was founded a few years later by Charles T. Yerkes, Chicago traction-system magnate whose career formed the basis for a trilogy of novels by Theodore Dreiser.[21]

In 1875, when the Lick trustees sought advice on the kind of telescope to be constructed for the California observatory, they naturally turned to Simon Newcomb, chief astronomer with the United States Naval Observatory in Washington. Two years previously, Newcomb had supervised the construction of the Navy Observatory's 26-inch object-glass; and, in his opinion, the "success of the Washington telescope excited such interest the world over as to give a new impetus to the construction of such instruments." [22] Newcomb's major field was celestial mechanics. While not indifferent to the newer astrophysical investigations, he expended his own efforts on mathematical astronomy in order to prepare the most exact tables possible for the motion of heavenly bodies. The motion of the moon was a lifelong concern of his; and in order to correct errors in the tables of lunar positions he delved into the old records of European observatories, pushing his researches back to the middle of the seventeenth century. In 1877, he became superintendent of the *Nautical Almanac* Office, responsible for preparing the *American Ephemeris*, an astronomical almanac containing, among other things, data on the past and future positions of stars and planets for the use of astronomers and navigators. Distressed by the confusion pervading the field of exact astronomy, he at once launched an ambitious program involving a discussion of all observations of value on the positions of the sun, moon, planets, and bright fixed stars made at the leading observatories of the world from 1750 onward. The magnitude of the task he had set himself was tremendous; but for more than twenty years he persisted in his efforts to bring precision into the calculations of the positions and motions of heavenly bodies and to "start the exact astronomy of the twentieth century on one basis for the whole world." [23] Newcomb's labors won universal respect among scientists. Einstein called him "the last of the great masters who . . . calculated with painstaking care the motions of the solar system," and regarded his work as "of monumental importance to astronomy." [24] Newcomb was once offered a position at Harvard and, though urged to take the opportunity to escape Washington politics, he elected to remain in government service. As he explained later, "I was still pervaded by the optimism of youth in everything that concerned the future of our government, and did not believe that, with the growth of intelligence in our country, an absence of touch between the scientific and literary classes on the one side, and 'politics' on the other, could continue." [25]

Like Newcomb, Samuel P. Langley, who became secretary of the Smithsonian Institution in 1887, found his work in Washington stimulating, as did his distinguished predecessors at the Smithsonian, Joseph Henry, the physicist (secretary from 1846 to 1878), and Spencer F. Baird, the zoologist (secretary from 1878 to 1887). Langley attracted public notice because of his pioneering work in aviation, but his achievements in astronomy were also notable. Unlike Newcomb, Langley was interested mainly in the physical characteristics of heavenly bodies, and his special field was that of solar radiation. While director of the Allegheny Observatory in Pennsylvania (1867–87), he invented an instrument which was to come into worldwide use, the bolometer, a kind of electrical thermometer for measuring the distribution of heat in the spectrum of the sun. With this instrument, capable of measuring differences in temperature as small as one-millionth of a degree, Langley investigated the distribution of radiation over the sun's surface and in sunspots, the solar energy spectrum and its extension toward the infrared, and the lunar energy spectrum and the temperature of the moon. He became increasingly absorbed in the problem of measuring the amount of heat which the earth receives from the sun and the effects of fluctuations of solar radiation upon the earth's atmosphere. His researches had a direct bearing on the development of an accurate system of weather forecasting. "If the observation of the amount of heat the sun sends the earth is among the most difficult in astronomical physics," he said, "it may also be termed the fundamental problem of meteorology or the science of weather." [26]

Not long after he left Allegheny Observatory to take up his duties with the Smithsonian, Langley heard a paper at the annual meeting of the A.A.A.S. in Buffalo concerning the flight of birds and arousing his interest in the mechanics of flight. He at once embarked on a series of experiments in what he called "aerodynamics," and in 1891 he announced that it was possible "to construct machines that would give such velocities to inclined surfaces that bodies definitely heavier than air could be sustained upon it and moved through it with great velocity, and capable of carrying other than their own weight." [27] While in Washington he constructed several model flying machines and on May 6, 1896, flew one of his models successfully for a distance of 3,000 feet. He could then safely declare that the new age of aviation was at hand.[28] Assisted by the war department, he was later persuaded to construct man-carrying airplanes. His experiments were unsuccessful, and it was left to the Wright brothers to make the first successful piloted flights. But Wilbur Wright acknowledged Langley's pioneer work.[29]

Because he attempted to put his theories about the mechanics of flight into actual practice, Langley was far better known, at least for a time, to the American public than his fellow physicists and astronomers. Even more celebrated, of course, both during the Gilded Age and ever since, were such inventors as Alexander Graham Bell and Thomas A. Edison. The relevance to everyday living of the telephone, the electric light bulb, and the many other practical inventions made by Americans during the period, was immediately apparent. The significance for human life of the fundamental researches of American physicists and astronomers, couched, as they were, in the abstractions of mathematics, was difficult for the layman to grasp. Scientists like Gibbs and Rowland and Pickering were indifferent to public fame; and since the tradition of popular pride in the achievements of theoretical scientists had not developed in the United States as it had in Europe, they were largely unknown outside of scientific circles. Hence the myth, persistent even today, that American talents lay almost exclusively in applied rather than pure science.[30] But American genius shone quite brightly in physics and astronomy (though it lagged considerably behind Europe in mathematics and chemistry) during this period; and recognition of this genius frequently came first in Europe. Students of American culture have still to do full justice to American contributions to science in the Gilded Age.

If the new ideas appearing in physics and astronomy, both here and abroad, left the American reading public largely untouched, the same was not true of the ideas set forth by Charles Darwin in his two most famous books, *Origin of Species* (1859) and *The Descent of Man* (1871). The impact of Darwinism on American popular, as well as scientific, thinking was prompt and profound; and historians of ideas in America have understandably placed major emphasis on this aspect of American thought during the Gilded Age. The importance of Darwin's transmutation theory for botany, zoology, geology, and biology was obvious; and unless American toilers in these fields were to remain simply fact-finders and classifiers it was urgent that they test the natural selection hypothesis in their own work. The shattering effect of Darwinian evolution upon traditional religious thought, taking for granted, as it did, the special creation and immutability of species and the uniqueness of man, was also apparent. It was necessary for American theologians to rethink their positions in the light of the new evolutionary concepts. The bearing of evolution upon the natural law tradition in American philosophy, moreover, had ultimately to be faced. Indeed, any American who thought seriously at all about the nature and destiny of man must familiarize himself with Darwin's work. Where Gibbs's and Michelson's work was a closed book for most Americans, *Origin of Species* could be read and generally understood by educated laymen; and the great debate over Darwinism which commenced among American scientists shortly after the publication of *Origin* soon spread to nonscientific circles throughout the land.

The number of American scientists of consequence who rejected Darwinism outright was not large and, as Darwin had expected generally when he first announced his views to the world, it was the older scientists who were least receptive to his conclusions. Edward Hitchcock, Massachusetts geologist and, for a time, president of Amherst College, had published a book in 1852 reconciling geology with the Scriptures, and saw no reason to modify his outlook. He remained a strict creationist and publicly opposed the doctrine of evolution. Timothy A. Conrad, Pennsylvania conchologist and paleontologist who also bitterly opposed evolution, predicted that Darwin's "wild speculations" would soon be forgotten.[31] Matthew F. Maury, the naval officer who had done so much to create and develop the science of oceanography, firmly rejected Darwinism as being incompatible with the Bible: "The Bible, they say, was not written for scientific purposes and is therefore no authority in matters of science. I beg pardon. The Bible is authority for everything it touches. The agents concerned in the physical economy of our planets are ministers of Him who made it and the Bible." [32]

By far the most famous and influential anti-Darwinist, however, was the Swiss-born Louis Agassiz, professor of natural history at Harvard. His work in ichthyology, paleontology, and glacial geology had earned him high esteem among scientists everywhere, including Darwin. Agassiz was no biblical literalist like Maury; he had, in fact, little interest in organized religion. His opposition to Darwin rested largely on a philosophy of nature which he had formulated as a young man in Europe and which in some respects resembled the transcendentalism of Ralph Waldo Emerson. For Agassiz, every specific form of plant and animal represented "a thought of God" at the moment of creation; and their structural affinities were "associations of ideas in the Divine Mind," not evidences of community of descent. "The study of nature," he said, "is an intercourse with the highest mind." [33] His exhibits in the Harvard Museum of Comparative Zoology were intended to reflect the permanence of species. Darwin's *Origin* he regarded as "mischievous in its tendency"; and in lectures, popular articles, and books, he waged a militant campaign against Darwinism and on behalf of his own version of special creationism.[34] In the last article he wrote on the subject, shortly before his death in December, 1873, he did concede that Darwin "brought to the subject a vast amount of well-arranged information"; but, to the very end, he insisted, "there is no evidence of a direct descent of later from earlier species in the geological succession of animals." [35] His Harvard colleague Jeffries Wyman, anatomist and ethnologist who regarded the "immediate creation of species" as "preposterous," regretted that Agassiz used his immense learning and prestige to combat Darwin: "He was just the man who ought to have taken up the evolution theory and worked it into good shape, which his knowledge of embryology and palaeontology would have enabled him to do. He has lost a golden opportunity, but there is no use in talking of that." [36]

Wyman was too cautious and reserved to challenge Agassiz publicly; and it was Asa Gray, director of the Harvard herbarium and pioneer in the field of plant geography, who emerged as Darwin's leading champion in the United States during the years of controversy. Gray had been supplying Darwin with floristic data since 1855 (some of which was utilized in *Origin*). In 1857 he was one of the three men (Joseph D. Hooker and Charles Lyell were the others) to whom Darwin, before publishing *Origin*, confided his theory of the evolution of species by means of variation, struggle for existence, and natural selection. Gray had reservations about natural selection; as a purely mechanical explanation of the evolutionary process, its implications for religion troubled him. But he was determined that Darwin "shall have fair play" in the United States.[37] His long review of *Origin* for the *Journal of Science* in March, 1860, which Darwin called "by far the best which I have read," was sympathetic and perceptive.[38] Gray's efforts on Darwin's behalf in the 1860's and 1870's have been compared to those of Thomas Huxley in England. Gray debated Agassiz before the Cambridge Scientific Club and at meetings of the American Academy of Arts and Sciences in Boston. He prepared a series of articles for the *Atlantic* explaining Darwin's ideas to the general public (reprinted in England), lectured on Darwinism to the Yale Divinity School students, and wrote friendly notices of Darwin's later books for the *Journal of Science*. Gradually, however, he and Darwin parted company over the matter of design in nature. Like the majority of American scientists in the Gilded Age, Gray was a convinced theist, and the reconciliation of Darwinism with religion was a matter of some urgency for him. Darwin, who confessed to Gray that he was "in an utterly hopeless muddle" over the problem, eventually became an agnostic.[39] Gray came to look upon the evolutionary process as "the order or mode in which [the] Creator, in his own perfect wisdom, sees fit to act," thus, in effect, transforming natural selection into what might be called "supernatural selection." [40] The weakness in Gray's reasoning—the introduction of providential design into evolutionary development, as Darwin pointed out, made natural selection "entirely superfluous"—is obvious.[41] Nevertheless, the teleological interpretation of Darwinism did enable Gray to square his scientific with his religious conscience, and there can be no doubt of his sincere and courageous devotion to complete freedom of inquiry in natural science. As the Darwinian botanist Joseph Hooker told Huxley after Gray's death in 1888, Gray understood Darwinism "clearly, but sought to harmonize it with his prepossession, without disturbing its physical principles in any way. . . . He certainly showed far more knowledge and appreciation of the contents of the *Origin* than any of the reviewers and than any of the commentators, yourself excepted." [42]

More common among American scientists than Agassiz's uncompromising animosity and Gray's consistent friendliness to Darwinism was a gradual accommodation to some limited form of evolutionism. Arnold Guyot, the Princeton geographer who, like Agassiz, regarded nature as a manifestation of God, at first clung tenaciously to his belief in the constancy of species; in time, however, he came to accept with reservations the idea of evolution through natural causes, though he excepted man from the process. James Dwight Dana, Yale geologist who led the way in transforming American geology from a collection of isolated facts into a historical science, was similarly slow to assent to the new view of species. "Geology," he declared in 1871, "has brought to light no facts sustaining a theory that derives species from others." [43] In 1874, however, he conceded that the "evolution of the system of life went forward through the derivation of species from species," though he insisted there had been "abrupt transitions between species" and that for man "there was required . . . the special act of a Being above nature." [44] His final position appeared in a letter to a clergyman toward the end of his life: "While admitting the derivation of man from an inferior species, I believe that there was a Divine creative act at the origin of man; that the event was as truly a creation as if it had been from earth or inorganic matter to man." [45]

Joseph LeConte, Georgia-born geologist teaching at the University of California, confessed that as late as 1872 he was still a "reluctant evolutionist"; a few years later, however, he described himself as "an evolutionist, thorough and enthusiastic." [46] But his evolutionism, like that of perhaps most American scientists in the Gilded Age, could scarcely be called Darwinism. Though LeConte regarded the "law of derivation of forms from previous forms" as "certain as the law of gravitation," he emphasized "paroxysmal" rather than uniform changes in nature, placed great stress on the Lamarckian factor of the transmission of acquired characters, and he relegated natural selection to a relatively minor role in the development of organic life.[47] He also worked out an ambitious religious philosophy, based on both the immanence and transcendence of God in universal evolution, that even the absolute idealist, Josiah Royce, found little to his liking. The Michigan geologist Alexander Winchell made a similar religious adjustment to evolution, while George Frederick Wright, the Oberlin geologist-clergyman who was an expert in glaciation and who, like LeConte, wrote extensively on religion and evolution, declared: "There must be a divinity shaping the ends of organic life, let natural selection rough hew them as it will." [48]

On the other hand, William Keith Brooks, professor of morphology at Johns Hopkins and a specialist in marine zoology, insisted, "The term 'supernatural' is due to a misconception of nature; nature is everything that is." [49] Though pointing out that science throws no light on final cause or purpose, Brooks, a former student of Agassiz's, was an early convert to Darwinism and accepted a wide applicability of the principle of natural selection. Chauncey Wright, Cambridge mathematician and philosopher, was an even more thoroughgoing evolutionary naturalist; and he vigorously objected to all cosmic generalizations founded on evolution. Fully accepting the naturalistic assumptions of Darwinism, he proposed in 1873 a scientific explanation of the origin of human self-consciousness based on psychological antecedents in animal life. But Wright, who died in 1875 at the age of forty-five, was a rarity. The Gray (design) or the LeConte (immanence) versions of evolution, in the main, dominated the thinking of American scientists during the 1870's and 1880's, and these adaptations of Darwinism most influenced American theological and popular religious thinking about evolution during these decades.

Many American scientists, however, stayed aloof from the conflict between naturalism and supernaturalism, and, quietly pursuing their researches in botany, zoology, geology, and paleontology, accumulated data providing indispensable evidence for the validity of Darwin's theory. This was particularly true of American paleontologists. Joseph Leidy, usually regarded as the founder of vertebrate paleontology in the United States, has been called "a John the Baptist for Charles Darwin." [50] One of the first to exploit the rich fossil beds in the West, Leidy, even before Darwin announced his theory publicly, had been gathering a mass of information about the ancestral lineage of the horse, camel, rhinoceros, and other vertebrates long since extinct in the United States, that pointed unmistakably to evolutionary development. With Gray, Leidy was one of the first to accept Darwin, and upon publication of *Origin* he saw to it that Darwin was elected a member of the Academy of Natural Sciences of Philadelphia. Immensely pleased by this early recognition of his work, Darwin told Charles Lyell: "It shows that some Naturalists do not think me such a scientific profligate as many think me here." [51]

Even more important for Darwinism was the work of Othniel C. Marsh, who was appointed to the chair of paleontology at Yale in 1866, the first such chair to be established in the United States. In 1870, Marsh launched a series of expeditions to hunt for ancient fossils in the West which yielded invaluable evidence for the evolutionary theory. His discovery of birds possessing teeth and other reptilian characteristics established a genetic link between reptiles and birds which, according to Huxley, removed Darwin's theory "from the region of hypothesis to that of demonstrable fact." [52] Of Marsh's monograph of 1880 on the extinct toothed birds of North America, Darwin wrote to say: "Your work on these old birds, and on the many fossil animals of North America, has afforded the best support to the theory of Evolution, which has appeared within the last twenty years." [53] Equally impressive was Marsh's collection of fossil bones tracing the evolutionary changes which had occurred during the emergence of the modern horse. Huxley, who visited the United States in 1876, spent several days in New Haven examining the collection, which he called "the most wonderful thing I ever saw." [54] As Marsh brought out box after box of fossil-horse material, he cried: "I believe you are a magician. Whatever I want, you conjure it up." [55] For Huxley, Marsh's specimens "demonstrated the evolution of the horse beyond question, and for the first time indicated the direct line of descent of an existing animal." [56] Marsh, known as the "Big Bone Chief" among Indians in the West, regarded his discoveries as "the stepping stones by which the evolutionist of to-day leads the doubting brother across the shallow remnant of the gulf once thought impassable," and was a firm exponent of natural selection.[57] "To doubt evolution to-day," he told the A.A.A.S. in 1877, "is to doubt science, and science is only another name for truth." [58] Edward D. Cope of Philadelphia, Marsh's great rival in the "boneyards" of the West, was a Lamarckian rather than a Darwinian; but his fossil collections and his classifications of extinct vertebrates in the western United States contributed enormously to the advance of evolutionary science.

Reviewing "Fifty Years of American Science" for the *Atlantic* in September, 1898, W. J. McGee pointed out that Darwinism had "wrought, within a quarter-century, the most profound revolution in the history of human thought." Then he added: "Yet the revolution would have been long delayed had Englishmen alone contributed to it, or even men of Continental Europe; for, with a half dozen exceptions, the earliest and strongest apostles were Americans." [59] His appraisal of the achievements of American scientists in other fields, particularly physics (though he overlooked Gibbs), astronomy, geology, and technology, was similarly enthusiastic, though he did not ignore the fact that the most basic scientific generalizations had been made by European scientists. "Most of the advances began in Europe," he admitted, but he insisted that they had been "hastened in America." "The world has moved forward as it never did before," he concluded. "Yet fully half the progress of the world, during the last fifty years, has been wrought through the unprecedented energy of American enterprise and genius, guided by American science." [60] McGee wrote partly out of a strong sense of national pride; but he was also motivated by admiration for "the straightforward and unselfish habit of thought fostered by scientific methods" and a wish to encourage these methods in all areas of

American life. He hoped that the "sense of right thinking" which is the "essence of science" would lead ultimately to "the elevation of moral character" in the United States.[61] Essentially an evolutionary optimist, McGee looked to the future with confidence.

Henry Adams, a conscientious observer of scientific developments here and abroad in the late nineteenth century, could not share McGee's sanguine expectations. He was chiefly impressed by the austere implications for human life of the scientific laws formulated during his lifetime. McGee had had nothing to say about the second law of thermodynamics (the law which states that entropy, dissipation of energy, tends to a maximum in the universe), but Adams was more struck by this law than by evolutionary law. Holding, like McGee, that science should be extended to the humanities, Adams proposed a re-evaluation of human life in the light of the second law. Man, he suggested, was a "thermodynamic mechanism" who by progressively untapping the energies latent in nature for his own use and misuse was contributing mightily to the dispersion of energy and hastening the day when energy in the solar system would be at too low a level to sustain life. Thermodynamics led Adams to Gibbs (who actually suggested certain limitations of the second law) and to the Phase Rule. For Gibbs's three phases (solid, liquid, gaseous) Adams substituted historical stages (religious, mechanical, electrical) based upon the kind and amount of energy being used up by man. "From the physicist's point of view," wrote Adams, "man, as a conscious and constant, single, natural force, seems to have no function except that of dissipating or degrading energy. . . . [He] does more to dissipate and waste nature's economies than all the rest of the animal or vegetable life has ever done to save them." [62]

For Adams, the twentieth century was to be one of unprecedented violence and destruction as man careened thoughtlessly but inevitably, in accordance with the second law, down the road to ultimate extinction. Few Americans shared Adams' pessimism. Like McGee, most Americans, including men of science, saw in the scientific advances of the late nineteenth century limitless opportunities for human progress. John Fiske's "cosmic philosophy," which saw the "perfecting of Humanity" as the goal of evolution, perhaps best reflected the exuberant spirit of the American people during the Gilded Age:

The future is lighted for us with radiant colours of hope. Strife and sorrow shall disappear. Peace and love shall reign supreme. The dream of poets, the lesson of priest and prophet, the inspiration of the great musician, is confirmed in the light of modern knowledge; and as we gird ourselves upward for the work of life, we may look forward to a time when in the truest sense the kingdoms of this world shall become the Kingdom of Christ.[63]

To William James, with his keen sensitivity to the ambiguities and recalcitrancies of the human situation, there was something distasteful, even callous, in the "sunny, skyblue" optimism of the Fiske variety. On the other hand, he could not help thinking that Henry Adams in his literalistic application of the law of entropy to human history was indulging himself in a kind of pessimistic frivolity over a "tragic subject." [64] James, who took his medical degree at Harvard in 1869 and who taught anatomy and physiology before moving into psychology and philosophy, had a thorough grasp of the scientific method. His "pragmatico-humanism," as he once called it, based on the science of the last half of the nineteenth century, was in many respects an effort to apply the scientific imagination to the basic questions of human existence.

But science, for James, did not consist of a body of immutable truths about reality; it was a purely human creation growing out of man's need to introduce some kind of useful order into the endless sequence of sense impressions which he experiences and which are the ultimate data for human knowledge. James did not believe that scientific laws were "exact copies of a definite code of non-human realities." They were rather "so much 'conceptual shorthand,' true so far as they are useful but no farther." "Our mind," he added, "has become tolerant of symbol instead of reproduction, of approximation instead of exactness, of plasticity instead of rigor." [65] For Adams, the abandonment of the belief that there were unchanging laws of nature, discoverable by man and inherent in the structure of things, meant confusion and chaos; for James, it meant challenge and adventure. It meant that the universe, so far as man can know it empirically, is open, plastic, unfinished, ever growing, and not to be confined within the bounds of any closed system of thought. James had a temperamental aversion to closed systems, scientific, religious, or philosophical, and he called them "block universes." Block universe theories pictured the universe as totally unified and inexorably shaped by a static plan or force of some kind —the will of God or Fate or the Absolute or Natural Law. Eliminating block universes, no matter how imposing in breadth of vision or attractive in aesthetic structure, meant freeing man from the bondage of determinism and enhancing his status and dignity as a creative thinker and actor in an ever changing universe. Evolutionary change was at the heart of James's philosophy. He was one of the first philosophers to realize that the Darwinian vision meant that fixity of natural laws, like fixity of species, must give way to a developmental view.

Like Darwin, James stressed the factor of variation in evolutionary development. He was particularly impressed by spontaneous variations in human thinking. Whatever unity there is in the universe, he insisted, has been introduced by man himself. When creative thinkers like Newton and Darwin select certain portions of reality and unify them into the law of gravitation and the law of natural selection, they are introducing something new into the universe with important consequences for the future. It is in such fashion that man participates creatively in the growth and development of the open universe. Even such common sense categories as "things," "minds," "bodies," and "causes," James suggested, were creations of "prehistoric geniuses whose names the night of antiquity has covered up; they may have been verified by the immediate facts of experience which they first fitted; and then from fact to fact and from man to man they may have *spread*, until all language rested upon them and we are now incapable of thinking naturally in any other terms." [66] But man's creative insights must be verified by experience; they must put him into fruitful relations with reality and satisfy some human need, physical or mental. This was James's humanism. The validity of ideas depends upon the degree to which they have satisfactory consequences when put into practice. This was James's pragmatism. Truth in ideas, said James, means *"that*

*ideas (which themselves are but parts of our experience) become
true just in so far as they help us to get into satisfactory relations
with other parts of our experience;* to summarize them and get about
among them by conceptual short-cuts instead of following the
interminable succession of particular phenomena." [67]

James believed that man has as much right to adopt "working
hypotheses," subject to the test of experience, in religion as in
science. Religion was a serious interest of his and, like Asa Gray, he
wanted to effect a reconciliation between religion and science that
would not do violence to pragmatically validated scientific ideas.
The LeConte-Fiske notion of a God immanent in creation did not
appeal to James; it seemed to imprison man in a closed universe and
deprive him of his freedom and responsibility. Nor was Gray's
argument from design intellectually convincing to James: "From
the order of the world, there is no path to God by coercive reasoning, or even by strong analogy or induction." But religion, like
science, James pointed out, satisfied certain human needs and must
be taken seriously by the pragmatic humanist. Where science satisfied the intellectual and aesthetic passion for order and unity and
economy of thought, religion fulfilled the emotional need for some
kind of moral meaning in the universe at large. In times of trouble,
religion offered comfort and consolation; in times of heroic endeavor (James's perennial mood), religion supplied the assurance
that the struggle for high moral ideals, against overwhelming odds,
was not pointless.

> That we believe in God . . . is not due to our logic, but to
> our emotional wants. . . . The world is a datum, a gift to
> man. Man stands and asks himself, 'What is it?' Science says
> molecules. Religion says God. Both are hypotheses. Science
> says, 'You can't deduce or explain anything by yours.' Reli-
> gion says, 'You can't inspire or console by yours.' What is
> *worth* most, is, after all, the question. Molecules can do certain
> things for us. God can do other things. *Which things* are worth
> the most? [68]

Both were worthwhile for James, but though he speculated endlessly on religion, he made no extensive use himself of what he called
the "will to believe." He did, however, dislike scientific determin-

ism. He thought that it not only deprived human life of any ethical significance, but also erected provisional and approximate scientific formulations about reality into final truths. He was convinced that there were aspects of human life (of which religion takes account) that always escape our impersonal scientific generalizations. In the deep privacy of every individual's heart there were unsharable experiences and voiceless intuitions that our abstract concepts can never quite define. To *be*, he once said, was more important than to *define being*. There was an unmistakable existentialist strain in James's thinking that passed almost unnoticed in his lifetime.

Critics of James have singled out for special attack his "pragmatic method," that is, his insistence that ideas be judged by their effectiveness in enabling us to cope with reality. (Michelson, for example, found the concept of ether totally ineffective while Gibbs found immense "cash value," to use James's expression, in understanding nature by means of the Phase Rule.) Vulgarized and caricatured to mean a justification for an ethic of sheer expediency and self-aggrandizement, James's philosophy has been interpreted as a perfect reflection of the materialistic ethos of Gilded Age America. James, according to Lewis Mumford, "was only warming over again in philosophy the hash of everyday experience in the Gilded Age." [69] But James was, in fact, a man with the highest moral and intellectual ideals, an indefatigable searcher for human understanding, and a courageous champion of ideas and causes that were unpopular and unconventional during his lifetime. [70]

But James was not alone in abhorring the acquisitive spirit of his age. Henry Adams was similarly alienated. Joseph Henry, the dedicated director of the Smithsonian Institution (who regarded an invitation for him to endorse a commercial product as an attempt at bribery), lamented that Americans honored wealth, political power, and military achievement, but gave little recognition to intellectual and scientific distinction. Whatever the shortcomings of their public image, or their lack of recognition, America's great scientists of the Gilded Age toiled ceaselessly to add to man's knowledge and understanding of the world in which he lived. Their goal was truth, and the thing they respected most was the scientific mind which admitted human imperfection and strove for perfection. [71]

Few ages or generations have held up the scientist and philosopher as great popular heroes. Their work, requiring as it does seclusion, time, and complex thought and labor, does not easily lend itself to public glamor. In this the Gilded Age differed little from other eras; yet perhaps it is too harsh a judgement to agree with the scientists that they lacked communication with their age. Most great creative minds always feel this way, whether it be true or not. Science fascinated millions in the Gilded Age; a host of periodicals and books and even newspapers catered to the taste for applied science; lectures were seldom without audiences, even when competing with the more popular ballyhoo which every generation prizes. Few men on the street may have known the names of Gibbs and his fellow thinkers, but the results of their work were often known, even if in a diluted form. Scientists maintained wide and successful contacts among themselves and their peers abroad through university work, free publication, and scientific and professional organizations.

The findings of such men, who number many in the Gilded Age, ought not to be forgotten when that generation's accounts are cast up; for they were contributions not merely to one country or culture, but to knowledge itself. Surely it would be a mistake to assess the Gilded Age without remembering the freedom, if not the popular recognition, it accorded these men. And they were not without an audience or popular recognition. Their age was not always so crass as to ignore or stifle them or their findings; and when it was, surely they rose above it.

Notes to Chapters

I

An Age in Need of Reassessment
A View Beforehand

1. *See* Vernon Lewis Parrington, "The Beginnings of Critical Realism in America," in *Maincurrents in American Thought*, 3 vols. in 1 (New York, 1958).

2. *Ibid.*, p. 11.

3. *Ibid.*, p. 4.

4. *Ibid.*, p. 48.

5. *See* Charles A. Beard and Mary R. Beard, *The Rise of American Civilization*, 2 vols. in 1, rev. ed. (New York, 1937).

6 *See Ibid.*, II, 383, 388, 394, 395.

7. *Ibid.*, II, 411–16, 447ff, 455.

8. *See* his books, *The Robber Barons* (New York, 1934); *The Politicos* (New York, 1938); and *The President Makers* (New York, 1940). Space forbids any extended historiographic essay on the literature of the Gilded Age. There is but one full-length coverage, Ellis P. Oberholtzer, *The History of the United States Since the Civil War*, 5 vols. (New York, 1917–37). Though well written, this work suffers from acute bias and incomplete coverage. The last two volumes in the *History* of James Ford Rhodes also cover the period with less detail. There are any number of specialized monographs dealing with the period, many of them excellent in coverage and approach. The American Political Leaders series published by Dodd-Mead in the 1930's contains many excellent biographies of leading men of the time. The most provocative work on the period by a recent scholar has been done by Edward C. Kirkland, whose books are basic to any study of the Gilded Age. See especially his *Industry Comes of Age* (New York, 1961); *Dream and Thought in the Business Community 1860–1900* (Ithaca, New York, 1956); and *Business in the Gilded Age* (Madison, Wisconsin, 1952). His article, "The Robber Barons Revisited," *American Historical Review*, 66 (October 1960), pp. 68–73, is interesting. In economic history, Thomas C. Cochran has produced a number of works, the most helpful of which is probably *American Railroad Leaders* (Cambridge, Massachusetts, 1953); see also his "The Legend of the Robber Barons,"

Pennsylvania Magazine of History and Biography, 74 (July 1950), pp. 307–21. Social history has fared less well in coverage, but Irvin G. Wyllie, *The Self-Made Man in America* (New Brunswick, New Jersey, 1954), is a pioneer study. A neglected but exceedingly able and interesting book is Lewis Atherton, *Main Street on the Middle Border* (Bloomington, Indiana, 1954). In recent years, business history, focused to a large extent on this era, has come to the fore, producing a number of able works and guides. Two books of local history are important for their depth studies of society and culture, Bessie Louise Pierce, *A History of Chicago, Vol. III, 1871–1893* (New York, 1957); and Philip Jordan, *Ohio Comes of Age, 1873–1900* (Columbus, Ohio, 1943), which contains a wealth of information on an important state. Agriculture has been covered in a few detailed monographs, but the only general survey is Fred A. Shannon, *The Farmer's Last Frontier* (New York, 1945). Though somewhat outdated, Arthur M. Schlesinger, *The Rise of the City 1878–1898* (New York, 1933), is a stimulating and useful book, as is Ida Tarbell, *The Nationalizing of Big Business 1878–1898* (New York, 1936), though it suffers from an acute antibusiness bias. Further bibliographical aids can be gleaned easily from the footnotes of this volume.

9. Henry Adams, *The Education of Henry Adams* (Boston, 1918), pp. 373–74.

2

The Robber Baron in the Gilded Age
Entrepreneur or Iconoclast?

1. Charles F. Adams, Jr., and Henry Adams, *Chapters of the Erie and Other Essays* (Boston, 1871), p. 134.

2. Adolph Berle, Jr., and Gardiner Means, *The Modern Corporation and Private Property* (New York, 1932), pp. 10–17.

3. Cf. Frederick Jackson, *A Week in Wall Street by One Who Knows* (New York, 1841); James K. Medbery, *Men and Mysteries of Wall Street* (Hartford, 1870).

4. Adams and Adams, *Chapters of Erie*, p. 135.

5. Ray Stannard Baker, "What the United States Steel Corporation Really is and How it Works," *McClure's*, 18 (1901), p. 6.

6. Berle and Means, *The Modern Corporation*, pp. 2–6.

7. Charles Wallace Collins, *The Fourteenth Amendment and the States* (Boston, 1912).

8. *The Nation*, September 30, 1880, p. 232.

9. *Pollock vs. Farmers' Loan and Trust Co.*, 157 U.S. 429, 158 U.S. 601.

10. *Annual Report of the Secretary of the Treasury 1890* (Washington, 1890), p. xxi.

11. *Commercial and Financial Chronicle*, December 18, 1886, 739; *U.S. Census 1910* (Washington, 1913), VIII, 32–33; Willard Long Thorp, *Business Annals* (New York, 1926), 129–30.

12. Allan Nevins, *A Study in Power: John D. Rockefeller, Industrialist and Philanthropist*, 2 vols. (New York, 1953), II, 613.

13. James H. Bridge, *The Inside History of the Carnegie Steel Company* (New York, 1903), p. 295.

14. *Ibid.*, p. 364.

15. *The Tribune Monthly*, 4 (1892), p. 92; Sidney Ratner (ed.), *New Light on the History of Great American Fortunes* (New York, 1953), pp. xviii–xxiii; Tarbell, *The Nationalizing of Business*, p. 113.

16. David Graham Phillips, *The Shame of the Senate;* reprint from *Cosmopolitan*, 1906, pp. 2, 94.

17. *See* John Tipple, "Who Were the Robber Barons?" which is forthcoming.

18. *Commercial and Financial Chronicle*, 43 (March 27, 1886), p. 393.

19. James F. Hudson, *The Railways and the Republic* (New York, 1886), pp. 25–66; A. B. Stickney, *The Railway Problem* (St. Paul, 1891), pp. 27–35; Frank Parsons, *The Railways, the Trusts, and the People* (Philadelphia, 1906), pp. 25–56.

20. Henry Demarest Lloyd, *Lords of Industry* (New York, 1916), p. 2; Ida M. Tarbell, *The History of the Standard Oil Company*, 2 vols. (New York, 1904), II, 111.

21. *Report of the Special Committee on Railroads* (Albany, 1879), pp. 49–50. (*Hepburn Report.*)

22. Senate Reports, 49th Congress, 1st Session, no. 46, p. 199. (*Cullom Report*).

23. *New York Senate Report*, no. 50 (1888), p. 10.

24. *State of Ohio vs. Standard Oil Company*, 49 Ohio State 137.

25. *Report of the Commissioner of Corporations on the Petroleum Industry* (Washington, 1907), I, xvi. (*Smith Report*).

26. *Standard Oil Co. of New Jersey et al. vs. United States*, 221 U.S. 1.

27. Andrew Carnegie, "Wealth," *North American Review*, 168

(June 1889), pp. 657, 654; The *Gospel of Wealth* (New York, 1900), p. 5.

28. *Cullom Report*, appendix, pp. 213–15.

29. Ralph W. and Muriel E. Hidy, *Pioneering in Big Business 1882–1911* (New York, 1955), pp. 678–79; cf. 43.

30. John D. Rockefeller, *Random Reminiscences of Men and Events* (New York, 1909), p. 112.

31. John Bates Clark, "The Society of the Future," *Independent*, 53 (July 18, 1901), pp. 1649–51.

32. Carnegie, "Wealth," *North American Review*, 168 (June 1889), p. 655.

33. John Moody, *The Truth About the Trusts* (New York, 1904), p. v.

34. *See* appended testimony to *Cullom Report*.

35. William Graham Sumner, "The Concentration of Wealth: Its Economic Justification," *Essays of William Graham Sumner* (New Haven, 1934), II, 166.

36. This view had extensive support in the business world. For a useful compendium see James H. Bridge, *The Trust: Its Book* (New York, 1902). *See also* Jonathan P. Dolliver, "Facts About Trusts: Arguments for Protection," *American Industries*, 2 (May 16, 1904); Franklin Head (ed.), *Chicago Conference on Trusts* (Chicago, 1900).

37. J. C. Welch and J. N. Camden, "The Standard Oil Company," *North American Review*, 136 (February, 1883), pp. 181–200; Hidy and Hidy, *Pioneering in Big Business*, pp. 658, 680.

38. Rockefeller, *Reminiscences*, pp. 81–82. Copyright 1909, Doubleday & Co., Inc.; copyright renewed 1936, John D. Rockefeller. Quoted by permission.

39. Andrew Carnegie, "The Bugaboo of Trusts," *North American Review*, 148 (February 1889), pp. 141–42.

40. *Literary Digest*, 45 (December 28, 1912), p. 1213.

41. Kirkland, *Dream and Thought in the Business Community*, p. 27. (Cornell University Press.)

42. Hans B. Thorelli, *The Federal Antitrust Policy* (Baltimore, 1955), p. 66.

43. *See Ibid.*, pp. 500–54.

44. Henry Demarest Lloyd, *Wealth Against Commonwealth* (New York, 1899), p. 496.

45. Walton Hamilton and Irene Till, *Antitrust in Action* (Washington, 1940), p. 6.

46. Thorelli, *The Federal Antitrust Policy*, p. 556.

47. Frederick Pollock, *The Genius of the Common Law* (New York, 1912), p. 95.

48. Arthur T. Hadley, *Railroad Transportation: Its History and Its Laws* (New York, 1885), pp. 69–70.

49. Richard Hofstadter, *Social Darwinism in American Thought 1860–1915* (Philadelphia, 1945), p. 201.

50. John Lydenburg, "Pre-Mucking: A Study of Attitudes Toward Politics as Revealed in American Fiction from 1870 through 1901" (Cambridge: Harvard University, unpublished dissertation, 1946), p. 59.

51. Lloyd, *Wealth Against Commonwealth*, p. 496.

52. S. R. 59, January 10, 1900; B and D, 951.

53. Thurman W. Arnold, *The Folklore of Capitalism* (New Haven, 1937), p. 211.

54. *Santa Clara Co. vs. Southern Pacific Railroad Co.*, 118 U.S. 394.

55. Arnold, *The Folklore of Capitalism*, p. 189.

56. *See* H. S. Commager (ed.), *Documents of American History*, 2 vols. in 1 (New York, 1949), II, 78.

57. Adams and Adams, *Chapters of Erie*, pp. 96–99.

58. Mark Van Doren (ed.), *The Portable Walt Whitman* (New York, 1945), p. 400.

59. As quoted in Irvin G. Wyllie, *The Self-Made Man in America* (New Brunswick, N.J., 1954), p. 147. (By permission, Rutgers University Press.)

60. Edward Everett Cassady, "The Business Man in the American Novel: 1856 to 1903" (Berkeley: University of California, unpublished dissertation, 1939), p. 199.

61. Medbery, p. 282; Fowler, p. 299.

62. Thomas W. Lawson, *Frenzied Finance* (New York, 1905), p. 174.

63. *See Report of Governor Hughes' Committee on Speculation in Securities and Commodities* (Albany, 1909), pp. 4, 15; Alexander D. Noyes, "The Recent Economic History of the United States," *Quarterly Journal of Economics*, 19 (June 1905), pp. 167–209.

64. Lloyd, *Lords*, p. 341.

65. W. A. Croffutt, *The Vanderbilts and the Story of Their Fortune* (Chicago, 1886), p. 129.

66. Francis A. Walker, "Democracy and Wealth," *Forum*, 10 (September 1890), p. 245.

67. Joseph Dorfman, *The Economic Mind in American Civilization* (New York, 1949), III, 73.

68. Andrew Carnegie, *The Empire of Business* (New York, 1902), p. 140.

69. Henry George, *Progress and Poverty* (New York, 1880), pp. 174–75; Lyman Abbott, "Industrial Democracy," *Review of Reviews*, 4 (June 1890), p. 662.

70. Burton J. Hendrick, "The Vanderbilt Fortune," *McClure's Magazine*, 19 (November 1908), pp. 46–62.

71. New York State, *Assembly Documents*, 1867, No. 19, pp. 205–10.

72. John Tipple, "The Anatomy of Prejudice: The Critical Foundations of the Robber Baron Legend" (Stanford: Stanford University, unpublished dissertation, 1958), pp. 15–17.

73. Frederick A. Cleveland and Fred W. Powell, *Railroad Promotion and Capitalization in the United States* (New York 1909), p. 141.

74. New York State, *Assembly Documents, op. cit.*

75. As quoted in Edward Stanwood, *A History of Presidential Elections* (Boston, 1892), pp. 474–78.

3

The Worker's Search for Power
Labor in the Gilded Age

1. *See* John R. Commons, *et al.* (eds.), *A Documentary History of American Industrial Society* (New York, 1958), IX, i–viii.

2. *See* Thomas C. Cochran, "The Social Sciences and the Problem of Historical Synthesis," in Fritz Stern (ed.), *The Varieties of History* (New York, 1956), pp. 352–56; Frank Tannenbaum, *A Philosophy of Labor* (New York, 1952), p. 68; John Hall, "The Knights of St. Crispin in Massachusetts, 1869–1878," *Journal of Economic History*, 17 (June 1958), pp. 174–75.

3. The literature is voluminous, if not always accurate or comprehensive; *see* Harold Williamson (ed.), *The Growth of the American Economy* (New York, 1951), p. 462; Anthony Bimba, *The Molly Maguires* (New York, 1932); J. Walter Coleman, *The Molly Maguire Riots* (Richmond, Va., 1936); George McNeil (ed.), *The Labor Movement* (New York, 1892), pp. 241–67; Andrew Roy, *A History of the Coal Miners of the United States* (Columbus, 1903); John R. Commons, *et al.*, *History of Labor in the United States* (New York, 1918), II, 179–80; McAlister Coleman, *Men and Coal* (New York, 1943), pp. 42–44;

Arthur Suffern, *Conciliation and Arbitration in the Coal Industry of America* (Boston, 1915), pp. 7–17.

4. Richard Lester, *Economics of Labor* (New York: Macmillan Co., 1947), p. 545.

5. Herbert Harris, *American Labor* (New Haven, 1938), p. 75.

6. Selig Perlman, "Upheaval and Reorganization Since 1876," in Commons *et al.*, *History of Labor*, II, 196.

7. J. A. Schumpeter, "The Problem of Classes," in Reinhard Bendix and Seymour Lipset (eds.), *Class, Status and Power* (Glencoe: Free Press, 1953), p. 79.

8. *Loc. cit.*

9. *See* Adna Weber, *The Growth of Large Cities in the Nineteenth Century* (New York, 1899), pp. 433–34.

10. *Chicago Times*, May 22, 1876.

11. *New York Times*, November 20, 1876.

12. *Chicago Tribune*, July 4, 1876.

13. Samuel Lane Loomis, *Modern Cities and Their Religious Problems* (New York, 1887), pp. 60–61, 63–66.

14. *See* Massachusetts Bureau of Labor Statistics, *Second Annual Report 1870–1871* (Boston, 1871), p. 475.

15. See e.g., Louis Wirth, "Urbanism as a Way of Life," in Paul Hatt and Albert Reiss, Jr. (eds.), *Cities and Society* (Glencoe, 1957), pp. 36–63; Bert F. Hoselitz, "The City, the Factory, and Economic Growth," *American Economic Review*, 45 (May 1955), pp. 166–84.

16. "The Distribution of Wealth," *Cooper's New Monthly*, 1 (July 1874), pp. 7–9.

17. *Iron Molder's Journal* (January 1874), p. 204.

18. *See* Ohio Bureau of Labor Statistics, *First Annual Report 1877* (Columbus, 1878), pp. 156–92.

19. A. Ross Eckler, "A Measure of the Severity of Depression, 1873–1932," *Review of Economic Statistics*, 15 (May 1933), pp. 75–81; O. V. Wells, "The Depression of 1873–1879," *Agricultural History*, 11 (July 1937), pp. 237–49; Rendigs Fels, "American Business Cycles, 1865–1879," *American Economic Review*, 41 (September 1951), pp. 325–49: Alvin Hansen, *Business Cycles and National Income* (New York, 1951), pp. 24–26, 39–41.

20. T. E. Burton, *Financial Crises and Periods of Industrial and Commercial Depression* (New York, 1908), p. 344.

21. *Annual Report of the Secretary of the American Iron and Steel Association of the Year 1874* (Philadelphia, 1875), pp. 4–5.

22. New York Association for Improving the Condition of the Poor, *Thirty-first Annual Report* (New York, 1874), p. 28.

23. *New York Graphic*, January 14, 1874.

24. *American Manufacturer*, October 30, 1873.

25. *Annual Report of the Secretary of the American Iron and Steel Association for the Year 1874*, pp. 12, 81–82.

26. See *Vulcan Record*, 1 (September 1874), pp. 12–14.

27. *New York Times*, October 27, November 2, 15, 1873.

28. *Chicago Times*, October 3, November 3, 1873.

29. See *Iron Molder's Journal*, 1 (December 1873), p. 161; *Iron Age*, May 26, 1874, p. 14.

30. *Annual Report of the Secretary of the American Iron and Steel Association for the Year 1874*, pp. 81–82.

31. *See* Herbert Gutman, "Trouble on the Railroads in 1873–1874: Prelude to the 1877 Crisis?" *Labor History*, 2 (Spring 1962), pp. 215–35; *Cincinnati Enquirer*, February–March, 1874; *Chicago Times*, November 12, 1873; *Chicago Tribune*, November 10–20, 1874.

32. *Workingman's Advocate*, March 28, June 27–July 4, 1874; John James, "The Miner's Strike in the Hocking Valley," *Cooper's New Monthly*, 1 (July 1874), p. 4.

33. *Chicago Tribune*, April 23, 1874; *Workingman's Advocate*, July 11–18, 1874; *New York World*, July 23, 1874.

34. *Workingman's Advocate*, March 28, 1874; *Chicago Times*, November 7–9, 1874; *Cincinnati Commercial*, February 11, 1874; *Iron Age*, August 13, 1874, p. 14.

35. *See* Herbert G. Gutman, "Two Lockouts in Pennsylvania, 1873–1874," *The Pennsylvania Magazine of History and Biography*, 83 (July 1959), pp. 317–18, 322–26.

36. *Iron Molder's Journal* (December 1874), p. 138.

37. *Chicago Tribune*, November 19, 1874.

38. *Workingman's Advocate*, April 14, 1874.

39. *Ibid.*

40. *Cincinnati Commercial*, January 18, 1874.

41. *Workingman's Advocate*, September 5–12, November 7, 28, 1874.

42. *Iron Molder's Journal* (December 1874), p. 138.

43. *Frostburg Mining Journal*, November 25 , 1876.

44. *Cooper's New Monthly*, 1 (January 1874), p. 16.

45. *Iron Age*, March 5, 1874; *Cincinnati Commercial*, January 29, February 3, 1874.

46. *Portsmouth Times*, February 7, 1874.

47. *See* Herbert G. Gutman, "The Braidwood Lockout of 1874," *Journal of the Illinois State Historical Society*, 53 (Spring 1960), pp. 5–28.

48. *See* Herbert G. Gutman, "An Iron Workers' Strike in the Ohio Valley, 1873–1874," *Ohio Historical Quarterly*, 68 (October 1959), pp. 353–70.

49. *See* Herbert G. Gutman, "Reconstruction in Ohio: Negroes in the Hocking Valley Coal Mines in 1873 and 1874," *Labor History*, 3 (Fall 1962), pp. 243–64.

50. *Cincinnati Commercial*, May 23, June 4, 1874; Edward Wieck, *The American Miners' Association* (New York, 1940), p. 141.

51. *Cincinnati Commercial*, May 23, 1874; *Hocking Sentinel*, December 25, 1873, January 8, 22, February 12, 26, March 5, 1874.

52. *Logan Republican*, April 4, 1874.

53. *Cincinnati Commercial*, May 23, 1874; *Workingman's Advocate*, May 23, 1874.

54. *Athens Messenger*, May 7, 1874.

55. *Hocking Sentinel*, April 1, 1874; *Chicago Tribune*, June 30, 1874.

56. *Cincinnati Commercial*, June 13, 14, 15, 1874; *New Lexington Democratic Herald*, June 18, 1874.

57. *Cleveland Leader*, July 7, 1874.

58. *Cincinnati Commercial*, October 3, 1874, March 22, 1875; *New Lexington Democratic Herald*, March 25, 1875; *Hocking Sentinel*, March 4, 25, 1875; *Ohio State Journal*, April 1, 1875.

59. *New York Graphic*, November 10, 1873; *Chicago Tribune*, December 23, 1873; New York Association for Improving the Condition of the Poor, *Thirtieth Annual Report, 1873* (New York, 1873), p. 41ff.

60. *New York Sun*, October 23, November 4, November 20–December 20, 1873; *Chicago Times*, December 1–31, 1873.

61. *New York World*, December 27, 1873; see sources in note 60.

62. *New York Tribune*, December 12, 1873.

63. *Ibid.*, December 12, 1873.

64. *Chicago Times*, December 23, 30, 1873; *Chicago Tribune*, December 23–30, 1873.

65. *See Chicago Tribune*, December 29, 1873; Thurlow Weed to the Editor, *New York Tribune*, December 20, 1873; *Cumberland* (Maryland) *Civilian and Times*, February 12, 1874.

66. *New York Tribune*, June 22, 1874.

67. *Chicago Times*, August 26, 1874.

68. *New York Herald*, November 2, 1873; *New York Times*, June 3, 1874; *Cleveland Leader*, June 18, 1874; *Chicago Tribune*, April 15, 1874.

69. *Pittsburgh Post*, November 21–30, 1873.

70. *Cleveland Plain Dealer*, May 7–11, 1874.

71. *New York Toiler*, August 22, 1874; *New York Sun*, July 6, 1874; Board of Health of the City of New York, *Fourth Annual Report, May 1, 1873 to April 30, 1874* (New York, 1874), pp. 96–97.

72. *New York Times*, June 25–30, 1874; *New York Tribune*, June 2–24, 1874.

73. *New York Sun*, June 2, 10, 1874; *New York World*, July 23–24, 1874.

74. *Chicago Times*, May 22, 1876; *Iron Age*, April 27, 1876, p. 24.

75. *See* Herbert Gutman, "Two Lockouts in Pennsylvania, 1873–1874," *loc. cit.*; and Herbert Gutman, "Trouble on the Railroads in 1873–1874: Prelude to the 1877 Crisis?" *loc. cit.*

76. *See* Louis Hartz, *The Liberal Tradition in America* (New York, 1955), 110–13, 189–227; Richard Hofstadter, *The American Political Tradition and the Men Who Made It* (New York, 1948), v–ix; John Higham (ed.), *The Reconstruction of American History* (New York, 1962), pp. 21–24, 119–56.

77. *See* Cochran, *Railroad Leaders*, p. 181.

4

Spoilsmen and Reformers

Civil Service Reform and Public Morality

1. I am grateful to the University of Illinois Press for permission to reprint portions of my book, *Outlawing the Spoils* (Urbana, 1961). I am also grateful to the editor of *The Historian* for permission to reprint portions of my article: "An Analysis of Civil Service Reformers," *The Historian*, 23 (November 1960), pp. 54–78. *See* Charles Francis Adams, Jr., and Henry Adams, *Chapters of Erie and Other Essays* (Ithaca, 1960); Ishbel Ross, *Proud Kate* (New York, 1953), pp. 246–49; W. A. Swanberg, *Jim Fisk* (New York, 1959); Robert Shaplen, *Free Love and Heavenly Sinners* (New York, 1954).

2. *The Nation*, 4 (April 11, 1867), p. 286.

3. C. Vann Woodward, *Origins of the New South 1877–1913* (Baton Rouge, 1951), pp. 66–74; Albert R. Kitzhaber, "Götterdämmerung in Topeka: The Downfall of Senator Pomeroy," *Kansas Historical Quarterly*, 18 (August 1950), pp. 243–78.

4. *See* John W. Pratt, "Boss Tweed's Public Welfare Program,"

New-York Historical Society Quarterly, 45 (October 1961), pp. 396–411, for a more charitable view of Tweed.

5. William L. Riordan, *Plunkitt of Tammany Hall* (New York, 1948), pp. 3–8.

6. Rollo Ogden (ed.), *Life and Letters of Edwin Lawrence Godkin* (New York, 1907); William M. Armstrong, *E. L. Godkin and American Foreign Policy 1865–1900* (New York, 1957).

7. *See* U.S. Revenue Commission, "Revenue System of the United States," *House Executive Documents*, 39th Congress, 1st session, VII, No. 34, 44–51; Charles Eliot Norton (ed.), *Orations and Addresses of George William Curtis* (New York, 1894), II, 39; W. W. Belknap to John A. Logan, August 15, 1872, Logan papers, Library of Congress; "Senator Trumbull and the Revenue," *Harper's Weekly*, 16 (September 7, 1872), p. 690; Curtis to Belknap, August 25, 1872, and Curtis, Cattell, *et al.*, to Logan, September [?], 1872, Logan papers. For another exaggeration of statistics by reformers *see Congressional Globe*, 41st Congress, 3rd session, 400, 459–460, 666. In fairness to Johnson the improvement of the Internal Revenue Service, no doubt, resulted more from the drastic elimination and simplification of excise taxes than from Grant.

8. Norton to Godkin, November 3, 1871, Godkin papers, Harvard University.

9. *See* Kermit Vanderbilt, *Charles Eliot Norton* (Cambridge, 1959); and Sara Norton and M. A. DeWolfe Howe (eds.), *Letters of Charles Eliot Norton* (Boston, 1913); Norton to Godkin, July 20, 1866, Godkin papers.

10. Norton to Godkin, March 13, 1867, May 30, 1868, Godkin papers; Norton to Curtis, July 24, 1868, Norton papers, Harvard University; Norton to Curtis, January 29, 1869, *Ibid.*; Curtis to Norton, March 13, 1869, Curtis papers, Harvard University; Norton to Curtis, July 22, 1869, Norton papers.

11. *See* Gordon Milne, *George William Curtis and the Genteel Tradition* (Bloomington, 1956), and Hoogenboom, *Outlawing the Spoils*, *passim.*

12. *The Nation*, 3 (November 1, 1866), p. 341; *Ibid.* (November 29, 1866), p. 422; Curtis to Norton, January 2, 1867, Curtis papers; "Reform of the Civil Service," *Harper's Weekly*, 11 (March 2, 1867), p. 130.

13. Curtis to Norton, September 17, 1870, Curtis papers.

14. *The Nation*, 16 (February 20, 1873), pp. 126–27; *Ibid.*, 16 (March 20, 1873), p. 189.

15. Curtis to Norton, September 19, 1873, Curtis papers; "The Prospects of Civil Service Reform," *Harper's Weekly*, 17 (October 25, 1873), p. 938.

16. Henry Adams to Charles Francis Adams, Jr., February 23, and April 29, 1869, and Henry Adams to Charles M. Gaskell, April 19 and June 20, 1869, in Worthington Chauncey Ford (ed.), *Letters of Henry Adams 1858–1891* (Boston, 1930), pp. 152, 156–57, 161–62. (By permission, Houghton Mifflin Company.)

17. Henry Adams to Edward Atkinson, February 1, 1869, and Henry Adams to Gaskell, August 27, 1869, *Ibid.*, pp. 151, 165–66.

18. Henry Brooks Adams, "Civil Service Reform," *North American Review*, 109 (October 1869), pp. 443–75; *The Nation*, 9 (November 11, 1869), p. 415.

19. *See* Hoogenboom, *Outlawing the Spoils, passim.*

20. Julius Bing, "Our Civil Service," *Putnam's Magazine*, new series, 2 (August 1868), p. 233.

21. Joint Select Committee on Retrenchment, "Civil Service of the United States," *House Reports*, 40th Congress, 2nd session, II, No. 47, 2, 7. Civil servants may actually have numbered 70,000 in 1867. Civil service statistics are frequently contradictory and must be used with caution. See Paul P. Van Riper, *History of the United States Civil Service* (Evanston, 1958), pp. 56–59.

22. Leonard D. White, *The Jacksonians* (New York, 1954), pp. 394–98. These generalizations on the personnel system of 1860 are applicable five years later.

23. Joint Select Committee on Retrenchment, "Civil Service of the United States," pp. 23, 40, 203.

24. *Ibid.*, 40.

25. "Civil Service Reform," I, 27, 31–35, 91–92, III, 558–559, Elliott papers, library of the U.S. Civil Service Commission, Washington, D.C.

26. *See Congressional Record*, 47th Congress, 1st session, 79–85.

27. George F. Howe, *Chester A. Arthur* (New York, 1934), pp. 48–49.

28. Joint Select Committee on Retrenchment, "Report," *Senate Reports*, 41st Congress, 3rd session, No. 380, 1–2.

29. *The Nation*, 14 (January 11, 1872), p. 17. *See also* William J. Hartman, "Politics and Patronage: The New York Customs House 1852–1902" (New York: Columbia University, unpublished dissertation, 1952), pp. 165–72. For the report based upon the hearings see

Committee on Investigation and Retrenchment, "Reports," *Senate Reports*, 42nd Congress, 2nd session, IV (in 3 parts), No. 227.

30. Richard Lowitt, *A Merchant Prince of the Nineteenth Century: William E. Dodge* (New York, 1954), pp. 275–83. *See also* "The Extraordinary Element in the Case of Phelps, Dodge & Co.," *The Nation*, 16 (May 1, 1873), pp. 297–99; *ibid.* (April 24, 1873), p. 278; *ibid.*, 17 (August 28, 1873), p. 138; *ibid.*, 18 (January 8, 1874), pp. 21–22.

31. *See* Hartman, "Politics and Patronage," pp. 186–91; Leonard D. White, *The Republican Era* (New York, 1958), pp. 123–26.

32. Hayes to Merritt, February 4, 1879, Hayes papers, Hayes Library, Fremont, Ohio.

33. Silas W. Burt, "A Brief History of the Civil Service Reform Movement in the United States," pp. K-L, in the Burt Writings, New York Public Library.

34. Dorman B. Eaton, "Civil Service Reform in the New York City Post Office and Custom House," *House Executive Documents*, 46th Congress, 3rd session, XXVIII, No. 94, 35–37; Curtis to Burt, August 18, 1879, Burt Collection, New-York Historical Society; *New York Times*, July 9, 1879.

35. Eaton, "Civil Service Reform," pp. 39–43.

36. *See* Ari Hoogenboom, "The Pendleton Act and the Civil Service," *American Historical Review*, 64 (January 1959), pp. 301–18.

5

The Republican Party Revisited
1877–1897

1. James Bryce, *The American Commonwealth*, 2 vols. (New York, 1895), II, 3–4.

2. *Ibid.*, pp. 4–5.

3. Henry Adams, *The Education of Henry Adams* (Boston and New York, popular edition, 1927), p. 294.

4. *Ibid.*, p. 355.

5. Beard and Beard, *Rise of American Civilization*, II, 341; Henry Steele Commager and Samuel Eliot Morison, *The Growth of the American Republic*, 2 vols. (New York, 1952), II, 214.

6. Robert McCloskey, *American Conservatism in the Age of Enterprise* (Cambridge, 1951), pp. 1–21.

7. Leonard D. White, *The Republican Era, 1869–1901* (New York, 1958), pp. 21, 24, 41.

8. Hanna Grace Roach, "Sectionalism in Congress, 1870–1890," *American Political Science Review,* 19 (1925), pp. 500–26.

9. E. Pendleton Herring, *The Politics of Democracy* (New York, 1940), p. 102.

10. Andrew McLaughlin, "The Significance of Political Parties," *Atlantic Monthly,* 101 (1908), pp. 145–56.

11. Connecticut, New Jersey, New York, Ohio, Indiana, and Illinois.

12. *New York Tribune,* March 13, 1877.

13. *Washington National Republican,* March 27, 1877.

14. Vincent P. De Santis, *Republicans Face the Southern Question* (Baltimore, 1959).

15. C. Vann Woodward, *Reunion and Reaction* (Boston, 1951), p. 25.

16. *New York Tribune,* April 2, 1877.

17. Kirk Porter, *National Party Platforms* (New York, 1924), pp. 95, 111, 133–36.

18. *New Orleans Times-Democrat,* October 2, 1894.

19. *The Nation,* 24 (April 5, 1877), p. 202.

20. Gunner Myrdal, *An American Dilemma* (New York, 1944), pp. 226, 738–39; Paul H. Buck, *The Road to Reunion* (Boston, 1937), pp. 283–96.

21. *The Louisianan,* November 3, 1877; Benjamin Quarles, *Frederick Douglass* (Washington, 1948), pp. 334–35.

6

Greenbackers, Goldbugs and Silverites
Currency Reform and Politics, 1860–1897

1. Bray Hammond, *Banks and Politics in America* (Princeton, 1957), pp. 722–23.

2. John Sherman, *Recollections of Forty Years in the House, Senate and Cabinet,* 2 vols. (New York, 1895), I, 290.

3. A. B. Hart, *Salmon Portland Chase* (Boston, 1899), p. 223; Hugh McCulloch, *Men and Measures of Half a Century* (New York, 1889), pp. 168–70.

4. *Ibid.,* pp. 163–65.

5. Andrew M. Davis, *Origins of the National Banking System* (Washington, 1910), p. 97; A. Barton Hepburn, *A History of the Currency of the United States* (New York, 1915), pp. 307, 310; Sherman, *Recollections*, I, 271, 287.

6. Connecticut alone had more national bank notes in circulation than Michigan, Iowa, Minnesota, Kansas, and Kentucky combined; Rhode Island had $77 per capita and Arkansas $0.13. Gilbert C. Fite and Jim E. Reese, *An Economic History of the United States* (Boston, 1959), p. 468.

7. James W. Gleed, "Western Mortgages," *Forum*, 9 (March 1890), pp. 93–105.

8. *See* Ellis P. Oberholtzer, *Jay Cooke*, 2 vols. (Philadelphia, 1907), I, 121–574; Henrietta M. Larson, *Jay Cooke* (Cambridge, 1936).

9. Alexander D. Noyes, *Forty Years of American Finance* (New York, 1909), pp. 123–26.

10. Horace White, "A Plan for a Permanent Banking System," *Forum*, 12 (December 1891), pp. 477–82; Hepburn, *Currency*, pp. 332, 342, 357–58.

11. Treasury notes in the form of "bills of credit" had been issued in the administrations of Monroe, Van Buren, Tyler, Polk, and Buchanan. Although not made legal tender they were still receivable for public dues. John Jay Knox, *United States Notes* (New York, 1884), pp. 21–79.

12. Hepburn, *Currency*, pp. 186–91; Edwin W. Kemmerer, *Money* (New York, 1935), pp. 238–43; Robert P. Sharkey, *Money, Class, and Party* (Baltimore, 1959), pp. 15–16, 29–50.

13. Knox, *United States Notes*, pp. 80–147.

14. Wesley Mitchell, *A History of the Greenbacks* (Chicago, 1903), pp. 10–15; Sharkey, *Money, Class, and Party*, pp. 18–19.

15. Hepburn, *Currency*, pp. 205–07; Rendigs Fels, *American Business Cycles, 1865–1897* (Chapel Hill, 1959), pp. 55–136.

16. Paul Studenski and Herman E. Kroos, *Financial History of the United States* (New York, 1952), p. 147; Sharkey, *Money, Class, and Party*, pp. 51–55.

17. McCulloch, *Men and Measures*, pp. 204–09; Noyes, *Forty Years*, pp. 11–16.

18. Hepburn, *Currency*, pp. 209–11; Chester MacA. Destler, "The Origin and Character of the Pendleton Plan," *Mississippi Valley Historical Review*, 24 (September 1937), pp. 171–84; Max L. Shipley, "The Background and Legal Aspects of the Pendleton Plan," *Ibid.*, 24 (December 1937), pp. 329–40.

19. Knox, *United States Notes*, pp. 156–66; Gerald T. Dunne, *Monetary Decisions of the Supreme Court* (New Brunswick, 1960).

20. Davis Rich Dewey, *Financial History of the United States* (New York, 1936), p. 370; George Anderson, "Western Attitude Toward National Banks, 1873–1874," *Mississippi Valley Historical Review*, 23 (September 1936), pp. 205–16; Chester MacA. Destler, "Western Radicalism, 1865–1901: Concepts and Origins," *Ibid.*, 31 (December 1944), pp. 335–68.

21. Dewey, *Financial History*, pp. 361–73; Matthew Josephson, *The Politicos, 1865–1896* (New York, 1938), p. 188.

22. Noyes, *Forty Years*, p. 21.

23. *Specie Resumption and Funding*, House Executive Document IX, 46th Congress, 2nd session; D. C. Barrett, *The Greenbacks and the Resumption of Specie Payment 1862–1879* (Cambridge, 1931); Sharkey, *Money, Class, and Party*, pp. 107–40.

24. John M. Willem, Jr., *The United States Trade Dollar* (New York, 1959), pp. 55–69, 111–24.

25. Dewey, *Financial History*, p. 403; Hepburn, *Currency*, pp. 270–73; Noyes, *Forty Years*, pp. 135–36; *History of the Coinage Act of 1873*, Senate Misc. Document No. 132, 41st Congress, 2nd session.

26. Great Britain was already on the gold standard. In 1871 the newly formed German nation and Holland and Spain adopted gold. Then the Latin Monetary Union—France, Belgium, Switzerland, and Greece—suspended the free minting of silver. The formation of the Scandinavian Monetary Confederation in 1873 resulted in the adoption of the gold standard by Sweden, Norway, and Denmark. Thus by the end of the 1870's practically every important European country had stopped minting silver.

27. *Senate Report No. 703*, 44th Congress, 3rd session.

28. David S. Muzzey, *James G. Blaine* (New York, 1934), pp. 137–38; Charles Richard Williams, *Rutherford Birchard Hayes*, 2 vols. (New York, 1914), II, 129–36; Leland L. Sage, *William Boyd Allison* (Iowa City, 1952); Jeanette P. Nichols, "John Sherman and the Silver Drive of 1877–1878: The Origins of a Gigantic Subsidy," *Ohio Archeological and Historical Quarterly*, 46 (April 1938), pp. 148–65.

29. *See* Noyes, *Forty Years*, p. 74.

30. Allan Nevins, *Grover Cleveland* (New York, 1933), p. 202.

31. Hepburn, *Currency*, pp. 290–98; Noyes, *Forty Years*, pp. 88–102.

32. *Report of the Director of the Mint, 1890* (Washington, 1891), p. 12; Fels, *American Business Cycles*, pp. 137–58.

33. Nevins, *Cleveland*, pp. 202–03.

34. James A. Barnes, *John G. Carlisle* (New York, 1931), p. 89; Alexander C. Flick and Gustav S. Lobrano, *Samuel Jones Tilden* (New York, 1939), p. 492; Robert McElroy, *Grover Cleveland*, 2 vols. (New York, 1923), I, 107–09; Nevins, *Grover Cleveland*, p. 204.

35. Flick and Lobrano, *Samuel Jones Tilden*, p. 492.

36. Williams, *Rutherford Birchard Hayes*, II, 368–69.

37. Muzzey, *James G. Blaine*, p. 348; Dewey, *Financial History*, p. 409–10.

38. Nevins, *Grover Cleveland*, pp. 266–79; Henry D. Russell, *International Monetary Conferences* (New York, 1898).

39. *See* Sidney Fine, *Laissez-Faire and the Welfare State* (Ann Arbor, 1956), pp. 301–02; John D. Hicks, *The Populist Revolt* (Minneapolis, 1931), pp. 54–95; Shannon, *The Farmer's Last Frontier*, pp. 148–96, 291–95.

40. *Proceedings of the First National Silver Convention* (St. Louis, 1889).

41. Noyes, *Forty Years*, pp. 139–47.

42. Sherman, *Recollections*, II, 1125, 1148, 1175–98.

43. Edward Stanwood, *History of the Presidency from 1897 to 1909* (New York, 1912), p. 490.

44. William A. Robinson, *Thomas B. Reed* (New York, 1930), pp. 242–45.

45. Fred Wellborn, "The Influence of the Silver-Republican Senators, 1889–1891," *Mississippi Valley Historical Review*, 14 (March 1928), pp. 462–80; Elmer Ellis, *Henry Moore Teller* (Caldwell, Idaho, 1941), pp. 188–97.

46. Frank W. Taussig, *The Silver Situation in the United States* (New York, 1896), pp. 10, 50; Fels, *American Business Cycles*, pp. 159–78.

47. Kemmerer, *Money*, pp. 359–64; L. A. Garnett, "The Crux of the Money Controversy: Has Gold Risen," *Forum*, 18 (January 1895), pp. 573–86, held an opposite view.

48. In simple terms, the quantity theory of money states that if the supply of money increases more rapidly than the supply of goods and services, prices will tend to rise. If, on the other hand, the volume of goods and services increases faster than the supply of money, prices will fall. The relation between money and prices may be stated as an equation, $P = MV/Q$, in which P stands for the general price level, M for the amount of money and credit, V for the velocity of circulation, and Q for the supply of goods. An increase in the velocity of

circulation tends to increase purchasing power, a decline in velocity to decrease it. However, easy money groups concentrated on the volume of money rather than on its velocity of circulation. *See* Milton Friedman, "The Quantity Theory of Money: A Restatement," in Milton Friedman (ed.), *Studies in the Quantity Theory of Money* (Chicago, 1958), pp. 3–21; Richard T. Selden, "Monetary Velocity in the United States," *Ibid.*, pp. 179–233; Alvin H. Hansen, *Monetary Theory and Fiscal Policy* (New York, 1949), pp. 43–53.

49. Sherman, *Recollections*, II, 1070.

50. *See* Thomas G. Shearman, "The Owners of the United States," *Forum*, 8 (November 1889), pp. 262–73; G. B. Spahr, *The Present Distribution of Wealth in the United States* (New York, 1896), p. 69.

51. Jeannette P. Nichols, "Bryan's Benefactor: Coin Harvey and His World," *Ohio Historical Quarterly*, 67 (October 1958), pp. 299–325; Fels, *American Business Cycles*, pp. 179–92.

52. Samuel P. Hays, *The Response to Industrialism* (Chicago, 1959); Horace S. Merrill, *Bourbon Democracy of the Middlewest, 1865–1896* (Baton Rouge, 1953).

53. Chester MacA. Destler, "The Labor-Populist Alliance in Illinois in 1894," *Mississippi Valley Historical Review*, 37 (March 1941), pp. 589–602; and "The Influence of Edward Kellogg upon American Radicalism, 1865–1896," *Journal of Political Economy*, 40 (June 1932), No. 3.

54. *See* A. L. Diggs, "The Farmers' Alliance and Some of Its Leaders," *Arena*, 5 (April 1892), pp. 590–604.

55. *Omaha World-Herald*, June 6, 1895; *Chicago Tribune*, June 2–7, 1895; Richard Hofstadter, *The Age of Reform* (New York, 1955); Henry Nash Smith, *Virgin Land* (Cambridge, 1950).

56. Claudius O. Johnson, "The Story of Silver Politics in Idaho, 1892–1902," *Pacific Northwest Quarterly*, 33 (July 1942), pp. 283–96.

57. Solon J. Buck, *The Granger Movement* (Cambridge, 1913), and *The Agrarian Crusade* (New Haven, 1920).

58. Fred E. Haynes, *James Baird Weaver* (Iowa City, 1919); Howard P. Nash, Jr., *Third Parties in American Politics* (Washington, 1959), pp. 148–63, 170–76; Allan Nevins, *Abram S. Hewitt with Some Account of Peter Cooper* (New York, 1935), pp. 282–89; Ellis B. Usher, *The Greenback Movement of 1875–1884 and Wisconsin's Part in it* (Milwaukee, 1911).

59. William A. Peffer, "The Farmer's Defensive Movement," *Forum*, 8 (December 1889), pp. 464–73, and *The Farmer's Side* (New York, 1891).

60. John D. Hicks, "The Birth of the Populist Party," *Minnesota History*, 9 (1928), pp. 219–47; Chester MacA. Destler, "Agricultural Readjustment and Agrarian Unrest in Illinois," *Agricultural History* (April 1947).

61. Paul H. Douglas, *Real Wages in the United States 1890–1926* (Boston, 1930), pp. 389–400; James C. Malin, "The Farmers' Alliance Subtreasury Plan and European Precedents," *Mississippi Valley Historical Review*, 31 (September 1944), pp. 255–60.

62. The immensity of the literature may be gleaned by noting that twenty-four articles appeared in the *Forum* and in the *North American Review* alone between 1890 and 1896 by men whose names started with A through M.

63. *Congressional Record*, 52nd Congress, 1st session, 23:13–14.

64. *Ibid.*, 23:656.

65 *Ibid.*, 23:5084–5085.

66. Noyes, *Forty Years*, pp. 176–77.

67. *Congressional Record*, 52nd Congress, 1st session, 24:1377–1382, 2121–2185, 2235–2239; *Omaha World-Herald*, February 10–12, 14, March 2, 1893; W. J. Bryan, *The First Battle* (Chicago, 1897), pp. 76–77.

68. A. T. Volwiler, "Tariff Strategy and Propaganda in the United States, 1887–1888," *American Historical Review*, 36 (October 1930), pp. 76–96; Sharkey, *Money, Class, and Party*, pp. 141–71.

69. Paolo E. Coletta, "The Morning Star of the Reformation: William Jennings Bryan's First Congressional Campaign," *Nebraska History*, 37 (June 1956), pp. 103–19, and "William Jennings Bryan's Second Congressional Campaign," *Ibid.*, 40 (September 1959), pp. 275–91; Parker, *Recollections of Grover Cleveland*, pp. 208–09.

70. Paolo Coletta, "Bryan, Cleveland and the Disrupted Democracy, 1890–1896," *Nebraska History*, 41 (March 1960), pp. 1–27.

71. Theodore Saloutous, *Farmer Movements in the South 1865–1933* (Berkeley, 1960); Sharkey, *Money, Class, and Party*, pp. 221–75.

72. In 1866 the currency in circulation was about $940 million and bank deposits about $758 million. By 1914 the figures were respectively $2 billion and $18 billion. Fite and Reese, *Economic History of the United States*, pp. 466–67.

73. J. Laurence Laughlin, *Facts About Money* (Chicago, 1895); Hepburn, *Currency*, pp. 363–64; Kemmerer, *Money*, pp. 369–71.

74. Between May and October 1893 loans in the national banks contracted by $317.8 million and individual deposits by $298.8 million.

75. Wholesale prices based on an index of 100 for 1873 fell to 65.0

in 1894, 63.3 in 1895, and 61.1 in 1896. By 1894 the price of silver had fallen to 50 cents, and the ratio of silver to gold was 32 to 1.

76. Charles Foster, "The Brussels Conference Reviewed," *North American Review*, 156 (April 1893), pp. 493–500; William E. Russell, "Political Causes of the Business Depression," *Ibid.*, 157 (December 1893), pp. 641–52.

77. See *Congressional Record*, 53rd Congress, 1st session, 25:400–411; *Omaha World-Herald*, May 5, 6, July 23–30, August 17, 23, 1893; *Omaha Bee, August* 17, 21, 23, 1893.

78. The seigniorage represented the gain which the government enjoyed when it purchased bullion at a lower price than the value stamped on the metal.

79. *Omaha World-Herald*, June 30–November 2, 1893; Jeannette P. Nichols, "The Politics and Personalities of Silver Repeal in the United States Senate," *American Historical Review*, 41 (October 1935), pp. 26–53, and "John Sherman: A Study in Inflation," *Mississippi Valley Historical Review*, 21 (September 1934), pp. 181–94; Richard P. Bland, "A Janus-Faced Statute," *North American Review*, 151 (September 1890), pp. 344–53.

80. Hepburn, *Currency*, pp. 351–53; Noyes, *Forty Years*, pp. 203–06; Fels, *American Business Cycles*, pp. 193–219.

81. See Grover Cleveland, *Presidential Problems* (New York, 1904); Nevins, *Grover Cleveland;* and Barnes, *John G. Carlisle.*

82. See Horace S. Merrill, *Bourbon Leader: Grover Cleveland and the Democratic Party* (Boston, 1957), pp. 168–207.

83. James A. Barnes, "Myths of the Bryan Campaign," *Mississippi Valley Historical Review*, 34 (December 1947), pp. 367–404; Gilbert C. Fite, "Republican Strategy and the Farm Vote in the Presidential Campaign of 1896," *American Historical Review*, 65 (July 1960), pp. 787–806.

84. See J. Laurence Laughlin, "Gold and Prices, 1890–1907," *Journal of Political Economy*, 17 (September 1909), pp. 257–71.

7
Rumblings Beneath the Surface
America's Outward Thrust, 1865–1890

1. See e.g., Samuel F. Bemis, *A Diplomatic History of the United States* (4th ed., New York, 1955), p. 432; Thomas A. Bailey, *A Diplo-*

matic History of the American People (6th ed., New York, 1958), p. 391; Julius W. Pratt, *A History of United States Foreign Policy* (New York, 1955), pp. 367–68; Julius W. Pratt, *America's Colonial Experiment* (New York, 1950), p. 11.

2. T. C. Smith, "Expansion After the Civil War, 1865–1871," *Political Science Quarterly*, 16 (1901), pp. 412–36; Donald Dozer, "Anti-expansionism during the Johnson Administration," *Pacific Historical Review*, 12 (1943), pp. 253–75.

3. Henry Cabot Lodge, *The Life of George Washington*, 2 vols. (Boston, 1889), II, p. 129.

4. *Papers Relating to the Foreign Relations of the United States, 1864*, IV, p. 20; hereafter cited as *For. Rel.*

5. James D. Richardson (comp.), *A Compilation of the Messages and Papers of the Presidents 1789–1897*, 10 vols. (Washington, 1896–99), VII, p. 495; VIII, p. 327.

6. *Hartford* (Connecticut) *Daily Courant*, March 22, 1882.

7. Kirk H. Porter and Donald B. Johnson (eds.), *National Party Platforms 1840–1956* (Urbana, 1956), pp. 37–85.

8. Foster Rhea Dulles, *America's Rise to World Power* (New York, 1954), p. xvii.

9. Joseph G. Whelan, "William Henry Seward, Expansionist" (Rochester: University of Rochester, unpublished dissertation, 1959), pp. 221–33.

10. Donald M. Dozer, "Anti-Imperialism in the United States 1865–1895" (Cambridge: Harvard University, unpublished dissertation, 1936), pp. 76, 82–114; Joe Patterson Smith, *The Republican Expansionists of the Early Reconstruction Era* (Chicago, 1933), pp. 117–24.

11. *Public Opinion*, 6 (February 9, 1889), p. 367; *New York Herald*, April 10, 1880.

12. *Congressional Record* (hereafter cited as *CR*), 48th Congress, 1st session, XV, part 6, Appendix, p. 431; *ibid.* XVIII, part 3, 49th Congress, 2nd session, Appendix, p. 93; *New York Tribune*, January 10, 1876, August 7, 1879; *New York Herald*, April 10, 1880.

13. *New York Tribune*, July 17, 1885; *New York Herald*, April 10, 1880; *The Nation*, 40 (June 11, 1885), p. 476.

14. "The Diplomatic Service," *The Nation*, 40 (June 11, 1885), p. 476; "An American Diplomat," *The Chautauquan*, 5 (June 1885), p. 549; *Springfield Daily Republican*, December 24, 1878.

15. John Macarthy, "A Dish of Diplomacy," *Catholic World*, 32 (October 1880), pp. 57–69; "Foreign Relations of the United States," *The Chautauquan*, 8 (November 1887), pp. 102–04.

16. *CR*, VII, part 2, 45th Congress, 2nd session, pp. 1608–22; *New York Herald*, April 10, 1880; *New York Tribune*, May 1, 1884.

17. However, Professor Bailey asserts that the United States became a world power with independence. Professor Ernest R. May feels that the United States became a power after the Venezuela crisis of 1895. *See* his *Imperial Democracy* (New York, 1961), chap. 1. *See also* T. A. Bailey, "America's Emergence as a World Power: The Myth and the Verity," *Pacific Historical Review*, 30 (February 1961), pp. 1–16; A. T. Volwiler, "The Early Empire Days of the United States," *West Virginia History*, 18 (January 1957), pp. 116–27.

18. *See* Hofstadter, *Social Darwinism*, p. 18.

19. John Fiske, "Manifest Destiny," *Harper's New Monthly Magazine*, 70 (March 1885), pp. 578–90.

20. Josiah Strong, *Our Country: Its Possible Future and Its Present Crisis* (New York, 1885), pp. 170–75.

21. Brooks Adams, *America's Economic Supremacy* (New York, 1900), pp. 26, 84–85; Brooks Adams, *The New Empire* (New York, 1902); Philip Africa, "The Historiography of Brooks Adams" (Rochester: University of Rochester, unpublished dissertation, 1954).

22. *Pittsburgh National Labor Tribune*, June 16, 1881; W. N. Lockington, "The Consolidation of Nationalities," *The American*, 16 (May 26, 1888), pp. 87–88.

23. Between 1870 and 1900 the total foreign trade jumped from about $913 million to almost two and a half billion dollars.

24. Kirkland, *Industry Comes of Age*, pp. 281–82; Richard E. Edmonds, "Our Exports of Breadstuffs," *International Review*, 11 (November 1881), pp. 450–62.

25. William Trimble, "Historical Aspects of the Surplus Food Production of the United States, 1862–1902," in *Annual Report of the American Historical Association*, 2 vols. (Washington, 1918), I, pp. 223–39; Morton Rothstein, "America in the International Rivalry for the British Wheat Market, 1860–1914," *Mississippi Valley Historical Review*, 47 (December 1960), pp. 401–18.

26. J. R. Lowell, *American Ideas for English Readers* (Boston, 1892), pp. 12–13.

27. Brainerd Dyer, *The Public Career of William M. Evarts* (Berkeley, 1933), pp. 234, 237; Andrew D. White to Blaine, June 17, 1881; *Diplomatic Despatches* (hereafter *Dip. Des.*), Germany, XXVIII, No. 212, National Archives.

28. Kirkland, *Industry Comes of Age*, pp. 290–95; *American Economist*, 6 (December 26, 1890), pp. 402–03.

29. *New York Daily Commercial Bulletin*, March 26, 1881; *New York Herald*, December 3, 1884.

30. *See* Edward J. Carroll, "The Foreign Relations of the United States with Tsarist Russia 1867–1900" (Washington: Georgetown University, unpublished dissertation, 1953), pp. 163–70, 172–75; *Consular Reports*, 6 (June 1882), pp. 161–62.

31. *See* Merle Curti, "America at the World Fairs 1851–1893," *American Historical Review*, 55 (July 1950), pp. 833–56.

32. *See* e.g., C. B. Norton to Frelinghuysen, July 8, 1884, *Misc. Letters, Department of State*, National Archives.

33. Jeanette Keim, *Forty Years of German-American Political Relations* (Philadelphia, 1919), p. 67; Louis L. Snyder, "The American-German Pork Dispute, 1879–1891," *Journal of Modern History*, 17 (1945), pp. 16–28; Elmer Ellis (ed.), *Finley P. Dunne's Mr. Dooley at His Best* (New York, 1938), p. 125. (By permission, Charles Scribner's Sons.)

34. Paul D. Dickens, *American Direct Investments in Foreign Countries* (Washington, 1930), pp. 37–49.

35. Delber Lee McKee, "The American Federation of Labor and American Foreign Policy 1886–1912" (Stanford: Stanford University, unpublished dissertation, 1952), pp. 14, 22, 24, 39, 42.

36. A. T. Mahan, "The United States Looking Outward," *Atlantic Monthly*, 66 (December 1890), pp. 816–24; W. B. Franklin, "National Defenses," *North American Review*, 137 (December 1883), pp. 594–604; *New York Times*, August 2, 1878.

37. *For. Rel.*, 1881, preface; *The Nation*, 33 (December 15, 1881), pp. 466–67; *Annual Report of the Secretary of the Navy 1881* (Washington, 1881), I, 3.

38. Robert Seager, II, "Ten Years Before Mahan: The Unofficial Case for the New Navy 1880–1890," *Mississippi Valley Historical Review*, 40 (December 1953), pp. 491–512.

39. R. W. Shufeldt, *The Relation of the Navy to the Commerce of the United States* (Washington, 1878).

40. John Roach, *The Successful Maritime Policy* . . . (New York, 1881); John Roach, *The American Carrying Trade* (New York, 1881); *New York Tribune*, October 7, 1880.

41. Bishop Charles H. Fowler, *Missionary Addresses* (Cincinnati and New York, 1906), p. 17; Reverend James S. Dennis, *Christian Missions and Social Progress*, 3 vols. (Chicago, Toronto, and New York, 1897–1906), III, pp. 248, 357, 386, 397.

42. American Board of Commissioners for Foreign Missions, *Annual*

Report 1889, xxxvi–xxxvii; "Africa," *Missionary Review*, 11 (January 1888), p. 52; Professor Kurtz (Johann Heinrich), *Church History*, 3 vols. (New York, 1889–90), III, 214ff.

43. Reverend James Johnston (ed.), *Report of the Centenary Conference on the Protestant Missions of the World*, 2 vols. (New York, 1888), I, 112, 138.

44. *Christian Standard*, 24 (March 9, 1889), p. 145; Augustus C. Thompson, *Future Probation and Foreign Missions* (Boston, 1886), p. 5.

45. *Statutes at Large . . .* , XV (July 27, 1868), p. 224.

46. *For Rel.*, 1885, pp. 855–59; Bayard to George Pendleton, September 7, 1885, *Instructions, Germany*, XVII, No. 43, National Archives.

47. *Cleveland Leader*, November 11, 1870.

48. Clark E. Persinger, "Internationalism in the 60's," *Historical Outlook*, 20 (November 1929), pp. 324–27; Foster R. Dulles, *The American Red Cross* (New York, 1950), pp. 2, 8–15.

49. Clyde Kelly, *United States Postal Policy* (New York, 1931), pp. 218–21; John F. Sly, "The Genesis of the Universal Postal Union," *International Conciliation* (October 1927), pp. 393–443.

50. Matthew Josephson, *Portrait of the Artist as American* (New York, 1930), p. 289; Frank Luther Mott, *A History of American Magazines*, 4 vols. (Cambridge, 1930–57), III, p. 249.

51. Eugene L. Didier, "American Authors and Artists in Rome," *Lippincott's Magazine*, 34 (November 1884), pp. 491–95; "The American Colony in Paris," *ibid.*, 24 (September 1879), pp. 384–86.

52. The literature on James is very extensive, but *see* especially Percy Lubbock (ed.), *The Letters of Henry James* (New York, 1920); Van Wyck Brooks, *The Pilgrimage of Henry James* (New York, 1925).

53. Lowell, *American Ideas for English Readers*, pp. 59–62.

54. The literature on Hearn is extensive, but *see* especially Elizabeth Stevenson, *Lafcadio Hearn* (New York, 1961).

55. Samuel Clemens, *The Innocents Abroad* (Hartford, 1869), pp. 645, 650; William D. Howells, *Literature and Life-Studies: Writings* (New York, 1902), III, pp. 203, 204.

56. *See* Arthur Morgan, *The Philosophy of Edward Bellamy* (New York, 1945); Everett W. Fish, *Biography of Ignatius Donnelly* (Chicago, 1892).

57. "Going to Europe," *The Nation*, 10 (April 28, 1870), pp. 269–70; *Indianapolis Journal*, July 1, 1881.

58. Speech, Article and Book File (1888–90), Whitelaw Reid papers, Library of Congress.

59. *See* Jurgen Herbst, "Nineteenth Century German Scholarship in America" (Cambridge: Harvard University, unpublished dissertation, 1958), p. 38.

60. *See* Charles F. Hall, *Arctic Researches and Life among the Esquimaux* . . . (New York, 1865); A. D. W. Greely, *Three Years of Arctic Service* . . . *1881–1884* (New York, 1885).

61. Wayne D. Rasmussen, "United States Plant Explorers in South America During the Nineteenth Century" (Washington: George Washington University, unpublished dissertation, 1950), pp. 321–22, 365–75.

62. America always regarded European colonial ambitions with a jaundiced eye; *see* for example, Evarts to A. D. White, August 6, 1880, *Instructions to Germany*, XVI, No. 128; *New York Herald*, August 15, 1889; *New York Times*, June 17, 1883; Bayard to McLane, December 21, 1888, *Instructions to France*, XXI, No. 214.

63. Mott, *History of American Magazines*, III, pp. 248–50, 278–79; IV, pp. 134–35, 223.

64. James Eckman, "The British Traveler in America 1875–1920" (Washington: Georgetown University, unpublished dissertation, 1946).

65. I. Joel Larus, "The Origin and Development of the 1891 Copyright Law of the United States" (New York: Columbia University, unpublished dissertation, 1960); Warren B. Bezanson, "The American Struggle for International Copyright 1866–1891" (College Park: University of Maryland, unpublished dissertation, 1953).

66. Morrell Heald, "Business Attitudes Toward Immigration, 1880–1900," *Journal of Economic History*, 13 (Summer 1953), pp. 291–304; Charlotte Erickson, *American Industry and the European Immigrant, 1860–1885* (Cambridge, 1957), pp. vii, 86.

67. Florence E. Gibson, *The Attitudes of the New York Irish Toward State and National Affairs 1848–1892* (New York, 1951), pp. 327–49.

68. Herbert Millington, *American Diplomacy and the War of the Pacific* (New York, 1948), pp. 9, 34, 53; Russell H. Bastert, "A New Approach to the Origins of Blaine's Pan-American Policy," *Hispanic American Historical Review*, 39 (August 1959), pp. 375–412.

69. *Annual Report of the Secretary of the Navy 1880*, pp. 24–26, 34.

70. Blaine to Logan, May 7, 1881, *Instructions to Central America*, XVIII, No. 145.

71. *For. Rel.*, 1881, p. 761; John W. Foster, *Diplomatic Memoirs*, 2 vols. (New York, 1909), I, pp. 92–93.

72. *Senate Executive Doc.*, *64*, 49th Congress, 2nd session, p. 15; "Annexation of Cuba," *Public Opinion*, 3 (October 8, 1887), p. 551.

73. *Chicago Tribune*, February 11, 1880, April 24, 1883; *New York Times*, March 9, 1880; "The Monroe Doctrine," *Catholic World*, 31 (April 1880), pp. 116–33.

74. *New York Herald*, February 14, 1880; *The Nation*, 30 (February 5, 1880), pp. 90–91.

75. Richardson, *Messages and Papers*, VII, pp. 585–86; VIII, p. 327; Charles R. Williams (ed.), *Diary and Letters of Rutherford Birchard Hayes*, 5 vols. (Columbus, 1934), III, pp. 586–88; Carnegie to Blaine, January 14, 1882, Blaine papers, Library of Congress.

76. Payson to Thomas M. Dawson, July 1, 1880, *Consular Instructions*, *Apia*, XCVI, No. 60; *New York Times*, January 27, 1889; *Samoan Times*, September 21, 1878.

77. Bates to Bayard, December 10, 1886, *Special Agents*, Department of State, XXXIII; Goward to Seward, December 28, 1878, *ibid.*, XIII.

78. Sylvia Masterman, *Origins of International Rivalry in Samoa 1845–1884* (Stanford, 1934), p. 106; *Reports of the Diplomatic Bureau*, IV (March 30, 1880), no. 1010, Dept. of State.

79. Dawson, "American Trade with Samoa," *Consular Reports* (August 11, 1882), No. 25.

80. Charles C. Tansill, *The Foreign Policy of Thomas F. Bayard* (New York, 1940), p. 373; *New York Herald*, July 25, September 12, 1887.

81. "Reciprocity in Congress," *Bradstreet's*, 5 (March 18, 1882), pp. 162–63; Sylvester K. Stevens, *American Expansion in Hawaii, 1842–1898* (Harrisburg, Pa., 1945).

82. H. C. Lodge, "The Fisheries Question," *North American Review*, 146 (February 1888), pp. 121–30; Goldwin Smith, "Canada and the United States," *ibid.*, 131 (July 1880), pp. 14–25.

83. *See* Donald F. Warner, *The Idea of Continental Union* (Louisville, Ky., 1960).

84. *New York Times*, May 29, 1887; "Canadian Commerce," *Commercial and Financial Chronicle*, 33 (July 30, 1881), pp. 114–15.

85. *New York Times*, January 1, 1883; *New York Herald*, November 4, 1887.

86. *CR*, XIX, part 6, 50th Congress, 1st session, p. 5197.

87. *Reports of the Diplomatic Bureau*, V, No. 61½ (May 1, 1881); *New York Herald*, September 2, November 21, 1887.

88. *New York Herald*, June 19, 1833; Bayard to R. D. Hubbard, August 19, 1885, *Instructions, to Japan*, III, No. 11.

89. "Japan," *Missionary Herald*, 66 (March 1870), pp. 74–77; *New York Herald*, June 21, 1889.

90. *Cleveland Leader*, January 26, 1870; James B. Angell, "The Diplomatic Relations between the United States and China," *Journal of the Social Sciences*, 17 (May 1883), pp. 24–36.

91. George W. Seward to Evarts, March 22, 1878, *Dip. Des., China*, XLVII, No. 425.

92. "The Beginnings of Medical Work in Korea," *Korean Repository*, 1 (December 1892), pp. 353–58; Charles O. Paullin, *Diplomatic Negotiations of American Naval Officers* (Baltimore, 1912), p. 309; Charles O. Paullin, *The Opening of Korea by Commodore Shufeldt* (Boston, 1910).

93. *New York Herald*, September 10, 1883; *Senate Executive Doc.*, No. 47, 48th Congress, 2nd session.

94. Tansill, *Thomas F. Bayard*, pp. 427–28.

95. "China and the United States," *Atlantic Monthly*, 59 (May 1887), pp. 586–90; Harold J. Noble, "The United States and Sino-Korean Relations, 1885–1887," *Pacific Historical Review*, 2 (1933), pp. 292–304.

96. Gilbert Haven, "America in Africa," *North American Review*, 125 (July 1877), pp. 147–58; "The Congo Commission," *Bradstreet's*, 10 (September 6, 1884), p. 146.

97. *New York Herald*, September 6, 1879; Richardson, *Messages and Papers*, VIII, pp. 175–76.

98. Frelinghuysen to Tisdel, September 8, 1884, *Special Missions, Department of State*, III, No. 1; Tisdel to Frelinghuysen, November 23, 1884, *Special Agents*, Dept. of State, XXXII.

99. *Reports of the Diplomatic Bureau*, III, no. 32 (August 14, 1879).

100. Frelinghuysen to Kasson, October 15, 1884, *Instructions to Germany*, XVII, No. 345; Edward Younger, *John A. Kasson* (Iowa City, 1955), pp. 324–37.

101. *New York Herald*, August 30, 1889; *Harford Daily Courant*, January 24, 1885.

102. Dozer, "Anti-Imperialism in the United States," *passim*.

103. A. T. Mahan, *From Sail to Steam* (New York, 1907), p. 324.

8
Gilt, Gingerbread and Realism
The Public and Its Taste

1. *See* e.g., Carl Bode, *The Anatomy of Popular Culture, 1840–1861* (Berkeley, 1959).

2. Morison and Commager, *Growth of the American Republic*, II, 266–68.

3. John D. Hicks, *A Short History of American Democracy* (Boston, 1949), pp. 460–61.

4. Wesley Gewehr, *et al.*, *The United States* (New York, 1960), p. 381.

5. *See* Richard Current, T. Harry Williams, and Frank Friedel, *American History: A Survey* (New York, 1961), pp. 561–85.

6. Bode, *The Anatomy of Popular Culture*, p. x.

7. Rosenberg and D. M. White (eds.), *Mass Culture* (Glencoe: Free Press, 1957), p. 50.

8. Bode, *Anatomy of Popular Culture*, p. ix.

9. Frank L. Mott, *Golden Multitudes* (New York, 1947), p. 85.

10. Russell Lynes, *The Tastemakers* (New York, 1949), pp. 65–66.

11. Mott, *Golden Multitudes*, p. 87.

12. Lynes, *The Tastemakers*, p. 80.

13. Lewis Mumford, *The Brown Decades* (New York: Dover, 1931), p. 109.

14. Morton Cronin, "Currier and Ives: A Content Analysis," *American Quarterly*, 4 (Winter 1952), pp. 317–30.

15. Lynes, *The Tastemakers*, p. 70.

16. Mott, *Golden Multitudes*, p. 125.

17. James D. Hart, *The Popular Book* (New York: Oxford University Press, 1950), p. 97.

18. Mott, *Golden Multitudes*, p. 136.

19. *New York Ledger*, January 4, 1868.

20. Hart, *The Popular Book*, pp. 99–100.

21. *Ibid.*, p. 164.

22. Harvey C. Minnich, *William Holmes McGuffey and His Readers* (New York, 1936), pp. 40, 89–90.

23. Harry F. Harrison as told to Karl Detzer, *Culture Under Canvas* (New York, 1958), p. xiii.

24. Hart, *The Popular Book*, p. 145; Harrison, *Culture Under Canvas*, p. xiv.

25. Hart, *The Popular Book*, pp. 145–46.

26. James M. Lee, *History of American Journalism* (New York, 1923), p. 352.

27. Mott, *History of American Magazines*, III, 5.

28. *Ibid.*, III, 5–9.

29. *Ibid.*, p. 10.

30. *New York Ledger*, March 14, 1885.

31. Mott, *History of American Magazines*, III, 6.

32. *Ibid.*, p. 42.

33. *Scribner's Magazine*, May, 1887.

34. William G. McLaughlin, Jr., *Modern Revivalism: Charles Grandison Finney to Billy Graham* (New York, 1959), p. 216.

35. Bernard A. Weisberger, *They Gathered at the River* (Boston, 1958), pp. 172–73.

36. Shaplen, *Free Love and Heavenly Sinners*, p. 5.

37. Victoria and Robert Ormond Case, *We Called It Culture* (New York, 1948), pp. 20–21.

38. *See* Lloyd Morris, *Curtain Time* (New York, 1953).

39. *Ibid.*, p. 231.

40. *Ibid.*, p. 235.

41. Carl Wittke, *Tambo and Bones* (Durham, N.C., 1930), pp. 38–86.

42. Cronin, "Currier and Ives," pp. 317–30.

43. As usual, an exception to the statement about anti-Catholicism can be found; in this case the excellent reception of the English translation of Ludovic Halevy, *L'Abbe Constantin*, certainly as Catholic in spirit as a book could be.

44. *See* Irving Wallace, *The Fabulous Showman* (New York, 1959).

45. *See* the comments on Ingersoll's career on the occasion of his death in 1899 in *Public Opinion*, 27 (September 14, 1899), p. 337.

46. Edward B. Marks, as told to Abbot J. Liebling, *They All Sang* (New York, 1934), pp. 43–49.

9

The Search for Reality
Writers and Their Literature

1. A few of the most important may be listed. E. H. Cady, *The Road to Realism* (Syracuse, 1956), and *The Realist at War* (Syracuse, 1958), a two-volume biography of Howells; Everett Carter, *Howells and the Age of Realism* (Philadelphia, 1954); H. N. Smith and W. M.

Gibson (eds.), *The Correspondence of Samuel L. Clemens and William Dean Howells 1872–1910*, 2 vols. (Cambridge, 1960); G. C. Bellamy, *Mark Twain as Literary Artist* (Norman, Okla., 1950); K. S. Lynn, *Mark Twain and Southwestern Humor* (Boston, 1959); R. Asselineau, *The Literary Reputation of Mark Twain from 1910–1950* (Paris, 1954); Walter Blair, *Mark Twain and Huck Finn* (Berkeley, 1960); F. O. Matthiessen and K. B. Murdock, (eds.), *The Notebooks of Henry James* (New York, 1947); F. W. Dupee, *Henry James* (New York, 1951); F. O. Matthiessen, *Henry James: The Major Phase* (New York, 1944), and *The James Family* (New York, 1947).

2. "Courage," *Rectorial Addresses, St. Andrews*, May 3, 1922.

3. Van Wyck Brooks, *The Opinions of Oliver Allston* (New York, 1941), p. 295.

4. Bernard Smith was partially correct in saying that literary criticism in the Gilded Age belonged to "Academy and Drawing Room," and Sinclair Lewis described it as "a chill and insignificant activity pursued by jealous spinsters, ex-baseball reporters, and acid professors." "The American Fear of Literature," *Why Sinclair Lewis Got the Nobel Prize* (New York, 1930), p. 20. Lewis was amusing, but the comment is hardly a serious one.

5. Twain, *The Innocents Abroad* (Hartford, Conn., 1871), preface.

6. *Atlantic Monthly*, 41 (January 1878), p. 132. *See also* T. S. Perry's comment in the *North American Review*, 111 (October 1872), p. 378: "The idealizing novelist will be the real novelist. All truth does not lie in facts."

7. *From Opitz to Lessing* (Boston, 1885), pp. 8–9.

8. *Atlantic Monthly*, 18 (October 1866), p. 48.

9. *French Poets and Novelists* (New York, 1878), p. 318.

10. Leon Edel, "The Enduring Fame of Henry James," *New York Times Book Review*, September 3, 1961, p. 1.

11. Mildred Howells (ed.), *Life in Letters of William Dean Howells*, 2 vols. (New York, 1928), I, 217.

12. *Their Wedding Journey* (Boston, 1871), chap. 3.

13. *Life in Letters*, I, 169.

14. *Hawthorne* (New York, 1879), p. 126.

15. *The Nation*, 24 (February 2, 1882), pp. 102–03.

16. Percy Lubbock (ed.), *Letters of Henry James*, 2 vols. (New York, 1920), I, 105.

17. "Henry James, Jr." *Century*, 25 (November 1882), p. 29.

18. *Partial Portraits* (New York, 1888), p. 399.

19. "Literary Essays," in *Writings of Mark Twain* (New York, 1918), pp. 152–53.

20. *Century*, 28 (August 1884), p. 632.

21. Mott, *Golden Multitudes, passim.* Mott estimates the total sales of Alger's novels at about 16 million. Some have put it at 100 million, which seems greatly exaggerated. A recent Alger collector and bibliographer, Frank Gruber, *Horatio Alger, Jr., a Biography and Bibliography*, calls Alger hyperbolically "the best selling author of all time" and estimates total sales at about 300 million. The figure seems vastly disproportionate.

22. "The Art of Fiction," *Partial Portraits*, p. 382.

23. In the *Galaxy* (1870): "One can deliver a satire with telling force through the insidious medium of a travesty, if he is careful not to overwhelm the satire with the extraneous interest of the travesty and so bury it from the reader's sight and leave him a joked and defrauded victim, when the honest intent was to add to either his knowledge or his wisdom."

24. In 1877 he wrote to Howells: "Delicacy—a sad false delicacy—robs literature of the two best things among its belongings. Family circle narrative and obscene stories." A. B. Paine (ed.), *Mark Twain's Letters*, 2 vols. (New York, 1917), p. 310.

10

New Men and New Ideas
Science and the American Mind

1. Henry Adams, *The Education of Henry Adams* (New York, 1931), p. 377.

2. Sir J. J. Thomson, *Recollections and Reflections* (New York, 1937), p. 185–86.

3. J. G. Crowther, *Famous American Men of Science* (New York, 1937), pp. 230–31.

4. Muriel Rukeyser, *Willard Gibbs* (New York, 1942), p. 266.

5. *Ibid.*, p. 251.

6. *See* D. S. Jordan (ed.), *American Men of Science* (New York, 1910), p. 351.

7. Bernard Jaffe, *Men of Science in America* (New York: Simon and Schuster, Inc., 1944), p. 327.

8. *Ibid.*, p. 328.

9. *Ibid.*, p. 329.

10. Rukeyser, *Willard Gibbs*, p. 280.

11. Thomas C. Mendenhall, "Henry Augustus Rowland," *National*

Academy of Science Biographical Memoirs (Washington, 1905), V, 131.

12. Jordan, *Men of Science*, p. 417.

13. Mendenhall, "Henry August Rowland," p. 133.

14. Jordan, *Men of Science*, p. 420.

15. Jaffe, *Men of Science in America*, p. 375.

16. *Ibid.*, p. 361.

17. Robert A. Millikan, "Albert Abraham Michelson," *National Academy of Sciences Biographical Memoirs* (Washington, 1938), XIX, 136.

18. Isaac Asimov, *The Intelligent Man's Guide to Science*, 2 vols. (New York, 1960), I, 277.

19. Jaffe, *Men of Science in America*, p. 372.

20. Joel H. Metcalf, "Edward Charles Pickering," *Proceedings of the American Academy of Arts and Sciences*, 57 (November 1922), p. 502.

21. Simon Newcomb, *The Reminiscences of an Astronomer* (Boston, 1903), p. 182.

22. *Ibid.*, p. 144.

23. *Ibid.*, p. 229.

24. "Einstein's Appreciation of Simon Newcomb," *Science*, 69 (March 1, 1929), p. 249.

25. Newcomb, *Reminiscences*, p. 213.

26. Jaffe, *Men of Science in America*, p. 337.

27. *Ibid.*, p. 340.

28. S. P. Langley, "The Flying-Machine," *McClure's Magazine*, 9 (June 1897), p. 660.

29. Jaffe, *Men of Science in America*, p. 346.

30. Cf. Thomas A. Bailey, *The American Pageant* (Boston, 1956), p. 553.

31. George P. Merrill, *The First One Hundred Years of American Geology* (New Haven, 1924), p. 201.

32. Jaffe, *Men of Science in America*, p. 248.

33. Jordan, *Men of Science*, p. 167.

34. *American Journal of Science*, 30, 2nd ser. (November 1860), p. 154.

35. Louis Agassiz, "Evolution and Permanence of Type," *Atlantic Monthly*, 33 (January 1874), pp. 94, 101.

36. Jordan, *Men of Science*, p. 194.

37. Francis Darwin (ed.), *The Life and Letters of Charles Darwin*, 2 vols. (New York, 1898), II, 63.

38. *Ibid.*, II, 80.

39. *Ibid.*, II, 146.

40. Asa Gray, *Darwiniana* (New York, 1876, 1889), p. 67.

41. Francis Darwin (ed.), *More Letters of Charles Darwin*, 2 vols. (London, 1903), I, 191.

42. Leonard Huxley, *Life and Letters of Thomas Henry Huxley*, 2 vols. (London, 1900), II, 193.

43. Jordan, *Men of Science*, p. 250.

44. *Ibid.*

45. Daniel Coit Gilman, *The Life of James Dwight Dana* (New York, 1899), p. 188.

46. William D. Armes (ed.), *The Autobiography of Joseph LeConte* (New York, 1903), p. 336.

47. Joseph LeConte, *Evolution* (New York, 1888, 1897), pp. 65–66.

48. G. Frederick Wright, *Studies in Science and Religion* (Andover, Mass., 1882), p. 117.

49. Jordan, *Men of Science*, p. 451.

50. Henry Fairfield Osborn, *Impressions of Great Naturalists* (New York, 1928), p. 158.

51. Darwin, *Letters*, II, 100.

52. *Ibid.*, II, 417n.

53. *Ibid.*, II, 417.

54. Huxley, *Letters*, I, 463.

55. *Ibid.*, I, 495.

56. O. C. Marsh, "Thomas Henry Huxley," *American Journal of Science*, 50, 3rd ser. (1895), p. 181.

57. Charles Schuchert and Clare Mae Levine, *O. C. Marsh: Pioneer in Paleontology* (New Haven, 1940), p. 232.

58. *Ibid.*, p. 240.

59. W. J. McGee, "Fifty Years of American Science," *Atlantic Monthly*, 82 (September 1898), p. 317.

60. *Ibid.*, p. 308.

61. *Ibid.*, p. 320.

62. Henry Adams, *The Degradation of the Democratic Dogma* (New York, Capricorn Books, 1958), pp. 212.

63. John Fiske, *The Destiny of Man* (Boston, 1884, 1912), pp. 118–19.

64. Henry James (ed.), *The Letters of William James*, 2 vols. (Boston, 1920), II, 344.

65. William James, *Pragmatism and Four Essays from the Meaning of Truth* (New York, Meridian Books, 1955), p. 233.

66. *Ibid.*, p. 121.

67. *Ibid.*, p. 49.

68. Ralph Barton Perry, *The Thought and Character of William James*, 2 vols. (Boston, 1935), I, 493.

69. Lewis Mumford, *The Golden Day* (New York, 1926), p. 95.

70. *See* John Dewey, "Pragmatic America," *New Republic*, 30 (April 12, 1922), p. 185.

71. Jordan, *Men of Science*, pp. 420–21.

Contributors

PAUL F. BOLLER, JR., earned his doctorate in American Studies at Yale University, and has taught history at Southern Methodist University. He is now at the University of Texas. An expert on American cultural and intellectual history, he has written many articles and reviews for magazines such as *Southwest Review*, *Journal of Negro History*, and the *William and Mary Quarterly*. He was a contributor to *The Impact of Darwinian Thought on American Life and Culture* (Austin, 1959), and is the author of *George Washington and Religion* (Dallas, 1963).

PAOLO ENRICO COLETTA has published many articles and reviews in such journals as *Pacific Historical Review*, *Nebraska History*, the *Proceedings* of the U.S. Naval Institute, and other publications. He is contributing editor of a symposium on William Jennings Bryan and of a similar work on William McKinley; he is engaged in a volume of essays on American secretaries of the navy. He is co-author of *Geography and Naval Power* (Annapolis, 1953 and 1958), and is at present writing a definitive biography of William Jennings Bryan. He teaches history at the U.S. Naval Academy at Annapolis.

VINCENT P. DE SANTIS received his doctorate at Johns Hopkins University and is a recognized authority on American political party development in the late nineteenth century. He has held fellowships from the Guggenheim Foundation and the American Philosophical Society. He has published articles and reviews in many important historical and political science journals. He is the author of *Republicans Face the Southern Question* (Baltimore, 1959), and is at present engaged in a general study of American party politics in the late nineteenth century. He is head of the history department at Notre Dame University.

ROBERT FALK received his doctorate at the University of Wisconsin and has taught at Wisconsin, Michigan State University, Rutgers University, and the University of California at Los Angeles, where he is associate professor of English. He has published many important works on American literature and cultural and intellectual history in the late nineteenth century. He is at present engaged in a broad study of American literature in the age of Howells and James.

HERBERT GUTMAN received his doctorate at the University of Wisconsin where he held a fellowship from the Social Science Research Council and began his studies of late nineteenth-century American labor. He is associate editor of *Labor History*, and has published many articles in journals such as the *Ohio Historical Quarterly*, *Labor History*, and the *Pennsylvania Magazine of History and Biography*. He is now writing a history of labor in the Gilded Age and teaching at Fairleigh Dickinson University. In September, 1963, he was named an associate professor of history at the State University of New York at Buffalo.

ARI HOOGENBOOM received his graduate training at Columbia University. He has taught at Columbia, Texas Western College, and at Pennsylvania State University, where he is associate professor of history. He has contributed to many national journals and reviews, and is the author of a basic monograph dealing with the Gilded Age, *Outlawing the Spoils* (Urbana, Ill., 1961). He is now writing a biography of Gustavus Vasa Fox and a history of Pennsylvania.

H. WAYNE MORGAN received his doctorate at the University of California, Los Angeles, and has taught at UCLA, San Jose State College in California, and at the University of Texas, where he is at present a member of the history department. He has written many articles and reviews and is the author of *Eugene V. Debs: Socialist for President* (Syracuse, 1962), *Writers in Transition* (New York, 1963), and *William McKinley and His America*, a definitive biography of the twenty-fifth president (Syracuse, 1963). He is at present engaged in writing a general history of the United States in the Gilded Age.

MILTON PLESUR received his graduate degree from the University of Rochester. He has taught at Rochester, at the State University of New York College in Buffalo, and at the University of Buffalo, where he is at present assistant professor of history and assistant dean of the University College. He has published a number of important articles on American foreign policy in the late nineteenth century, and is at work on a study of American foreign policy and intellectual trends, 1865–90.

ROBERT R. ROBERTS received his doctorate at the University of Chicago, and has specialized in the history of American religious thought and American social history. He has taught at Mankato State College in Minnesota and at San Jose State College, where he was an associate professor of history. In June, 1963, he became professor of history and chairman of the Social Science Division at the San Bernardino-Riverside

State College, California. He is at present writing a study of the life and thought of Washington Gladden, prominent Social Gospelite.

JOHN TIPPLE received his graduate degree at Stanford University and is at present associate professor of history at Los Angeles State College. He has written many articles and reviews on the history of American business and the ideas of American enterprise. He is the author of *Problems of Progress: Andrew Carnegie and Henry George* (Cleveland, 1960), and *The New Order: Alexander Hamilton and Thomas Jefferson* (Cleveland, 1961). He is at present working on a two-volume intellectual history of the United States, to be published shortly.

Index

Adams, Brooks, 6, 143
Adams, Charles Francis, Jr., 14, 31–32, 69, 78–79
Adams, Henry, 6, 14, 69, 79, 83, 143, 154; on the Gilded Age, 11, 72, 92; on U. S. Grant, 78–79; on the powers of the president, 98; on science and history, 238–39
Adams, Herbert Baxter, 156
Adee, Alvee A., 162
Africa, American interest in, 166ff.
Agassiz, Louis, 232
Aldrich, Nelson W., 129
Alger, Horatio, 8, 33, 198, 199, 216, 217–18
Allen, Horace N., 151
Allen, William, 58, 60
Allison, William Boyd, 122
Altgeld, John Peter, 129
American Bimetallic Union, 129
Ames, Oakes, 70
Anarchists, 7
Arnold, Matthew, 158
Arthur, Chester A., 6, 77, 107, 123; as collector of the Port of New York, 84, 86, 87
Asimov, Isaac, 227
Austen, Jane, 208

Baird, Spencer, 229
"Baltimore Plan," 115
Barnard, Edward E., 228
Barnum, P. T., 193
Bayard, Thomas F., 152, 162
Beard, Charles A., 3ff., 92
Beecher, Henry Ward, 69, 170, 187–88
Bellamy, Edward, 155, 218, 219
Bing, Julius, 80
Blaine, James G., 6, 93, 97, 160–62; and naval construction, 150
Bland, Richard P., 122, 125–26, 132, 136
Bland, Thomas A., 32

Bland-Allison Act (1878), 123, 125
Bode, Carl, 170–71, 172
Boutwell, George S., 79, 121; as an administrator, 83–84
Brooks, Van Wyck, 197, 214, 218–19
Brooks, William Keith, 235
Bryan, William Jennings, 129, 130, 134, 138
Bryce, James, 91–92, 102, 158–59
Burgess, John W., 156
Burke, Edmund, 100
Burlingame Treaty (1868), 164
Burt, Silas W., 88–89
Butler, Benjamin F., 162

Cable, G. W., 202
Canada, and annexation to the U.S., 162ff.
Cannon, Joseph G., 99
Carlisle, John G., 133, 135
Carnegie, Andrew, 10, 17–18, 35, 161, 180; on competition, 25; on millionaires, 34; and role of wealth, 23
Chandler, William E., 97
Chase, Salmon P., 111–12, 116
Chautauqua movement, 8, 171–72, 188–90
Chinese immigration, 164ff.
Cleveland, Grover, 123–25, 129, 132–38, 141, 161, 163
Cobb, Sylvanus, Jr., 177
Colfax, Schuyler, 89
Communists, 7
Conkling, Roscoe, 6, 69, 76–77, 87, 97
Conrad, Timothy, 232
Conwell, Russell, 172, 180, 189
Cooke, Jay, 114
Cooper, Peter, 6
Cope, Edward D., 237
Corporate system, 16–17
Cox, Samuel S., 152
Crane, Stephen, 219
Credit Mobilier, 9, 70
Crisp, Charles, 132–33

Cullom Committee, 22
Currier, Nathaniel, 176
Curtis, G. W., 72, 74, 75–78, 79, 83, 88

Dana, James Dwight, 234
Darrow, Clarence, 129
Darwinism, 231ff.
De Forest, John W., 197, 199, 219
De Long, G. W., 156
Diaz, Porfirio, 160
Dickens, Charles, 172, 174, 204
Diplomatic service, 142ff.
Donnelly, Ignatius, 130, 155
Douglass, Frederick, 109
Drew, Daniel, 10

Eaton, Dorman B., 89
Eggleston, Edward, 8
Eliot, George, 204, 205, 208
Elliott, E. B., 83
Ely, Richard T., 156
Evarts, William M., 145

Fish, Hamilton, 75
Fisher, Irving, 222
Fisk, James, 10, 38, 69, 70, 72, 74, 170
Fiske, John, 238–39; on expansion, 143
Foster, Charles, 134
Fourteenth Amendment, 17

Garfield, James A., 90; on silver legislation, 99, 123
Garland, Hamlin, 8, 219
Gibbs, Josiah Willard, 221–24, 238, 242
Gilbert, William S., 191
Gilman, Daniel Coit, 225
Godkin, E. L., 4, 6, 72, 74, 184
Gompers, Samuel, 129
Gospel of wealth, 28
Gould, Jay, 10, 35, 70
Grant, U. S., 6, 9, 17, 75, 77, 78–79, 83, 85, 98, 103, 106, 141; and finance, 117, 118; and political corruption, 70–72
Gray, Asa, 233–34
Greeley, Horace, 6
Greely, Adolfus W., 157
Greenback Labor party, 131
Greenbackers, 7

Greenbacks, 116ff.
Grinnell, Moses, 85
Guyot, Arnold, 234

Hall, Charles F., 156
Hamilton, Alexander, nationalism of in Gilded Age, 7
Hancock, Winfield Scott, 93
Harris, Joel Chandler, 197, 202, 209
Harrison, Benjamin, 108, 144; and silver legislation, 126, 129, 132
Harte, Bret, 154, 181–82, 197, 198, 200, 202–03, 208, 210–11, 218, 219
Hayes, Rutherford B., 6, 93–94, 125, 141, 161, 164; administration of the customhouse, 87–88; difficulties as president, 97; and silver legislation, 122–25, 132; and the South, 105, 107, 109
Haymarket Riot, 38
Hearn, Lafcadio, 154
Henry, Joseph, 229, 242
Hepburn Committee, 22
Hewitt, Abram S., 124–25
Hitchcock, Edward, 231–32
Hoar, Ebenezer Rockwood, 79
Hoar, George F., 98
Hobson, John, 42
Holmes, Mary J., 176
Homestead Strike, 38
Howells, William Dean, 8, 154, 196–214, passim
Humorous fiction, 181–82, 209–11
Hunt, William H., 149
Hunter, William, 81–82
Huntington, Collis P., 35

Immigrants, as strikebreakers, 46ff.
Imperialists, 143–44
Indian Frauds, 9
Individualism, 18–20
Internal improvements, 6
Isthmian canal, 161ff.
Ives, James Merritt, 176

James, Henry, 154, 196–220, passim
James, Thomas L., 89
James, William, 4, 9, 239ff.
Jefferson, Joseph, 172
Jenckes, Thomas A., 80–81

Jewett, Sarah Orne, 197, 202
Johns Hopkins University, 9, 156, 225
Johnson, Andrew, 72–73, 75, 83, 98, 117
Josephson, Matthew, 5ff.

Kasson, John A., 167
Knox, John Jay, 121

Langley, Samuel P., 229–30
Lanier, Sidney, 209
Lawson, Thomas W., 33
Lease, Mary E., 130
LeChatelier, Henry Louis, 231
LeConte, Joseph, 235
Leet, George, 85–86
Legal Tender Act (1862), 115–16
Leidy, Joseph, 236
Lick, James, 228
Lincoln, Abraham: and national banking system, 111, 115; tradition of, 93
Lloyd, Henry D., 22, 129; on free competition, 28; on trusts, 34
Local color in fiction, 202–04
Lodge, Henry Cabot, 140
Logan, John, 97
Lowell, James Russell, 74, 145, 154, 158

McCulloch, Hugh, 112, 116–17
McGee, W. J., 237–38
McGuffey, William H., influence of readers, 179–80
McKinley, William, 6, 93–94, 98, 141, 168; on silver legislation, 99, 126, 138
McKinley Tariff (1890), 126–28
Magazines, 8
Mahan, A. T., 143, 149; on imperialism, 167–68
Mahone, William, 94
Mansfield, Josie, 69
Marble, Manton, 124
Marsh, Othniel C., 236–37
Maury, Matthew F., 232
Maxwell, Clerk, 222, 224
Mellon, Andrew W., 70
Merritt, Edwain A., 87–89
Michelson, Albert A., 226

Mill, John Stuart, 28
Millionaires, numbers of, 17
Miners' National Association, 57
Minstrel shows, 192
Molly Maguires, 38
Moody, Dwight L., 170, 172, 186–87
Morgan, J. P., 18, 21, 35; on trusts, 26
Morley, Edward A., 227
Murphy, Thomas, 84, 85–86

Nast, Thomas, 4, 6
National Labor Reform party, 130–31
National Silver party, 129
Naval construction, 148ff.
Negroes: as strikebreakers, 46ff., 56; and Republican party, 107–08
New York Italian Labor Company, 66–68
Newcomb, Simon, 228–29
Norton, Charles Eliot, 73–75, 76, 79, 83

Ohio Valley Iron Association, 52
Operetta, 191–92
Ostwald, Wilhelm, 234

Pan-Americanism, 159ff.
Panic of 1873, 17, 44ff.
Parrington, Vernon L., 2ff., 170
Patronage, and Republican party, 102–04
Peary, Robert Edwin, 156
Peffer, William A., 130
Peirce, Charles S., 4, 9, 224
Pendleton Act (1883), 90
Peoples' party, 131ff.
Periodical literature, 182–86
Perkins, Charles, 24
Perry, Thomas, 204
Pickering, Edward, 227
Pinkerton, Allan, 50
Plunkitt, G. W., 70–71
Pomeroy, Samuel Clarke, 70
Postal rates, 153
Powderly, Terence V., 129
Powell, John Wesley, 156
Prohibitionists, 7
Pullman Strike, 38

Quantity theory of money, 262, 48n

Randall, Samuel, 124
Ray, Patrick H., 157
Reade, Charles, 177
Realism in literature, 200ff.
Rebates, 24
Reed, Thomas, 144
Ricardo, David, 28
Richardson, William A., 70
Rockefeller, John D., 10, 17–18, 35, 37, 38; and Standard Oil Company, 22–24, 26; on necessity for trusts, 26
Rogers, H. H., 22
Rogers, John, 176
Roosevelt, Franklin Delano, 155
Roosevelt, Theodore, 143
Rowland, Henry A., 224–25
Royce, Josiah, 9

Sanborn, John D., 70
Sankey, Ira D., 170, 186–87
Schumpeter, Joseph, 40
Schwab, Charles, 18
Scott, Tom, 35
Seward, William H., on expansion, 140–42
Sharpe, George, 77
Shepherd, Boss, 69
Sherman, John, 98, 112, 116, 118–19, 122, 123, 126, 129, 132
Sherman Anti-Trust Act (1890), 30
Sherman Silver Purchase Act (1890): passage of, 126–29; repeal of, 132–36
Shufeldt, Robert W., 164–66
Simpson, Jerry, 130
Single-tax, 28
Sloane Physics Laboratory, 222
Smiles, Samuel, 180
Smith, Adam, 28
Social Darwinism, 4; and politics, 95
Social gospel, 28
Socialists, 7
Sons of Vulcan, 45
Southworth, Mrs. E. D. E. N., 173, 176–77

Specie Resumption Act (1875, 1879), 118–19
Spencer, Charles, 77
Sprague, Kate Chase, 69
Stanford, Leland, 35
Stanley, Henry M., 156
Star Route Frauds, 9
Strong, Josiah, 143
Sturtevant, John M., 34
Sullivan, Sir Arthur, 191
Sumner, Charles, 162
Sumner, William G., 25
Swank, James M., 45
Swift, Alexander, 52ff.

Tariff, 6
Taxation, 17
Teller, Henry M., 127
Theater, 172–74; on national tours, 189–91
Tilden, Samuel, 124
Tracy, Benjamin F., 150
Trollope, 204, 208
Trumbull, Lyman, 72, 129
Twain, Mark (Samuel L. Clemens): coins term "the Gilded Age," 1; as a writer, 8, 154, 170, 181, 196–203 passim, 208, 210–11, 214–20 passim
Tweed Ring, 69

Vanderbilt, Cornelius, 10, 34, 38; on law, 35–36

Wallace, Lew, 179, 198
Warner, A. J., 124
Watson, Tom, 130
Weaver, James B., 130, 136
Weights and measures, 153–54
Whisky Ring, 9
White, Andrew D., 145
Whitman, Walt, 32, 198, 200
Wilson Tariff Bill (1894), 129
Windom, William, 126, 129
Wolcott, Edward O., 127
Woolson, Catherine Anne, 197, 202
Wright, Chauncey, 235
Wyman, Jeffries, 232–33

Young, Charles A., 227–28